Dr. Ray M. Frank

DELIVER ME

RICHARD EXLEY

THOMAS NELSON PUBLISHERS
Nashville

Published in Nashville, Tennessee, by Thomas Nelson, Inc.

Unless otherwise noted, Scripture quotations are from THE NEW KING JAMES VERSION. Copyright © 1979, 1980, 1982, 1990, Thomas Nelson, Inc., Publishers.

Scripture quotations noted KJV are from the KING JAMES VERSION.

Scripture quotations noted NIV are from the HOLY BIBLE: NEW INTERNATIONAL VERSION®. Copyright © 1973, 1978, 1984 by International Bible Society. Used by Permission of Zondervan Publishing House. All rights reserved.

Scripture quotations noted TLB are from THE LIVING BIBLE, copyright 1971 by Tyndale House Publishers, Wheaton, IL. Used by permission.

Scripture quotations noted Jerusalem Bible are from THE JERUSALEM BIBLE. Copyright © 1966 by Darton, Longman & Todd Ltd. And Doubleday & Company, Inc. Used by permission.

Scripture quotations noted J. B. PHILLIPS are from J.B. PHILLIPS: THE NEW TESTAMENT IN MODERN ENGLISH, Revised Edition. Copyright © J.B. Phillips 1958, 1960, 1972. Used by permission of Macmillan Publishing Co., Inc.

Scripture quotations noted RSV are from the REVISED STANDARD VERSION of the Bible. Copyright © 1946, 1952, 1971, 1973 by the Division of Christian Education of the National Council of the Churches of Christ in the U.S.A. Used by permission.

The names and some personal information of individuals in the stories I have related in *Deliver Me* have been changed except for public figures whose stories are a matter of public record.

ISBN 0-7852-7112-0 (hc)

Printed in the United States of America

Dedication

To Jesus Christ, who "was in all points tempted as we are, yet without sin." May Your kingdom come and may Your will be done on earth as it is in heaven.

All stories related in *Deliver Me* are true. I have, however, changed the names of the participants, except for those public figures whose stories are already a matter of public record, in order to protect their privacy.

CONTENTS

ACKNOWLEDGMENTS

The writing of a book is always a team effort involving far more people than just the author. In the case of *Deliver Me* this was especially true. First I would like to thank my agent, Sealy Yates, and his assistant, Tom Thompson, for introducing me to the wonderful people at Thomas Nelson. Without them there would have been no book.

To Rolf Zettersten, Curtis Lundgren, Cindy Blades, and the entire team at Thomas Nelson Publishers. Your dedicated efforts turned my dream into reality.

To Rick Nash, editor and friend. Because of you, *Deliver Me* comes much closer to being the book I envisioned it could be. Thanks for stretching me—as a writer and a thinker.

To my brother Robert Exley, Ph.D., who read the manuscript and made invaluable suggestions.

To all who helped me with the research, especially Douglas Baker, a son-in-law extraordinaire.

To Leah Starr, the best daughter a father could ever have. Thanks for your constant encouragement, especially when it seemed I would never get finished.

To Brenda Starr, my wife and forever friend. Thanks for all the hours you have spent listening to me read my "day's work." You are truly a gift from God and the joy of my life.

INTRODUCTION

The Parable of the Geese[1]

We have been flying since the first hint of daylight and the sun is now far down in the western sky as we circle the body of water far below us. Though we have ridden a fierce north wind most of the day, weariness makes our wings heavy. Twice we have bypassed promising lakes after being alerted to danger by our experienced leader. He is a magnificent bird well past his prime, but he can still fly with the best of the young geese. He has been my mate for many winters. For the most part we have had a good life—flying north to Canada in the spring to hatch our young, and then back south with the first hint of winter—but twice we lost offspring to the deadly guns of the hunters.

Through the driving snow I now see a cluster of geese huddled against a marshy bank at the far end of the lake. Being surrounded by grain fields, it promises not only a sheltered resting place but sustenance as well. We will not find a better place to spend the night, of that I am sure.

Mordecai leads us in a wide circle around the end of the lake and the adjoining field, alert for any sign of danger. Though I see nothing to cause alarm, I cannot shake a nagging sense of dread. From the lake below comes the faint honking of geese at rest. It is the "all clear" signal, but I take no comfort in it, nor does Mordecai.

Well do I remember another day not much different from this. We had ridden a cold front out of Canada and as the sun slid far down the curve of the earth we set our wings and began the long glide toward the water below. We were about to touch down when two hunters emerged from beneath a sheet of white canvas with guns blazing. Instantly Mordecai veered left, his wide wings clawing the heavy air as he fought for height. Our firstborn was flying on his right wing, just behind him, in tight formation. When Mordecai veered left he followed, taking the full load of shot intended for his father. I watched in helplessness and rage as his lifeless body folded and plunged into the water below. Other birds were dying, too, five in all, but I had eyes only for my firstborn.

The hunters' guns continued to boom a moment more, spitting orange flame and deadly shot into the indigo sky above the slate-colored lake. I took a couple of pellets in one leg, sending a flash of burning pain to explode in my brain, but it was nothing compared to the awful ache in my heart. Riding the winds I followed the others into the safety of the wide sky, but when they turned south I lingered behind. After they were gone I continued to circle overhead, just out of range of the guns below. I watched as the hunters began slapping each other on the back and shouting with glee before splashing through the frigid water to collect their prey.

This is on my mind as Mordecai leads us in ever tightening circles, and on his as well, I am sure. He has never been able to forgive himself for that earlier debacle, though what he could have done differently I do not know. The fact that our firstborn took the shot intended for him has been nearly more than he can bear.

Although everything appears to be in order, Mordecai hesitates still, generating a rumble of protests from some of the young males. They resent Mordecai's caution, but those of us who have known the terror of the hunters' guns appreciate it. Suddenly Absalom, a two-year-old goose of magnificent proportions, breaks formation and begins a long glide toward the water below. For a moment no one follows, then four or five of the younger birds give chase. Mordecai hisses a stern warning while the flock emits a scolding chorus. Both are ignored.

As the renegade geese near the water the marsh grass seems to explode, ripping the pale evening sky with jagged apricot flashes. Absalom takes a full load in his chest and explodes in a tangled mass of blood and feathers. Behind him the young geese veer off in all directions, frantically pounding their wings in a desperate attempt to escape the hunters' rain of death. Some hug the water, while others seek the safety of the sky.

Jonathan takes a hit in his left wing and lurches crazily before plunging into the lake. Abigail is down, as is Esther. Only Obadiah escapes and he carries pellets in his legs. The hunters emerge from a well-concealed blind clothed from head to toe in camouflage gear.

One of them spots Jonathan who is trying to hide in the tall marsh grass. Taking aim he shoots him and Jonathan dies while we watch in stunned disbelief.

There is nothing we can do so Mordecai turns once more toward the south and we fall into formation, death having left several jagged holes. Below us the hunters remove their decoys, collect the bodies of our fallen comrades, and troop across the field to their 4x4.

As a boy I considered hunting geese a great sport, a rite of passage to manhood if you please, so I could hardly wait until I was old enough to go on my first goose hunt. In preparation I read everything I could find on goose hunting. I learned that the most successful goose hunters utilize blinds, decoys, and goose calls. The blind is constructed from materials indigenous to the area where they will be hunting. Often it is prepared well in advance of hunting season so the geese can become accustomed to it. On the day of the hunt the hunters usually arrive well before daylight. Quietly they position their decoys to resemble geese who are feeding or at rest. Once they are in place, the hunters retreat into the blind where they are able to watch for incoming geese without being seen. When a high-flying flock is spotted, one of the hunters uses a goose call to lure them in by imitating the "all clear" honk of the geese.

By nature geese are wary and will circle for a long time before landing to feed. As they circle they are constantly alert for anything that might signal danger—an unnatural goose call, a poorly positioned decoy, or the premature movement of a hunter in the blind. The skillful hunter patiently works his goose call, enticing the flock ever closer. If the hunter is successful in deceiving them, the geese will eventually set their wings and glide toward the decoys. Of course when they come within range, the hunters begin shooting from their blind, making short work of those magnificent birds.

Now that I am grown, I no longer think of hunting geese as sport; rather, I see it as a parable of temptation. Like the goose hunters of my childhood, the tempter studies his unsuspecting prey. With clever genius he builds his blinds and sets his decoys, ever luring the unsuspecting toward the trap he has prepared.

Satan is the master of deception and is so identified throughout Scripture. In Genesis he is called a serpent, and he is described as being "more cunning than any beast of the field" (Gen. 3:1)—

and he is after *you*. Like the goose hunter, he wears camouflage gear. The apostle Paul says that he "transforms himself into an angel of light" (2 Cor. 11:14), and he warns us not to be ignorant of his devices (2 Cor. 2:11). In Ephesians we are told to "put on the whole armor of God, that [we] may be able to stand against the wiles of the devil" (Eph. 6:11).

Did you notice the descriptive language the Scriptures use? Satan is ever so cunning, and we are warned against his devices, tricks, and intrigues. Even as the goose hunter employs the same deceptions again and again, so does Satan. It is critical to learn from the experience of those who have gone before, as well as from our own temptations. In Scripture we see the heroes of faith brought face-to-face with Satan's subtle snares time after time. Notice how the enemy tempted Joseph, how he tricked Samson, how he ensnared David. We can learn from their mistakes. And once we recognize his alluring devices, we can stand firm against him, and he will flee from us (James 4:7). Failing here, however, the believer risks becoming ensnared in the devil's carefully laid trap.

*In reality God is more anxious to forgive us
than we are to be forgiven.*

According to the Scriptures Satan's most ingenious deceptions have their roots in spiritual things: false prophets (Matt. 7:15), deceitful workers (2 Cor. 11:13)—that is, those who pretend to be followers of Christ in order to infiltrate the fellowship and lead others astray—and lying miracles (2 Thess. 2:9). These all look like the real thing, they sound like the real thing, and up to a point they even act like the real thing, *but they are counterfeit.* Like the decoys set out by the goose hunters they look real enough on the outside, especially from a distance, "but inwardly they are ravenous wolves" (Matt. 7:15). Make no mistake—Satan means to ruin you! He comes only to steal and kill and destroy (John 10:10).

It should come as no surprise that temptation is rooted in deception. It could hardly be otherwise. If we could see sin as it really is *in the end,* it would scarcely be tempting. For instance, had Lot been able to see the tragedies that would befall him in Sodom, he would not have been tempted to pitch his tent near there, no matter how fertile and well-watered the plain. Had Samson known his relationship with Delilah would end in betrayal, blindness, and imprisonment, chances are he would never have gone to her, no matter how beguiling her beauty. Nor would David have invited Bathsheba into his palace, had he known his affair with her was going to end with the murder of her husband, the death of the child conceived during their illicit tryst, and turmoil without end in both his family and his kingdom.

Who would ever be tempted to try cocaine if, instead of the promised highs and the supposed popularity, we were shown the inevitable consequences of addiction—financial ruin, marital conflict, and personal tragedy? What teenage girl would seek love in the backseat of a car if she knew her quest was going to end, not in the security she seeks, but in the ongoing tragedy of abortion?

The hidden costs of sin are just that—hidden. With consummate skill the tempter creates a mesmerizing illusion. He positions his decoys in a place that offers the very things we need—i.e., food, shelter, and companionship. He does not necessarily entice us with bad things, at least not at first; rather, he tempts us to satisfy a legitimate need in an inappropriate way. Hear him as he whispers his beguiling lies: "You will not *surely* die," he says, "but you will become like God. You will be the master of your own destiny" (see Gen. 3:4–5).

He is the master of the half-truth, the short view, sin's immediate benefit. God, on the other hand, deals with the whole truth—the long view. Ultimately *God's truth* is our only defense against the lies and deceptions of the enemy.

To escape the tempter's snare we must know the truth about sin. It is *never* without consequences. There are no extenuating circumstances. "The soul who sins shall die" (Ezek. 18:4). No matter how tired or hungry those geese are, if they are fooled by the hunters' decoys they are going to be killed or wounded.

"Do not be deceived, God is not mocked; for whatever a man sows, that he will also reap. For he who sows to his flesh will of the flesh reap corruption, but he who sows to the Spirit will of the Spirit reap everlasting life" (Gal. 6:7–8).

To escape the tempter's snare we must know the truth about ourselves. As painfully humbling as it may be, we must come to grips with our capacity for sin. Given the right circumstances we are all capable of unspeakable evil. Only as we acknowledge this tragic truth will we take the steps necessary to protect ourselves from the evil within. Only as we acknowledge our weakness will we find strength in Christ to withstand the enemy.

To escape the tempter's snare we must know the truth about God. Satan wants us to believe that God is hard-hearted, that He is quick to judge and slow to forgive. Nothing could be further from the truth. "The steadfast love of the LORD never ceases, his mercies never come to an end; they are new every morning" (Lam. 3:22–23 RSV). No matter how miserably we might have failed, no matter how far we might have fallen, He stands ready to forgive us. As David testified, "The mercy of the LORD is from everlasting to everlasting" (Ps. 103:17).

If Satan cannot get us to believe that God is hard-hearted, then he will try to convince us that He is a soft touch, that God will grant us a special dispensation because of our "unique" circumstances. That just isn't true! Although the grace of God is inexhaustible we must not allow ourselves to be deceived into believing that we can abuse it without suffering the consequences.

To escape the tempter's snare we must know the truth about forgiveness. We do not have to prove ourselves, or earn God's forgiveness, or promise to never sin again.

"If we confess our sins," writes John the Beloved, "He is faithful and just to forgive us our sins and to cleanse us from all unrighteousness" (1 John 1:9).

To escape the tempter's snare we must know the truth about temptation. It is not a sin, no matter how unclean it may make us feel. Nor should we ever feel guilty for being tempted. If Jesus was not above temptation then how can we expect to escape the attack of the enemy of our souls? Temptation is simply a fact of life. There are some things we can do to minimize its power, but we will never totally escape it in this life. Having said that, let me hasten to add that we should always seek to avoid temptation, and we should ever pray, "Do not lead us into temptation, / But deliver us from the evil one" (Matt. 6:13).

Temptation does not come from God, nor is it unique or irresistible. The apostle Paul says, "Remember this—the wrong desires [temptations] that come into your life aren't anything new and different. Many others have faced exactly the same problems before you. And no temptation is irresistible. You can trust God to keep the temptation from becoming so strong that you can't stand up against it, for he has promised this and will do what he says. He will show you how to escape temptation's power so that you can bear up patiently against it" (1 Cor. 10:13 TLB).

Experience has taught me that in the early moments of temptation the way of escape is broad and easy to find. The longer I delay, however, the narrower the way of escape becomes, and the harder it is to find. Consider the parable of the geese. When they first see the decoys and hear the hunters' goose calls, escape is easy. The whole sky is open to them. However, once they come within range of the hunters' guns their options narrow. Escape is still possible, but now they must flee through a hail of steel shot. The moral of the goose story is simple: He who is serious about escaping temptation will act quickly.

To escape the tempter's snare we must know the truth about God's faithfulness. Not only is He faithful to provide a way of escape, but He will also use the very temptation the enemy intended for our destruction to produce spiritual maturity in us. I best understand how God does this when I compare it to the way an expert in self-defense uses his opponent's weight and momentum against him. In the same way God turns the enemy's attack to our advantage. God is not the source of our temptation, nor does He will it, but when the enemy tempts us, God works in our situation to help us grow in grace. Therefore James writes, "My brethren, count it all joy when you fall into various trials, knowing that the testing of your faith produces patience. But let patience have its perfect work, that you may be perfect and complete, lacking nothing. . . . Blessed is the man who endures temptation; for when he has been proved, he will receive the crown of life which the Lord has promised to those who love Him" (James 1:2–4, 12).

A friend comes to mind whose spiritual condition once seemed hopeless. Although he was reared in a Christian home he fell prey to temptation during his teen years and embarked on a twenty-year odyssey of disobedience. His first marriage ended in divorce, as did his second, leaving him bitter and disillusioned. In desperation he turned to the pursuit of education in an attempt to rebuild his flagging self-esteem. He excelled in his studies and soon earned his Ph.D. Unfortunately, or perhaps I should say fortunately, his scholastic achievements did nothing to ease his hurting soul. As he piled success upon success his spiritual pain only became more pronounced.

One night the Lord appeared to him in a dream, bringing him a message of unconditional love as well as a terrifying warning. Though the enemy tried to convince him it was nothing but a dream, the man knew better. For too many years he had been deceived by Satan's lies, and now he was having no part of it. God had spoken to him, and he was determined to obey.

The following Sunday he took his family to church, where the Lord met him in a remarkable way. God's love washed over him in waves, healing his deep wounds, forgiving his sins, and restoring his soul. Today he is a spiritual leader in his church, and his family is serving the Lord faithfully.

While I celebrate his restoration I cannot help grieving over all those wasted years. Had he known the truth about God and temptation he may well have escaped the tempter's snare during his teen years. Or at least he could have been restored early in life rather than living in disobedience for nearly a quarter century. That is why I am writing this book. I want to show you how to resist temptation, though if we are painfully honest with ourselves, we have to admit that there are times we don't want to resist temptation until it is too late. I'm going to show you what's behind that and how to get it behind you. And even if you feel like Tonya Harding—banned for life—I'm going to show you the way to restoration. "God does not take away a life; but He devises means, so that His banished ones are not expelled from Him" (2 Sam. 14:14).

THE TRUTH
ABOUT TEMPTATION

The root cause of virtually all spiritual failure is disobedience in the little things. Though it may not seem significant at the time, each disobedience, no matter how small, is like a fissure in the wall of a person's soul. Through each tiny crack the acid of evil seeps in and begins to eat away at the foundations of his spiritual character. Over a period of time his spiritual will is compromised and when a crisis of temptation arises he simply does not have the will to resist. To the undiscerning it may appear that he was brought down by that final crisis, but in reality it was the dry rot of disobedience that did him in.

By the same token, each act of obedience, no matter how small, reinforces the foundation of a person's spiritual character. Day by day he is "... strengthened with might through His spirit in the inner man...."(Eph. 3:16). When a potentially overwhelming temptation arises he is prepared, for having been obedient in the face of seemingly insignificant temptations, he is now able to be obedient in the moment of crisis.

1

THE ROOTS OF
TEMPTATION

As the clerk is ringing up my purchases at the checkout counter, she discovers one of the items is not marked. Since she is the only employee on duty, she excuses herself and makes her way to the back of the store to check on the price. Standing alone at the counter, while waiting for her to return, my eyes are drawn to a display of scissors. There are several different sizes. They all gleam brightly in the overhead lights, new and shiny.

Suddenly a voice inside my head seems to say, "Go ahead, take a pair. Slip them under your jacket. No one will see. No one will ever know."

Glancing over my shoulder, I locate the clerk kneeling before a bin at the rear of the store. Quickly I conclude that she is paying no attention to me, so intent is she on what she is doing. I let my eyes roam over the rows of merchandise to make sure no one is watching me. There are two or three other customers, but they all seem preoccupied with their own shopping.

Inside my head the voice urges me on. "Do it now before the clerk returns. Don't hesitate, or it will be too late."

Reaching out my hand I pick up the nearest pair of scissors. My mind is racing. I am an ordained minister, serving a local congregation. I am thirty-three years old, and to my knowledge I have never taken anything that did not belong to me, not even when I was a kid. Yet I now find myself in the grip of an almost overwhelming desire to steal a pair of scissors I don't need and can well afford to buy.

3

The voice inside my head is almost frantic. "This is your chance. Seize the moment. Be bold."

So intense is my struggle that my heart is pounding and my breath comes in ragged little gasps. I can feel the perspiration on my brow. Holding the scissors in my hand, I fight the desire to stuff them under my jacket.

Out of the corner of my eye I glimpse a movement. Realizing the clerk is returning, I carefully replace the scissors on the display, doing my best to appear nonchalant. Glancing at me she asks, "Are you all right? You look a little pale."

"I'm just fine, thank you. A little warm, maybe."

Taking out my wallet, I pay for my purchases and exit the store. Hurrying toward my car I experience a confusing mixture of shame and relief. Although I am thankful I have resisted the nearly overwhelming impulse to shoplift, I am absolutely mortified to think that I, a minister of the gospel, could be tempted with such a thing. To tell you the exact truth, I feel tainted. I feel guilty, as if I have done something sinfully wrong.

Thinking about that experience now, nearly twenty years removed, it seems almost bizarre. If Satan was serious about tripping me up, why would he choose something as silly as a pair of scissors? Or maybe that is just the point. Had he tempted me with embezzlement of church funds or armed robbery it would not have tempted me at all. But by suggesting something as silly as shoplifting, he caught me totally off guard. Almost before I knew what was happening I found myself in the grip of desire. Had I succumbed to temptation and been caught shoplifting, my ministry would have been ruined—over a pair of scissors!

It is no accident that the enemy first tempts us with seemingly insignificant things. He knows that each sinful act, no matter how small, is like a seed sown in the soil of our soul. At first it is so tiny, so apparently harmless, that we pay it no mind. In the darkness of our heart it germinates and sends out roots. Little by little, like tentacles, its roots wind their way into the deepest part of our being. Then one day, much to our chagrin, we find ourselves participating in sinful acts of which we could never have imagined ourselves capable.

For me the process began with a pair of scissors. For you it was probably something equally innocuous. Perhaps you were tempted to fudge on your expense account or to tell a little "white" lie, or some such thing. Often it is upon such little matters that our spiritual destiny hinges. If we remain faithful here, our spiritual character is reinforced. Conversely, if we fail here, we risk setting in motion a pattern of compromises that will eventually lead us to ruin.

No One Is Immune to Temptation

My experience with the scissors illustrates at least two important truths. First, none of us are above temptation. It matters not a whit whether we are a brand-new convert or a spiritually mature believer, we all hear the siren songs of the enemy. Only spiritual pride or scriptural ignorance could cause us to think otherwise. The biblical record is clear. Whether we are talking about patriarchs or prophets, kings or apostles, *all* have felt the none-too-subtle tug of temptation. And not infrequently even these heroes of the faith fell prey to temptation's sly enticements.

Abraham was called the friend of God, yet he lied to Pharaoh, telling him Sarah was his sister rather than his wife (Gen. 12:10–20). Jacob yielded to temptation so often it is hard to remember when he *didn't*. Moses, the lawgiver, lost his temper and killed an Egyptian (Ex. 2:11–12). David, the man after God's own heart, succumbed to vanity and took a census of the people (1 Chron. 21:1–8). Elijah, being a man subject to like passions as we are (James 5:17), fell into a near suicidal depression (1 Kings 19:4).

The New Testament record is hardly better. Yielding to pressure from their mother, James and John gave in to fleshly ambition and sought to be the greatest in the kingdom (Mark 10:35–41). Peter could not grasp the concepts of redemption and became the unwitting tool of the enemy (Matt. 16:21–23). Ananias and Sapphira lied to the Holy Spirit (Acts 5:1–10). Paul and Barnabas had a falling out over John Mark (Acts 15:36–41). Sexual sin abounded in the church at Corinth (1 Cor. 5). Hymenaeus and Alexander made shipwreck of their faith (1 Tim. 1:19–20). Hardly an unblemished record, yet we remember many of these as giants of the faith. They became heroes not because they were *perfect*, but because they *persevered*. And as they matured in the Lord their record improved. Although they never outgrew temptation, they did learn to overcome it.

Given these facts, we shouldn't really be surprised when we are accosted by sinful desires, regardless of the form they may take. No matter how spiritually mature we become, we will never escape the reach of temptation. Being tempted is not a sign of carnality as much as it is evidence of our humanity. On this fallen planet temptation is a fact of life!

Although we will never be immune to temptation, we should expect to leave some temptations behind as we mature, both physically and spiritually. For instance a man's sex drive peaks in late adolescence or early adulthood, making him especially vulnerable to sexual temptation during those years. As he reaches midlife and beyond his sex drive diminishes, making him less susceptible to temptations in this area. From a spiritual perspective we are continually being conformed to the image of Christ (Rom. 8:29), making the desires of the flesh less appealing. That is not to say that we will never be tempted with the things that haunted us earlier in life, but only that the nature of our temptations change. As we conquer one area in our life, the enemy attacks another. Early in our Christian walk we are often tempted with old vices, sinful habits from our not-too-distant past. As we mature in the Lord, our temptations become more subtle. Instead of being tempted with the lust of the flesh, we are now tempted with sins of the spirit—things like pride, self-righteousness, spiritual ambition, and judgmentalism.

When God forgives our sins He is done with them;
He never brings them up again!

Having said that, let me hasten to add that we must *always* be on guard against the old temptations. As soon as we begin to feel totally secure in a given area, the enemy will likely ambush us right there. That is one of the reasons, and there are many others, why spiritual leaders often fall in an area where they were sure they could not be compromised. "Therefore let him who thinks he stands take heed lest he fall" (1 Cor. 10:12).

Feeling Guilty

The second truth my experience highlights is temptation's power to make us feel guilty. Although I successfully resisted the impulse to steal a pair of scissors, I experienced no sense of victory.

Instead I felt ashamed, even unclean. Because of this, without realizing what was happening to me, I became the unwitting tool of the enemy. With a vengeance I berated myself: I was unfit for the ministry. I was a disgrace to the body of Christ. What kind of man was I if I could be tempted to steal a pair of scissors, for crying out loud? What did this say about me? What hidden sin lurked in the dark and unexplored corners of my heart?

In actuality my reaction says more about my spiritual condition than I initially realized. I feared I was unfit for the ministry because I could be tempted to thievery, when in truth, spiritual pride was my besetting sin. Only a spiritually arrogant person is shocked when he is tempted, thinking himself above the kind of petty sins that trouble other people. It pains me to admit this, but my shocked embarrassment is irrefutable evidence.

By the time I reached home I was thoroughly browbeaten. The enemy had stolen my victory! Having failed to get me to yield to temptation, the tempter now appealed to my spiritual pride, heaping loads of guilt upon me. Insidiously he suggested that if I were the kind of man I ought to be, I could not be tempted with such a paltry crime.

False Guilt

What we have here is a classic example of *false guilt*. This guilt is false because it is rooted in subjective feeling rather than objective fact. That is, it feels like the real thing, but it has no basis in reality. The feelings are *acute*, but they are not *accurate*.

How, you may be wondering, can a person distinguish between genuine guilt, which is the convicting work of the Holy Spirit, and false guilt, which is the condemning slur of the accuser of the brethren? The key is found in 2 Corinthians 7:10, which says, "Godly sorrow [conviction] produces repentance leading to salvation, not to be regretted; but the sorrow of the world [condemnation] produces death."

Genuine guilt comes from the Holy Spirit. It makes us painfully aware of our sinful failures, but even as it does, it motivates us to confess our sins and try again. We hear ourselves praying, "I know I've failed, but I will do better next time."

False guilt, on the other hand, tempts us to despair. It tells us that we will never be any different, that God is sick of our repeated

7

failures and ready to wash His hands of us. It tempts us to give up and drives us into hiding, away from God.

The convicting work of the Holy Spirit is always specific. When He convicts us of sin He puts His finger on it and identifies it so we can deal with it and get rid of it. Condemnation is vague, general. It leaves us feeling guilty and unworthy, but not able to identify a specific cause for our guilt. It tells us that we are unfit for the kingdom and that we will never be any different. It does not identify a particular sin, lest we deal with it and be delivered. In fact, the only time condemnation is specific is when the accuser condemns us of sins we've already confessed. Or, as in my case, when he tries to condemn us of things that aren't really sin at all.

Remember, if you are feeling guilty about a sin that you have already confessed, that feeling is not from God, so reject it. When God forgives our sins He is done with them; *He never brings them up again!* "As far as the east is from the west, / So far has He removed our transgressions from us" (Ps. 103:12).

Sometimes the guilty feelings persist even when we know they are not from God, even when we have done everything in our power to cast them out. Be encouraged. John tells us that even "if our heart condemns us, God is greater than our heart" (1 John 3:20).

In times like that we must choose to believe the truth of God's Word rather than our feelings, no matter how persistent they may be. When I speak of choosing to believe, I am talking about a course of action rather than mere mental assent. Because God's Word says I am forgiven, I now walk in that truth. I do the things a forgiven person would do. I worship. I serve. I witness, and I minister. By walking in the truth of God's Word I bring my feelings into agreement.

Temptation Is Not Sin

Unfortunately, I had only a limited understanding of these truths twenty years ago when I was doing battle with my tormenting thoughts, and my ignorance made the enemy's attack that much more effective. The struggle was not constant, but it did continue for nearly a month. Two or three days might go by without a conscious thought of the incident; then, for no apparent reason, I would find myself reliving the shameful experience all over again.

Talking with someone surely would have helped, but I could not bring myself to confide in anyone. That I could be tempted to steal a pair of scissors was simply too embarrassing to share. Thus we encounter another favorite tactic of the enemy—*isolation*. Satan knows his chances of bringing us down are much better if he can separate us from other believers.

Guilt continued to haunt me, and I could not seem to get over the feeling that I had done something wrong. On an intellectual level, I knew being tempted was not a sin, but I still *felt* sinful. Then one day as I was reading in Hebrews, a passage of Scripture seemed to leap off the page: "For we do not have a High Priest who cannot sympathize with our weaknesses, but was in all points tempted as we are, yet without sin" (Heb. 4:15). It was not an unfamiliar verse; in fact, I had committed it to memory years before. Still, familiar though it was, it was like a revelation to me. I understood, maybe for the first time ever, that Jesus truly experienced temptation.

Like many believers, I had accepted the fact of Jesus' temptation without really considering it. I had never truly allowed His temptations to be *real*. Somehow I just assumed that temptation was no big thing for Him, that He never had to struggle to do the right thing. Now I realized how wrong I had been. *Our Lord's battle against temptation was every bit as real as my own.* He *suffered* when He was tempted (Heb. 2:18). In fact the *Living Bible* suggests that His struggle against temptation in Gethsemane on the night He was betrayed was so severe that He sweat great drops of blood (Heb. 12:3–4).

The specific details of all the temptations that Jesus suffered during His lifetime are not recorded in Scripture. This, however, should not blind us to the fact that He was "in all points tempted as we are" (Heb. 4:15). In truth, the details are far less important than the fact that it happened. Jesus understood what happened to me in that hardware store because, at some point in His life, He experienced the same thing. Not the same details, but the same sort of temptation. He could identify with my feelings of self-doubt and unworthiness because He was also tempted with the same feelings.

Therefore we are encouraged to "come boldly to the throne of grace, that we may obtain mercy and find grace to help in time of need" (Heb. 4:16). We are not approaching a distant deity who knows nothing of our struggles, but One who was "in all things . . .

made like His brethren" (Heb. 2:17). And because "He Himself has suffered, being tempted, He is able to aid those who are tempted" (Heb. 2:18). Our boldness, our confidence, has nothing to do with who we are, but who He is, "a merciful and faithful High Priest" (Heb. 2:17). One who can "sympathize with our weaknesses" (Heb. 4:15).

As these truths became real to me I suddenly found myself thinking: *Why should I feel guilty about being tempted? Temptation isn't a sin. The Bible says as much right here. Jesus was tempted in every way "yet [was] without sin" (Heb. 4:15)! It isn't a sign of spiritual weakness. If Jesus, the righteous One, the only morally pure Man who ever walked the face of the earth, could be tempted in all points, great and small, then why should I feel guilty for being tempted with petty theft?*

For the first time in days I was free from my paralyzing self-doubt. Like the sun breaking through the gray overcast, I felt the warmth of God's presence fill my being. I wasn't a spiritual dunce. I wasn't an outcast. I was a child of God, beloved of the Father.

When Does Temptation Become a Sin?

Only one question remained, and I now turned my attention toward it: At what point does temptation become a sin? The most obvious answer, of course, is when a person yields to it, when he acts on his sinful desires. In my case, had I slipped those scissors under my jacket that would have been a sin. Even if I had never been found out, it still would have been a sin.

Although I resisted the temptation to steal, I was not yet out of the woods. Had I later regretted my decision and began imagining the thrill of possessing those scissors—fantasizing about the way they would feel in my hand, the kind of patterns I could cut with them, how proud I would be to show them off to my friends—that too would have been sin.

Sometimes we resist temptation not because we abhor sin, but simply because we lack the courage or the opportunity to act on our sinful desires. That being the case, we may develop an elaborate thought life in which we entertain our sinful fantasies. On the screen of our imagination we indulge in all manner of evil. Soon we are living a double life. Outwardly we appear to be spiritual persons, but in our thought life, we are something different.

And according to the Scriptures altogether, "As [a man] thinks in his heart, so is he" (Prov. 23:7).

Most of our spiritual battles are won or lost right here—in the arena of our heart and mind. If we will bring every thought and every feeling into obedience to Jesus Christ, our daily walk will be obedient as well. Conversely if we give our emotions and our imaginations free rein to entertain the tempting suggestions of the enemy, we will soon find ourselves living out our secret fantasies, regardless of how sinful they might be.

All that a person does, whether good or evil, originates in his heart. Jesus said, "A good man out of the good treasure of his heart brings forth good things, and an evil man out of the evil treasure brings forth evil things" (Matt. 12:35).

Initially our thoughts are nothing more than involuntary responses to external stimuli. Sometimes they are morally neutral, as when we respond to the beauty of a sunset, but more often than not they are either good or bad. For instance, when I read a great book, or listen to an inspiring piece of music, my thoughts naturally turn toward God. On the other hand, when I am bombarded by materialistic or sexual stimuli, my thoughts turn toward the gratification of those desires.

At this point my thoughts still fall within the realm of temptation. I can reject them, or I can make a place for them in my heart. If I refuse to allow them a lodging place they will soon wither and die, for they need my complicity to exist. They become sin only when I entertain them, only when I fantasize them into greater existence.

Jesus addressed this issue as well when He said:

> You have heard that it was said to those of old, "You shall not murder," and whoever murders will be in danger of the judgment. But I say to you that whoever is angry with his brother without a cause shall be in danger of the judgment. . . . You have heard that it was said to those of old, "You shall not commit adultery." But I say to you that whoever looks at a woman to lust for her has already committed adultery with her in his heart. *(Matt. 5:21–22, 27–28)*

By upping the ante, as it were, Jesus is not trying to make the spiritual life more difficult. Instead He is showing us how to deal with temptation the first moment it rears its ugly head. We can take a giant step toward overcoming temptation by refusing to entertain, even for a moment, any thought or feeling that is not honoring to Christ. On the other hand, if we allow our carnal thoughts free rein, they will soon dominate not only our thought life but our actions as well.

> Many a man has mistakenly assumed that he could reserve a part of his heart for weeds, only to discover that evil is a malignancy that invades every part of his being. In time its roots reach even into the most sacred areas of his life, choking out all that is good and decent. Ultimately, he finds himself behaving in ways which were once unthinkable to him.[1]

> Inevitably, the thoughts and feelings we harbor in our hearts become the attitudes and actions of our lives. Early on, they are just seeds scattered across the soil of our heart. With a minimum of effort we can sweep them away; but if we delay, or worse yet, if we nurture them, they will take root. Even then, we can uproot them; but if we do not act quickly they will overwhelm us.[2]

The person who is truly serious about overcoming temptation will "above all else, guard [his] heart, for it is the wellspring of life" (Prov. 4:23 NIV).

Reflecting on Him

1. *Nearly every one of us has experienced something similar to the episode described in the opening paragraphs of this chapter. How has "false guilt" interfered with your perception of yourself as an authentic Christian?*

2. *In your own words, what does it mean to say that "being tempted is not a sign of carnality as much as it is evidence of our humanity"?*

3. *Many of us harbor secret regrets about "lost opportunities" in our past where we successfully resisted temptation but still wonder what it would have been like to have yielded. Do you have similar thoughts and memories? In private, make a list of these "secret regrets" and confess them to God in prayer, asking Him to free you from these dangerous fantasies—you might want to burn the list or tear it up when you are finished.*

2

The Almighty "I"

Some years ago I worked with a recovering alcoholic named Jim. Like many alcoholics he had an insatiable need to talk, and daily he regaled me with his philosophy of life—not that I minded, for he was an interesting conversationalist. According to his way of thinking, all of humanity's problems revolved around what he called the big "I." He blamed it for all of his problems as well—financial woes, marital conflict, unemployment, and especially his drinking.

"I can stay sober," he said, "as long as I depend on a higher power to help me live my life. But if I ever let that *almighty 'I'* get the upper hand then I'm in trouble. Because it is *'I'* who gets confused. It is *'I'* who gets angry. It is *'I'* who gets frustrated, and it is *'I'* who gets drunk!"

Listening to him I realized that it's not only alcoholics who have "I" problems—the whole world does. It is at the root of every temptation we face and the cause of our downfall when we succumb. No one is immune, not even the most committed Christian. Without exception we all have to battle the almighty "I." Like the apostle Paul we find ourselves crying, "Oh, what a terrible predicament I'm in. Who will free me from my slavery to this deadly lower nature?" (Rom. 7:24 TLB).

That's the question, isn't it: Who will free us from our slavery to the almighty "I"? Who will deliver us from the egomaniac within? For our only hope of consistently overcoming temptation lies in defeating this deadly foe. "Thank God! It has been done by Jesus Christ our Lord. He has set [us] free" (Rom. 7:25 TLB).

That's the good news!

13

The bad news is that in spite of all that Jesus Christ has done, many of us experience no consistent victory over temptation. As a local pastor and the shepherd of men's souls, I've heard every excuse in the book, but at their core they are all the same: No one wants to take responsibility for his actions. No matter what a person does it is never his fault. As the wise man said, "A man's own folly ruins his life, yet his heart rages against the LORD" (Prov. 19:3 NIV).

The Blame Game

Blaming others, even God, is nothing new; it is as old as humankind. When God confronted Adam in the garden after he had yielded to temptation and eaten the forbidden fruit, Adam blamed Eve: "The woman you put here with me—she gave me some fruit from the tree, and I ate it" (Gen. 3:12 NIV). Eve in turn blamed the serpent: "The serpent deceived me, and I ate" (Gen. 3:13 NIV).

As you can see, when it comes to sin and temptation, we are all pretty good at passing the buck. No one wants to take the blame. Either the devil made us do it, or we were led astray by friends, or there were extenuating circumstances, or. . . . The list is endless, and while blame-shifting may temporarily ease our guilty conscience, it does nothing to help us overcome the almighty "I," or the temptations he is so prone to. In fact, it is counterproductive. As long as we blame others, we have no conscious need of God's help, thereby cutting ourselves off from the source of our strength. Conversely, the sooner we accept responsibility for our actions, the sooner we can draw upon the resources of God to overcome.

Seldom have I seen this principle more graphically displayed than in the case of a distraught wife who sought my pastoral counsel some years ago. Entering my office she took a seat on the couch and hung her head. For several seconds, perhaps as long as a minute or two, she said nothing. She simply sat there twisting a tissue as she fought to maintain her composure. Finally she took a deep breath and forced herself to look me in the eye.

In a halting voice she began, shame coloring every word. "I'm having an affair with a coworker, and Gary just found out about it. Last night he came home from work early and overheard me talking to Austin on the phone. At first I tried to deny everything, but it was no use. I know it's wrong. I know I shouldn't have done it, but my life has been so miserable."

Her voice trailed off, and she paused, waiting for the remonstration she was sure was coming. When I only nodded, she gathered her courage and plunged ahead, rationalization replacing her earlier shame. "Everyone thinks Gary is such a fine man, but they don't know him the way I do. They don't have to live with him. I don't suppose he is a bad man, not really—just insensitive, inattentive where I am concerned. Don't misunderstand me—he never forgets my birthday or our anniversary, but we never talk. He is always too busy, preoccupied with other things. And on those rare occasions when we do talk he doesn't talk to me. He talks past me, as if my thoughts and feelings are of no concern to him."

She spent the better part of an hour carefully cataloging all of Gary's faults before finally resting her case. As best I could determine it was not really forgiveness she sought, but vindication, for to her way of thinking all the fault was Gary's. If he had been more understanding she would not have been tempted by the attentions of another man. If he had spent more time with her, been more attentive to her needs, this terrible thing would never have happened to her.

At the root of every spiritual struggle, there are two forces at war: not so much good and evil, but God and self.

Gently, but firmly, I confronted her. "Marilyn," I said, "Gary's shortcomings as a husband undoubtedly contributed to the circumstances that made you vulnerable to temptation, but he is not responsible for your sinful actions. That decision was yours and yours alone. No matter Gary's behavior, you are still free to choose how you are going to live your life."

As I spoke I sensed her anger building. "You're a man," she blurted out, "so why am I surprised you don't understand? I should have known you would take Gary's side."

I let her fume for a couple of minutes before saying, "I'm not taking anyone's side, and I'm sure when you have had a chance to think about it, you will realize as much. What I'm trying to do is help you come to grips with a very difficult situation. If you continue to blame Gary for your actions no one can help you, not even God."

Opening the Bible I reminded her that King David was an adulterer. "Why," I asked her, "do you suppose we remember him as a man after God's own heart rather than as an unfaithful husband?"

After thinking about it for a moment she shrugged her shoulders.

"We remember David as a godly man," I said, "not because he never sinned, but because he knew how to find forgiveness. When Nathan the prophet told him, 'You are the man!' and that he was the one who took Uriah the Hittite's wife, and he was the one who killed him with the sword of the Ammonites, David did not try to pass the buck. He never blamed anyone but himself."

Glancing down at my open Bible, I read, "So David said to Nathan, 'I have sinned against the LORD'" (2 Sam. 12:13).

That's all I read, nothing more. We sat quietly while she pondered the words of Scripture. At last she lifted her head and made eye contact with me. Though she was making no sound, her shoulders were shaking and huge tears rolled down her cheeks, spoiling her perfect makeup. "You're right," she said. "I have no one to blame for my sinful disobedience except myself. Gary didn't make me do it. Austin didn't seduce me. I can't even blame the devil, though I'm sure he had a hand in it somewhere.

"As much as it pains me to admit it," she continued, "I *wanted* it to happen. I felt I deserved some excitement in my life. After thinking about Gary's needs and the kids' needs for more than twenty years, I decided it was time somebody looked after my needs, and I was going to be that somebody."

Having finally accepted the responsibility for her actions, Marilyn was able to call upon the name of the Lord and find forgiveness. That was just the first step in a long journey toward the healing of her marriage. With the help of a fine Christian counselor, she and Gary were able to rebuild their broken marriage, but for a while it was touch-and-go. Like most of us, they found it difficult to "own" their mistakes and take responsibility for overcoming temptation. It was easier to blame each other or play the part of a victim. But as they learned, easier is not necessarily better, and once they stopped playing the blame game, God was able to do a significant work in their lives and marriage.

Hopefully most of us will not have to experience a tragedy of that magnitude before we are willing to take responsibility for our behavior. By acknowledging that we are our own worst enemy when it comes to temptation, we can be about the business of overcoming the almighty "I"— what some have called the enemy within.

The Enemy Within

William Temple, in his commentary on John's gospel, writes, "There is only one sin, and it is characteristic of the whole world. It is the self-will which prefers 'my' way to God's—which puts 'me' in the centre where only God is in place."[1]

If that is the case, and I believe it is, then it must be equally true that there is only one temptation: the ever present temptation to choose my will over God's will, my way over God's way. At the root of every spiritual struggle, there are two forces at war: not so much good and evil, but God and self.

Although there is only one temptation, it wears many faces. And the enemy of our souls knows precisely which face is most appealing to each of us. Having made a study of human nature, he knows exactly how to approach us. Based on his understanding of our individual personalities he shapes temptation's face to fit our particular disposition. But strip away the facade, peel off the various masks, and at its core is the same old temptation to choose my will over God's will.

Return with me to humanity's first temptation. Hear the tempter say to Eve, "You will not surely die. For God knows that in the day you eat of it your eyes will be opened, and *you will be like God*, knowing good and evil" (Gen. 3:4–5, emphasis mine).

At the heart of every temptation, from then until now, is *the desire to become God*. We may call it by any number of names—individualism, self-determination, uniqueness, ambition—but at its core it is the same old obsession: Every one of us wants to be God. We all want to be in control. We want to make the rules and decide what is best for us. We don't want anyone telling us what to do or how to live our lives. It is the ultimate temptation, and it comes from within rather than without. Satan may fan the flames, but the embers of sinful egotism reside in our own hearts.

The truth of the matter is that when it comes to temptation we are our own worst enemy. The tempter has a part to play to be sure, as do friends and associates who influence us, but theirs is a bit part. *The lead role in temptation goes to the enemy within—self—the almighty "I"!* It is not the devil who leads us astray, but our own sinful desires. "But each one is tempted when he is drawn away by his own desires and enticed" (James 1:14).

Satan may fan the flames, but the embers of sinful egotism reside in our own hearts.

Although temptation may take many forms—"the lust of the flesh, the lust of the eyes, and the pride of life" (1 John 2:16)—at its core it is ever the same. *It is always rooted in our own evil desires, the product of our fallen nature.*

Those of us who are serious about overcoming temptation are deeply troubled by the evil within. Again and again we find ourselves crying from the depth of our souls, "Oh, what a terrible predicament I'm in. Who will free me from my slavery to this deadly lower nature?" (Rom. 7:24 TLB).

The Source of Our Victory

According to Romans 6, the source of our victory over temptation, whether it comes from within or without, is our identification with Jesus in His death and resurrection. "For we know that our old self [the almighty 'I'] was crucified with him so that the body of sin might be done away with, that we should no longer be slaves to sin" (Rom. 6:6 NIV).

Before our conversion to Jesus Christ the almighty "I" sits on the throne of our lives, dictating our sinful actions. But at the moment of conversion his stranglehold on our will is broken. Now we are free to choose whom we will serve: God or self. The only real power he now has over us is what we voluntarily give him. One night after talking with Jim (my friend who battled alcoholism) about these things, I had a dream in which there was only one character—me! Only there were two of us, twins, if you please, but not identical. The first me was the man I know, the man I was at the time—thirty-five years old, about five feet, nine inches tall, and maybe fifteen pounds overweight. The other me was the man

I once wanted to be—more than six feet tall, with the kind of body that only steroids and weights can produce.

God will not destroy the almighty "I" without our cooperation, and we cannot overcome him without God's direct intervention.

In my dream we were standing on the edge of a cliff overlooking the ocean. A hundred feet below, the surf beat itself into foamy spray against a wall of jagged rocks. The steroid me was holding the real me high above his head, as if he were going to hurl me to my death on the rocks far below. The real me, that is, the one I recognized, attempted to reason with the other me—that muscle-bound egomaniac—but to no avail.

I tried to tell him that he was throwing his life away. Why hurl me to my death, I reasoned, when he could use his enormous strength and agility to pursue a career as a professional athlete? He appeared not to hear me, or at least not to care, and death seemed imminent.

At that point I awoke in a cold sweat. Instantly I sensed that the dream was a warning from the Lord. Somehow I understood that the steroid me was my ego and my ambition, what Jim called the almighty "I." He was so powerful that I could not contend with him. He was immune to my most desperate and impassioned pleas. God was my only hope, and there beside my bed I cried out to Him:

Lord Jesus, deliver me from myself! Help me to lose my life that I might find it. To become the least, to become the servant of all, that I might become truly great in the kingdom of heaven. I yield myself to You, my personal dreams and desires, and all that I am, even my rights. Especially my rights! Make me the kind of man You want me to be. Let me decrease that You may increase. In Your holy name I pray. Amen.

Arising from my knees I sensed a new power within, a new freedom in Christ. The almighty "I" had been dealt a crushing blow. Although he was not yet destroyed, he was no longer the "strong man" holding me captive, and I was no longer at his mercy. He was still a deadly enemy to be sure, and not one to be taken lightly, but he was no longer in charge of my life. By both Scripture and experience I knew that I would have to contend with him all the days of my life, but with the help of the Holy Spirit I was confident of the outcome. "The God of peace [would] soon crush Satan under [my] feet" (Rom. 16:20 NIV), and the almighty "I" with him! For "He who is in [us] is greater than he who is in the world" (1 John 4:4).

The War Within

The dynamics of this ongoing conflict between the old man of sin and the new man of the spirit may be best understood if we will remember how children see the world, especially when they are very young. By nature they come into the world thinking everything revolves around themselves. Initially they think only in terms of "I," "me," "my," and "mine." One of our responsibilities as parents is to challenge their "me only" thinking at an early age, or else it will create serious problems during adolescence and beyond.

One of the ways we can help our children overcome their inherent selfishness is to discipline them consistently so that they come to understand that their selfish behavior has consequences. One couple I know utilizes "time out" effectively to accomplish this. When their preschool or elementary-age children misbehave, they are sent to their room for a predetermined amount of time to contemplate their actions. Before the child can resume his activities he is required to tell his mommy or daddy what he did wrong and to present a way to do it right the next time.

They combine this with positive reinforcement. Anytime anyone in the family (parents included) does something good—such as helping with the dishes without being asked or showing courtesy to another—they put a marble in the family marble jar. Once the jar is full, the entire family is rewarded by going out for pizza or ice cream.

Now let's apply this principle to our daily spiritual walk with its ongoing conflict between the almighty "I" and the new man of the spirit. At conversion Jesus takes the almighty "I" captive and assumes His rightful place on the throne of our lives. From His position of authority He now empowers us to "discipline" the almighty "I." We accomplish this as we daily resist life's little temptations, thus keeping this "naughty boy" in his room, as it were.

We do not allow him to come out and play. As a result his influence over us becomes progressively weaker.

Over a period of weeks, months, and years, this "naughty boy" is reduced to a mere shadow of his former self. He is still dangerous to be sure, but he no longer wields the power he once did. Consequently when a significant temptation comes he is in no condition to dominate our will and lead us into sin.

Life itself provides daily opportunities to practice the kind of self-denial that puts the almighty "I" in his place, especially as we interact with others. Arriving at the checkout line the same time as another customer affords us an opportunity to step back and let him go first. Being cut off by another driver in rush hour traffic provides us with an opportunity to exercise patience. Should a coworker slander us we have a choice; we can reciprocate in kind, or we can repay evil with good. Each time we exercise that kind of Spirit-directed self-control we drive a stake in the heart of our archenemy—the almighty "I."

The reason many of us know no consistent victory over sin and temptation is because we do not deal with it at the source. Instead of cutting our sinful desires off at the root by putting the almighty "I" to death, we do battle with the symptoms—lust, materialism, vain ambition, the abuse of power, etc. With superhuman effort we try to bring these degenerate desires under control, but to little avail. Try as we might we cannot long repress our sinful impulses. Although our efforts may be sincere, they are no more effective than the ministrations of a physician who treats the fever rather than the infection that is causing it. Cold packs and aspirin may temporarily lower the patient's temperature, but the fever will continue to plague him until the infection is cleared up.

When it comes to temptation, the root cause is not lust or greed or envy or jealousy, but our fallen nature—our predisposition to sin—what Jim referred to as the almighty "I." Until we do something about it, any victory we experience will be short-lived at best. But if we will daily crucify "the sinful nature [the almighty "I"] with its passions and desires" (Gal. 5:24 NIV), we will find that temptation no longer has the same power over us.

By practicing the spiritual disciplines of the Word, prayer, fellowship, worship, and obedience we can strengthen the new man of the spirit. By doing this consistently we will grow in grace, becoming more and more the victorious person God has destined us to be. In truth, overcoming temptation and the evil within is a cooperative effort between God and man. God *will not* destroy the almighty "I" without our cooperation, and we *cannot* overcome him without God's direct intervention. But together with God we can overcome temptation and live a victorious life. "So I say, live by the Spirit, and you will not gratify the desires of the sinful nature" (Gal. 5:16 NIV).

Reflecting on Him

1. *What face does the almighty "I" wear in your life? In a sense, what is your "spiritual Achilles heel" that you need help with?*

2. *If, as this chapter discusses, the real question is one of doing "my will" versus "God's will," what Scripture verses apply to your almighty "I"? For example, if you have trouble with being argumentative and constantly wanting your own way when dealing with others, then Ephesians 5:21 indicates God's will—"Submit to one another out of reverence for Christ" (NIV). Make a list of the verses that apply to your situation and refer to them when you are tempted.*

3

THE BIG LIE

Roy and Curt were avid hunters. For years they dreamed of hunting big game in Alaska, and now it was finally happening. After securing the services of a bush pilot they flew into the wilderness and set up camp. Once that was done the pilot flew out, promising to return in two weeks.

When he came back to fly them out he discovered he had a problem. Both hunters had filled their big game tags—each had shot an elk and a moose—and there was absolutely no way the pilot's plane was equipped to handle that much weight. As diplomatically as he could he explained the situation.

"Gentlemen," he said, "we've got a problem."

"And what might that be?" asked Curt.

"Your game puts our load way over the weight capacity of my plane. If we try to take it out we will never make it over that mountain at the far end of the lake."

"If you think we are going back without our game," Roy said, "you have another thing coming. We didn't come this far to leave our trophies hanging in a tree!"

"I guess I could make two trips," the pilot replied, "but of course that will cost you."

Looking at him as if he had lost his mind, Curt retorted, "There's no way we're going to pay for an extra trip. You will get all of our stuff on that plane and fly us out of here, or I'll know the reason why!"

"It can't be done," the pilot responded.

"What kind of rip-off is this?" Roy demanded. "We hunted this same place last year, and our pilot flew us out."

23

After considerable discussion the pilot reluctantly agreed to take the two hunters and all of their gear out in one trip, including their game. It took some doing, but they finally got everything into the plane and began taxiing down the lake for takeoff. At the last moment the plane lifted off the water, barely clearing the trees at the end of the lake. Desperately the pilot fought for altitude, but to no avail. As he had predicted, they failed to make it over the mountain.

Crawling out of the wreckage, Curt wiped the blood off of his face, looked around groggily, and asked, "Do you have any idea where we are?"

Roy studied the landscape briefly then replied, "I would say that we are about three hundred yards from where we crashed last year."

Part of the humor of this story comes from the fact that we can all identify with it. Like Roy and Curt we have all made the same dumb decision again and again, only to experience the same disappointing outcome. When it comes to temptation, however, it is not just disappointment we experience, but sinfulness with the accompanying consequences. If we don't learn from the past, we are doomed to repeat it.

Alluding to the Israelites' pilgrimage of faith, the apostle Paul urged us to learn from their mistakes. Although they experienced a special manifestation of God's presence, they nonetheless succumbed to temptation. They lusted after evil things. They worshiped false gods. They participated in sexual immorality, and they tempted God. "All these things happened to them as examples—as object lessons to us—*to warn us against doing the same things; they were written down so that we could read about them and learn from them in these last days as the world nears its end*" (1 Cor. 10:11 TLB).

The Big Lie

Although the Scriptures clearly state that "no temptation has overtaken you except such as is common to man" (1 Cor. 10:13), Satan still tries to convince us that our situation is unique. He tells us that no one has ever been involved in a situation quite like ours. It is not a new line, but it is an effective one. The person who wishes to justify his sinful desires is only too anxious to believe that his situation is the exception, especially if the devil sprinkles his arguments with scriptural references, as he did with Eve in the garden and with Jesus in the wilderness.

The tempter's spiel usually goes something like this:

> You are not a bad person. In fact, compared to most people you are remarkably moral. Under ordinary circumstances you would never consider such a thing, but these are not ordinary times. Of course you are uncomfortable. That's perfectly understandable. Still, it may be helpful to remember that the Scriptures are filled with the accounts of godly men and women who found it necessary to do things they normally would never consider doing.
>
> For instance, Moses told the children of Israel to "borrow" from their Egyptian taskmasters when they were preparing to flee Egypt. Then there's the case of Rahab the harlot. Though the commandments expressly forbid dishonesty, she was commended for lying to the king of Jericho regarding the spies who came into Jericho to spy out the land. All of which just goes to show you that unusual circumstances demand unusual responses.

Of course his pitch will be tailored to fit your personal situation. It will be artfully crafted, designed to push all of the right buttons. Often the deceiver's insidious suggestions seem to come to us as spontaneous thoughts. Let him prime the pump the least little bit, and our imaginations are capable of taking over and creating all kinds of compromising rationale. At other times he speaks to us through the music we listen to, or the books we read, or the movies we watch. And what powerful mediums these are. Thinking we are only being entertained, we lower our guard, never realizing the persuasive power they wield over both our thinking and our appetites.

His most persuasive suggestions, however, usually come from the lips of another—a professor we admire or a colleague we trust. One young man I know was led astray by his employer, a man he greatly admired. Jay was a believer and very big on grace, never missing an opportunity to expound on the freedom of the sons and daughters of God. He was death on legalism, making a mockery of those Christians who based their relationship to Christ on a long list of things they could and could not do. Quoting Scriptures like, "To the pure all things are pure" (Titus 1:15) and "All things are lawful for me" (1 Cor. 6:12), he encouraged his young friend to enjoy his "liberty" in Christ.

Unfortunately Christian liberty soon became license for that young man. Before long his conversation was sprinkled with profanity. He no longer felt it necessary to attend church regularly or to practice the disciplines of Bible reading and prayer. Soon he was experimenting with drugs and alcohol, leading to an addiction that he battles to this day.

As Haddon Robinson points out, when Satan tempts us, "he does not come in the form of a coiled snake. He does not approach with the roar of a lion. He does not come with the wail of a siren. He does not come waving a red flag. Satan simply slides into your life. When he appears he seems almost like a comfortable companion. There's nothing about him that you would dread."[1] That comes later—in the form of remorse and bitter regret.

Rationalization

Once the enemy convinces a person that his situation is unique, and therefore the exception to the rule, it is but a small step to rationalization. With a little help from the tempter he is soon justifying his sinful behavior. For instance, Jim Bakker, the founder of PTL, convinced himself that his illicit tryst with Jessica Hahn wasn't adultery at all. It was simply an attempt to make his wife, Tammy Faye, jealous and to restore her interest in their marriage. Later, when Jessica Hahn approached the ministry demanding a sizable sum of money to keep quiet about their sexual rendezvous, Richard Dortch initiated a cover-up. Like Bakker, he convinced himself that his inappropriate actions were justifiable under the circumstances. He was doing it to save the ministry. Of course, history has fully revealed their self-deception and the resulting consequences. Thankfully both men now understand their folly and have been fully restored, but what a terrible price they paid—public disgrace and imprisonment—for falling prey to the enemy's oldest deceit.[2]

The tempter customizes the process of rationalization for each individual. Based on our temperament and personal history, Satan designs a rational set of arguments to fit our situation. For the unhappy wife, rationalization may go something like this: "My husband doesn't understand me. He never listens to me. His work is more important than I am. It's all he ever wants to talk about."

Then she meets someone who excites her interest, someone who offers the attention she craves, and her rationalization takes a new twist. Now she justifies her budding relationship: "We are only friends, nothing more. The feelings I have for this man have nothing to do with my husband or my marriage. Why shouldn't I enjoy his company? After all, I have had little enough pleasure in my life the last few years." And out of that inner dialogue she finds "good, sound reasons—or reasons that sound good—for disobeying God."[3]

Many a man has thrown himself into his work at the expense of his family and his faith. His rationalization is different from that of the unhappy wife, but no less self-serving. He tells himself it is only for a time, that he is doing it for his family. To his way of thinking he is not being selfish, just conscientious. Once he gets established he will cut back, no more burning the midnight oil or working weekends. After he has made his mark he will have time for the children. They will do things together, go places as a family. Unfortunately by the time he gets established it is often too late. His work owns him, and his children are grown and gone, and maybe his wife is gone too.

For the midlife male, rationalization usually involves a preoccupation with self—my life, my needs, my desires. The enemy often tells him, "You have worked hard all your life, and what has it gotten you? Little or nothing. Less qualified men have been promoted over you. They have the positions you deserve, along with the perks that go with them. Your family sees you only as a money machine. Does your wife want a new outfit? You pay. Do the kids need braces? You pay. Is it time for them to go to college? You pay. Life's not fair. You deserve more than this. Why not think about your needs for a change?"

Of course when a man lets that kind of thinking go unchallenged he exposes himself to all manner of temptation. Now he sees his wife through new eyes. Gone is the youthful beauty he married, and in her place is a matronly woman who no longer excites him. Resentment tempts him. She has taken the best years of his life and given little in return. A sense of desperation grips him. He feels he must do something before it is too late. If he is not careful he may have an affair with a younger woman or quit his job. All because he has been deceived into thinking that life is passing him by. In truth, if he succumbs to this temptation, life *will* pass him by!

The Scriptures are emphatically clear. There are *no* extenuating circumstances, *no* unique situations whereby one can justify his sinful disobedience. "Let no one deceive you with empty words, for because of these things the wrath of God comes upon the sons of disobedience. Therefore do not be partakers with them" (Eph. 5:6–7).

Deceived

On May 19, 1986, a former staff member of Euzoa Bible Church in Steamboat Springs, Colorado, went to jail for embezzling almost $42,000 from the church over a six-year period.[4] When I first learned of his crime I remember thinking, *How could a minister do such a thing?*

I was tempted to conclude that he was an aberration, an impostor, an evil man masquerading as a minister. Such a conclusion made his sinful dishonesty easier to explain. Unfortunately it doesn't fit the facts.

More likely he was a sincere man. No better and no worse than the rest of us. Somewhere along the way he took a wrong turn. Probably it seemed insignificant at the time. Perhaps he padded his expense account or hedged on his income tax return. Or maybe he was short of cash and "borrowed" from church funds until payday. He intended to pay it back, but somehow he never got around to doing it. After a while it was easier just to pretend it had never happened.

Had Satan tempted him to steal $42,000 in one lump sum it is not likely that he would have succumbed. Undoubtedly he considered himself an honest man, and there would have been no way he could reconcile a theft of that magnitude with his image of himself. Therefore Satan tempted him with "insignificant" amounts— twenty dollars here, fifty dollars there. And most likely he convinced himself that it was just a loan; he would pay it back.

The devious ways in which Satan endeavors to entrap us were brought home to me yet again when I had lunch with a friend. Keith is the CEO of a company with annual sales totaling more than twenty million dollars. Over coffee he told me of making several purchases at a well-known office supply store. Arriving home he discovered that a Mont Blanc pen he had purchased was missing. After searching the car to no avail, he returned to the store and explained the situation. The salesclerk insisted that he had placed the pen in the bag and that there was nothing they could do about it. Keith then asked to speak to the manager.

When the manager arrived, Keith repeated his explanation, adding that his company had an account with the store totaling more than fifty thousand dollars in business annually. Of course the manager gave Keith another Mont Blanc pen at no charge and apologized profusely for any inconvenience they might have caused him.

Some weeks later Keith was giving his car a thorough cleaning when he found the original pen beneath a corner of the carpet under the front seat. Though he knew immediately that he should return the pen, he was tempted to keep it. No one would be the wiser. What would it hurt? The loss of one Mont Blanc pen was not going to bankrupt the office supply company. Besides, he reasoned, they should just give him the pen, considering the amount of business his company did with them.

Finally, character prevailed, and Keith returned the pen, to the amazement of the manager. A good thing, too, for there was more at stake here than just a pen. The enemy was making a play for his soul. If he could get Keith to compromise his integrity here, then maybe, just maybe, he could tempt him with something a little more serious next time.

Who knows, but that it was something as trivial as this that started the aforementioned minister down the path of crime that ultimately led to his imprisonment. It is safe, I am sure, to say he did not plan to embezzle from his church. After all, if a man plans to misappropriate funds there are plenty of places more lucrative than a country church. Undoubtedly he backed into it one small compromise at a time. Somewhere along the line he opened his heart to the enemy, and before he knew it he was in over his head. At the time of his resignation he told the congregation, "The depth of the deception is so ingrained, I do not know the scope of the amount of my stealing. I am dependent upon the elders and their audit to know the scope of my sin."[5]

Truth or Consequences

The believer's only defense against the lies of the deceiver is the truth of God's Word. Nothing else will sustain him in the hour of temptation. Not reason, or logic, or even conscience. These are simply no match for the evil one. Even Jesus, when doing battle with the tempter, did not defend Himself with anything but the Word. Three times the enemy attempted to deceive Him and three times He said, "It is written" (Matt. 4:4, 7, 10). If Jesus relied only upon the truth of God's Word, dare we do otherwise?

Conscience is a good thing, and every sincere believer knows its value. Still, our conscience is no match for the enemy. When it comes to discerning right from wrong, we cannot trust our conscience as the final authority. It is too subjective, too easily influenced by our thoughts and feelings.

Years ago a man sought my counsel. "Pastor," he said, "I've met a woman that I believe God wants me to marry. Although she is several years younger than I am, we have many things in common, including our faith."

It seemed he wanted to say more, but his voice trailed off. Hoping to make him feel more comfortable, I asked a few questions about their relationship. How had they met? Did she also feel it was God's will for them to marry? Had they set a date for the wedding?

We talked for a few minutes more, and though it appeared they had everything well thought out, I couldn't help feeling there was something troubling him, something he wasn't telling me.

Finally as he was preparing to leave he dropped the bombshell. "There is only one problem," he said. "She's already married."

Without a moment's hesitation, I opened my Bible and read Exodus 20:17: "You shall not covet your neighbor's house; *you shall not covet your neighbor's wife*, nor his male servant, nor his female servant, nor his ox, nor his donkey, nor anything that is your neighbor's" (emphasis mine).

He started to protest, but I held up my hand and asked him not to say anything until we had looked at a few more Scriptures. Handing him my Bible I asked him to read verse 14. He glanced at it and moved to return my Bible.

"Read it out loud, please."

Reluctantly he read, "You shall not commit adultery" (Ex. 20:14).

Turning to Proverbs 6, I asked him to read verses 27, 28, and 29: "Can a man take fire to his bosom, / And his clothes not be burned? / Can one walk on hot coals, / And his feet not be seared? / So is he who goes in to his neighbor's wife; / Whoever touches her shall not be innocent."

I then asked him to read verse 32: "Whoever commits adultery with a woman lacks understanding; / He who does so destroys his own soul."

Picking up another Bible from my desk I turned to the New Testament and read from Ephesians 5:3, 5–7 (NIV): "But among you there must not be even a hint of sexual immorality, or of any kind of impurity, or of greed, because these are improper for God's holy people. . . . For of this you can be sure: No immoral, impure or greedy person—such a man is an idolater—has any inheritance in the kingdom of Christ and of God. Let no one deceive you with empty words, for because of such things God's wrath comes on those who are disobedient. Therefore do not be partners with them.'"

The root cause of virtually all spiritual failure is disobedience in the little things.

Looking him in the eye I asked, "Do you understand what these verses mean?"

Ignoring my question he said, "But we've prayed about it, and we both feel it is God's will."

Curbing my growing impatience, I attempted to reason with him. "Help me to understand how you think it could possibly be God's will when the Scriptures explicitly forbid it."

"I don't know the Scriptures the way you do," he said, "but I'm sure there must be some explanation, something you are overlooking."

"Are you telling me that you believe God wants you to marry another man's wife in direct violation of His Word?"

"All I know is that we love each other, and that can't be wrong. She should never have married her husband in the first place. It was a mistake. It wasn't the Lord's will. She realizes that now."

I could see there was no reasoning with him, so I moved to bring our conversation to a close. "I can't stop you from doing what you've made up your mind to do, but I urge you to carefully consider your actions in light of God's Word."

Hoping to appease me he replied, "I promise you we will pray about it."

As he turned to leave I said, "A. W. Tozer says that we should never seek guidance about what God has already forbidden. In those instances, what we need is not guidance but obedience." I wish I could tell you that reason prevailed, but I cannot. After that visit to my office, neither of them ever attended our church again. Some weeks later I read of her divorce, and shortly thereafter they were married. I grieved for them, as any pastor would, but I was not surprised by their sinful choice.

Why, you may be wondering, do some people consistently overcome temptation while others repeatedly succumb? Undoubtedly there are a number of reasons, but at the top of the list is spiritual discipline. The person who wants to live an overcoming life doesn't live recklessly, then look for a miracle in the moment of crisis. Rather, he practices the spiritual disciplines of his Lord day by day, thus he is equipped to deal with temptation from a position of spiritual strength, not weakness.

The spiritual disciplines I am referring to include, but are not limited to, a consistent prayer life, daily reading and memorization of the Word, participation in public worship, and obedience in all things, large and small. These disciplines do not make a person spiritually strong in and of themselves; rather, they open him to the transforming power of the Holy Spirit. The disciplines are like paths that lead a person into the presence of God. And it is the manifest presence of the Spirit in a person's life that conforms him to the image of his Lord and empowers him to overcome temptation.

Dallas Willard, in his classic work, *The Spirit of the Disciplines,* says, "We can, through faith and grace, become like Christ by practicing the types of activities he engaged in, by arranging our whole lives around the activities he himself practiced in order to remain constantly at home in the fellowship of his father. . . . Such things as solitude and silence, prayer, simple and sacrificial living, intense study and meditation upon God's Word and God's ways, and service to others."[6]

While it is difficult to emphasize one discipline above another, I feel I must address the matter of obedience as being of utmost importance. *The root cause of virtually all spiritual failure is disobedience in the little things.* Though it may not seem significant at the time, each disobedience, no matter how small, is like a fissure in the wall of a person's soul. Through each tiny crack the acid of evil seeps in and begins to eat away at the foundations of his spiritual character. Over a period of time, his spiritual will is compromised, so that when a crisis of temptation arises he simply does not have the will to resist. To the undiscerning it may appear that he was brought down by that final crisis, but in reality it was the dry rot of disobedience that did him in.

By the same token, each act of obedience, no matter how small, reinforces the foundations of a person's spiritual character. Day by day he is "strengthened with might through His Spirit in the inner man" (Eph. 3:16). When a potentially overwhelming temptation arises he is prepared, for having been obedient in the face of seemingly insignificant temptations, he is now able to be obedient in the moment of crisis. Wisely, Dallas Willard concludes, "A successful performance at a moment of crisis rests largely and essentially upon the depths of a self wisely and rigorously prepared in the totality of its being—mind and body."[7] And obedience is at the heart of that preparation.

Reflecting on Him

1. *American folklore, with its emphasis on "rugged individualism," makes heroes out of individuals who willingly defy group norms in search of individual freedom and success. How does this cultural expectation make it difficult for Christians to accept the mandate to obey God?*

2. *Think of, or describe, an incident in your life where you have experienced feelings of resistance toward authority and anger simply because "no one is going to tell you what to do" — not even the preacher or the Bible. What actions (disciplines) of Jesus provide an example for you to follow so that you can overcome this natural tendency to resist authority?*

3. *What "little things" have you allowed to creep into your life? Identify the ways you have rationalized your actions.*

4

GOD IS FAITHFUL

For all practical purposes it seemed like any other Saturday morning. Neither Brad nor Susan had any way of knowing that their world was about to come crashing down around them. After a light breakfast of fruit and muffins, they took Brad's car to the garage to be serviced. On the way home Susan suggested that they stop at the supermarket and pick up some things for dinner, never realizing that tragedy awaited them.

Since their two-year-old son was asleep in his car seat, Susan decided to stay in the car with the children while Brad picked up the things on their list. Watching him enter the supermarket, shopping list in hand, she couldn't help thinking how blessed they were. Twelve years of marriage had brought them a modest four-bedroom home and three lovely children, not to mention lots of happiness. That Brad enjoyed his work in law enforcement was obvious to all who knew him. For her part, she loved being a wife and mother, though she had to admit that trying to keep up with three active children was a bit overwhelming at times.

Glancing toward the backseat she noted that their youngest was still asleep while his four-year-old brother entertained himself with a toy truck. Thankful for a few minutes of peace and quiet, she picked up her book and was soon engrossed in Patricia Cornwell's newest release. She could not have been reading for more than a few minutes when the sound of a gunshot exploded from the rear of the car.

Brad heard the shot as he was exiting the supermarket. Dropping the groceries he raced to the car and jerked the rear door open. The first thing he saw was his service pistol lying on the floorboard.

For a moment nothing seemed real—not the tearful explanations of his four-year-old: "I didn't mean to, Daddy. I didn't mean to," nor the bloody figure of his two-year-old son, Bobby, nor Susan's piercing shriek.

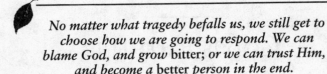

No matter what tragedy befalls us, we still get to choose how we are going to respond. We can blame God, and grow bitter; or we can trust Him, and become a better person in the end.

"Call 9-1-1!" he screamed as he lifted his dying son out of the car seat and cradled him in his arms. By the time the ambulance arrived, the little boy was dead.

Initially shock rendered everything unreal, and Brad and Susan clung desperately to each other. The next four or five days passed in a blur. There were the necessary details: funeral arrangements to be made, a casket to be selected, and a burial plot purchased. Once the funeral was over, however, reality set in and with a vengeance. Family and friends returned to their routines, leaving Brad and Susan to contend with their unspeakable loss and the guilt it birthed.

The shooting was a freak accident. No one's fault, really, yet Brad and Susan found more than enough blame to go around. Without intending to, they each found themselves blaming the other. Why, Susan wanted to know, had Brad left a loaded pistol under the driver's seat in her car without telling her? For his part, Brad couldn't believe that Susan could be in the same car with the children and yet be oblivious to what was going on in the backseat. What was she doing reading a book when she should have been watching them?

Beneath their anger toward each other there lay a deeper, more sinister anger—they were angry at God! At first they refused to acknowledge it, but that did not keep it from eating on their souls. Of course the tempter moved to take advantage of the situation, for there is nothing he likes better than to malign God's character. With insidious cruelty he whispered his malicious lies: "Given the circumstances of your situation you can only conclude that God has the power to prevent such tragedies, but He doesn't care enough to intervene. Or else He cares, but He is powerless to do anything about it. Either way He is hardly a God to be trusted."

In Susan's case his slanderous suggestions fell on deaf ears. Intuitively she understood that God was her only hope. Although she could not explain how He could allow such a terrible thing to happen, she was certain He was not at fault. The greater her grief, the more desperately she clung to Him. Of her it could be said, as it was of Job, "In all this [she] did not sin nor charge God with wrong" (Job 1:22).

Unfortunately Satan found a receptive subject in Brad. His tormented soul proved to be fertile soil for the lies of the enemy, and soon he wanted nothing more to do with God or His people. A few weeks after the funeral, he legally separated from Susan, having found her unwavering faith impossible to bear.

You may be wondering how Brad and Susan could have such diametrically opposite responses to their son's death—a good question and one that cuts to the heart of the issue. There is no easy answer, but experience has taught me that no matter what happens to us, we always have a choice. No matter what tragedy befalls us, we still get to choose how we are going to respond. We can blame God, as Brad did, and grow *bitter;* or we can trust Him, as Susan did, and become a *better* person in the end. VICTOR FRANKLE

The choice a person makes depends upon a number of factors, not the least of which is his perception of God. If he sees God as loving and compassionate, he will likely turn to Him in the hour of temptation and find grace to sustain himself. On the other hand, if he can be persuaded to doubt the goodness of God, he will not trust Him or turn to Him in his hour of need.

The Ultimate Temptation

The tempter's ultimate goal is not simply to solicit our disobedience, but to discredit the character of God. For, to borrow the words of Dr. Haddon Robinson, "Once the well is poisoned, all the water is polluted."[1] To that end the enemy attempts to fill our minds with all manner of evil concerning God.

How he works may best be understood by alluding to the Old Testament story of Ruth and Naomi. To escape the famine in Israel, Elimelech took his wife, Naomi, and his two sons and fled to the country of Moab. He died while in Moab, leaving Naomi to be cared for by their sons. Shortly thereafter, both boys married Moabite women. One of the women was named Orpah and the other, Ruth. For approximately ten years life was good, then both sons died, leaving Naomi alone in a foreign country. After considerable thought she decided to return to her own people.

It was a painful parting for Orpah and she wept bitterly, but it was impossible for Ruth. Desperately she clung to Naomi, pleading, "Entreat me not to leave you, / Or to turn back from following after you; / For wherever you go, / I will go; / And wherever you lodge, I will lodge; / Your people shall be my people, / And your God, my God. / Where you die, I will die, / And there will I be buried" (Ruth 1:16–17).

How Ruth's devotion must have warmed Naomi's heart.

But suppose someone whispered to Naomi, "Naomi, listen, Ruth's a gold digger. She's a manipulator. What Ruth, this Moabitess, really wants to do is get into Israel to marry a wealthy Jew. She knows you are her passport. She'll tell you anything to get a free pass into Israel." *If Naomi believes that, the well is poisoned.* Every good word Ruth speaks, Naomi now suspects. Every kind act Ruth does, Naomi will reject.[2]

Thus does Satan attempt to poison our minds against God. Drawing upon the disappointments and tragedies of life, he fills our minds with all manner of slanderous suggestions—"God is not to be trusted; God plays favorites; God is nothing more than a figment of our imagination"—and once the mind is poisoned all our thoughts are polluted.

If we believe his evil report, *although it is not true*, then God's goodness is suspect, even His very existence. Let misfortune strike, and we immediately conclude that God is against us. Let something happen to our mate, or one of our children, and straightaway we blame God. Like Martha we cry, "Lord, if You had been here, my brother would not have died" (John 11:21). And if we do not go so far as to blame Him, we do suspect Him. We doubt His concern for us. Like the disciples caught in a furious storm at sea, we cry, "Do You not care that we are perishing?" (Mark 4:38). We hear of someone who has experienced a miraculous recovery, and instead of being encouraged, we simply conclude that God plays favorites. Oh, yes, He will do it for someone else, but never for us.

Satan is pleased when he can lead us into disobedience, but that is a small thing compared to discrediting God. Disobedience can be forgiven, the wandering soul restored to fellowship, but if Satan can poison our hearts against God, we may be lost forever. To that end he applies all of his evil genius.

Turning Good into Evil

If Satan can cause us to doubt God's character then even God's blessings will be suspect. This point was driven home to me some years ago when I found myself leading the congregation I served in a major building program. For ten long years the congregation had worshiped in rented facilities, mostly public school auditoriums. That meant setting up on Sunday mornings before the service—hauling in sound equipment and musical instruments for the auditorium, as well as cribs and baby beds for the nursery, not to mention all the supplies for Sunday school and children's church—and then tearing it all down and packing it away on Sunday evenings after the service. A building of our own seemed an impossible dream until God gave us a financial miracle. Some stock in an oil company was sold in the church's name, and we received a check for $429,444.79! With that money we purchased 7.9 acres of land and began construction on a 23,000-square-foot facility.

Our congregation numbered only about 300 at that time and the cost of the total project was nearly 2.5 million dollars—quite a stretch for a church our size, especially back in 1984. We borrowed one million dollars and raised the balance of the money through a capital funds campaign. Still, as construction drew to a close, I realized that we were going to be somewhere between $40,000 and $50,000 short of having enough cash to pay all of the construction costs.

I tried to encourage myself in the Lord by remembering His supernatural provision, but it was no use. Every time I remembered the $429,444.79 check, the enemy would turn the tables on me. "You are on your own this time," he would whisper insidiously. "God has already given you more than your share of financial miracles. You have no right to expect any more help from Him." As a result, instead of being encouraged by God's past faithfulness, I found it a burden.

As we neared the completion of our new facilities, the financial pressures mounted, as did the enemy's attack against God's trustworthiness. Daily he tempted me to doubt the faithfulness of God. In the midst of that battle the Lord gave me a passage of

Scripture. While in prayer, I felt directed to Isaiah 65:21–24. Opening my Bible I read:

> They shall build houses and inhabit them;
> They shall plant vineyards and eat their fruit.
> They shall not build and another inhabit;
> They shall not plant and another eat;
> For as the days of a tree, so shall be the days of My people,
> And My elect shall long enjoy the work of their hands.
> They shall not labor in vain,
> Nor bring forth children for trouble;
> For they shall be the descendants of the blessed of the LORD,
> And their offspring with them.
> It shall come to pass
> That before they call, I will answer;
> And while they are still speaking, I will hear.

As I read that passage, faith leaped in my heart. Immediately I realized it was a word from the Lord for Christian Chapel. Let the enemy rage. Let him hurl his insidious lies against the Lord. Our future was secure! The Lord had spoken. Our labor would not be in vain. We would inhabit our new facilities, and we would long enjoy the work of our hands, and our children after us.

Divine Provision

On a Tuesday evening a few days later I had a most unusual experience. While sitting in the family room at our home, the Lord gave me a vision in which I saw our unfinished auditorium. It looked exactly as it was at the time, except in my vision the red exit lights were already installed above the doors. The auditorium was mostly dark, and I had to strain to see; still, I was able to make out the form of a man pushing a loaded wheelbarrow. I followed him as he took it to a room located on the left side of the platform. When he opened the door, light from the room spilled into the auditorium, and I realized that the wheelbarrow was filled with money, as was the room into which he wheeled it.

Then the vision was over, and the Spirit of the Lord came upon me, and I began to prophesy. Grabbing a pen I wrote, "The Lord is like a man working in the dark, storing up his plunder to be revealed in due season." The whole experience didn't last more than a minute or two, but I knew instantly it was assurance from the Lord regarding His provision for the financial needs of our church, especially as it related to our new facilities. By the Spirit I understood that when the red exit lights went up over the doors in the auditorium, God would manifest His provision. In my enthusiasm I shared the entire experience with our congregation. Excitedly I told them that when the exit lights were installed, God would supernaturally supply our financial needs.

Every day I drove to the construction site to see if the exit lights had been installed yet. A week passed, and then two weeks, and still no exit lights. Finally I asked the building contractor about them. To my chagrin he told me they were on back order and might not arrive for several weeks. And he was right. The exit lights were not installed until six weeks after we moved into our new building.

Well do I remember the morning I arrived at the church and saw the electricians installing them. A part of me rejoiced in anticipation of seeing the Lord's promised financial provision, but I was also assailed with self-doubt. I now questioned whether I had rightly interpreted the significance of the exit lights.

My stomach was in knots as I made my way toward my office. If God didn't come through with a sizable financial miracle *my* credibility would be shot. Although it had seemed like the right thing to do at the time, I now berated myself for my rashness in sharing the vision with the whole congregation.

As I passed my secretary's desk she stopped me. "I made another appointment for this afternoon," she told me. "A student from the Oral Roberts University School of Medicine called and asked to see you. She said it was urgent, but she wouldn't tell me what it was about. All she would say is that the Lord told her to come see you."

Oh, great, I thought, as I entered the office. *All I need is some student who thinks she has a word from the Lord for me.*

The morning passed quickly, and before I knew it my secretary was calling me on the intercom. "Your two o'clock appointment is here," she said.

Picking up the phone, I reminded her to buzz me in ten minutes. I had absolutely no intention of giving this student more than a few minutes of my time.

Entering my office the young woman took a seat and got right to the point. "Pastor Exley," she said, "my great-grandmother passed away recently, and the attorneys have just finished probating her will. Much to my surprise she left me $100,000. I received the check yesterday and during my devotional time the Lord told me to give the tithe to Christian Chapel."

With that, she reached into her purse and extracted a folded check, which she pushed across the desk toward me. Opening it I saw that it was made out to Christian Chapel in the amount of $10,000. Before I could say anything she stood to her feet and said, "If you will excuse me, I have an exam to study for."

After she left I sat at my desk marveling at the goodness of God. How foolish my earlier fears now seemed. How ridiculous the enemy's suggestion that God had no more miracles for us. We still needed more than $30,000, but now my faith was soaring. As I praised the Lord the words of Isaiah came to mind: "It shall come to pass / That *before they call*, I will answer; / And while they are still speaking, I will hear" (Isa. 65:24, emphasis mine).

Two days later another man, a member of our congregation, brought me a check for $33,000, which was the balance of his $50,000 capital funds pledge. When he presented the check he explained that after making his pledge the bottom fell out of the oil market. There was a glut of crude oil, and the price dropped from $20 a barrel to less than $12. As a result he lost a sizable sum of money and was unable to fully pay his pledge. Just the day before, he had received a $33,000 tax refund from the Internal Revenue Service. Although it would have provided needed capital for his business he felt it was only right that he use it to pay the balance of his pledge. After he left I could only marvel at his integrity. He was truly a man of his word.

Once more I praised the Lord for His faithfulness and His perfect timing. In less than forty-eight hours after the exit lights were installed we had the funds to pay all of our construction costs. *God was as good as His word!*

Even more important, the enemy's attack on God's credibility had been rebuffed. Satan had tempted me to doubt God's trustworthiness, but God proved He could be trusted. He would take care of His own. As Paul told the Corinthians, "God is faithful, who will not allow you to be tempted beyond what you are able, but with the temptation will also make the way of escape, that you may be able to bear it" (1 Cor. 10:13).

Never More Than We Can Bear

The tempter is relentless, and no matter how often he is rebuffed he never gives up. If he cannot make us doubt God in one area he will attack us in another, as my wife and I were soon to learn. In short order our family came under tremendous attack. My father underwent open-heart surgery. My wife, Brenda, was involved in a serious automobile accident that left her with a 30 percent permanent disability. Her sister's marriage ended after twenty-two years. And the big one—our only daughter went through a tragic divorce. Watching her suffer was nearly more than we could bear.

It has been noted that divorce is very much like a death, with two or three notable differences. Following the death of a spouse there is grief, but there is not a sense of rejection and loss of self-worth. Loneliness, yes, and loss, to be sure, but the memories of your years together are still intact, untainted. When two people divorce, they are left with nothing but the pain and a host of questions: Was it all a facade? Did he ever really love me? What things were really in his heart when we seemed so happy? Was he even then harboring secret doubts, unspoken desires?

Also when a spouse dies, he or she is dead and gone. When a couple divorces, the relationship is dead, love is dead, the marriage is dead, but the spouse is very much alive. Frequently the divorced person is required to deal with his or her ex-mate for years to come because of the children, and this continued contact can be emotionally wrenching.

Whatever form it takes, deliverance is always a manifestation of God's faithfulness.

Finally, if a person loses a spouse through death, he or she gets sympathy and emotional support during the time of bereavement, at least initially. Divorced persons, on the other hand, are often treated as if they are getting what they deserve. At best, they are left to find their own way—uncondemned perhaps, but ignored.

Leah experienced all of that and more. The plethora of emotions was absolutely overwhelming. The pain was all-consuming. It surrounded her, came at her from all sides. Sometimes it felt like failure—if only she had tried harder, been more accepting, more understanding. Sometimes it felt like the unpardonable sin, as if she would never be without shame again. And sometimes it felt like death. In fact her divorce *was* death: The death of her marriage. The death of her hopes and dreams. The death of what was and what could have been.

A Way of Escape

At times it literally seemed more than she could bear, and suicide tempted her with promises of sweet oblivion. One night, in absolute despair, she locked herself in the bathroom and cried out to God. Desperately she begged Him for some word of encouragement, for some evidence of His continuing love for her. "Help me, Jesus," she prayed, "or let me die. I can't go on like this. This pain is more than I can bear."

Her Bible was in her lap, and when she picked it up it fell open to Psalm 71. Glancing down her eyes were immediately drawn to verses 20 and 21. Through her tears she read, "Though you have made me see troubles, many and bitter, you will restore my life again; from the depths of the earth you will again bring me up. / You will increase my honor and comfort me once again" (NIV).

It was as if the Lord Himself had spoken to her. He had not forsaken her, nor rejected her. She was still His child, and He would restore her life again. God Himself promised to give her comfort, He would remove her shame and restore her honor.

Her pain didn't end that night, nor for a long time after that, *but her sense of hopelessness did.* When the pain returned, as it did from time to time, and the enemy tempted her to despair, she strengthened herself in the Lord. His Word became a way of escape for her. Psalm 71:20–21 became a rock for her to stand on. It was a light in a dark place, a very present help in time of trouble.

Several years have passed since that night, and Leah is now remarried. Recently we were talking when she said, "Dad, I've never been happier or more fulfilled in my life. God has truly restored my life." Pausing, she thought for a moment, then she concluded, "As terrible as my divorce was I would go through it all again if that's what it took to find the love and happiness I now have."

Of course the enemy would like you to believe that God plays favorites, that He ministered to Leah in the dark hour of temptation, but He doesn't care about you. Don't you believe it. What the

Me too Lord!

44

Lord did for Leah He will do for you! His promises are faithful and true. He "knows how to deliver the godly out of temptations" (2 Peter 2:9), and He will deliver you.

Sometimes God makes a way of escape through a special visitation of His Holy Spirit, as He did for me when He gave me the vision of a man with a wheelbarrow full of money. At other times He speaks through His Word, bringing hope and deliverance as he did for Leah in the dark hour of her despair. Others have been delivered from temptation through the counsel of a spiritual friend or through the intercessory prayers of a loved one. Whatever form it takes, deliverance is always a manifestation of God's faithfulness.

I am told that in a certain museum there is a painting called *Checkmate*. The artist painted a chessboard depicting a game in progress. Seated on one side of the board is a young man with a look of desperation on his face. Across from him sits Satan, leering sadistically. The game is over. Satan has won. The young man has been checkmated!

According to the story a certain man returned to the museum day after day. He would stand for hours before that painting, studying it in great detail. Finally, one day, he let out a shout. "It's not checkmate!" he cried. "It's not checkmate!"

Soon a crowd gathered to see what the commotion was all about. Excitedly he told them, "I'm a chess master. I've studied this picture for days now, and if the young man moves this piece to that square, he escapes checkmate."

Perhaps you feel checkmated at this time in your life. The enemy came against you, and not knowing how to resist him, you fell into his trap. Now your life is a mess. Your most important relationships are on the rocks, and your personal life is in shambles. With cunning cruelty the enemy suggests that God has washed His hands of you, that He wants nothing more to do with you. Now you find yourself tempted, not only to doubt God's love, but His very existence. From where you sit it looks like checkmate for sure.

Left to your own devices, it is over. But it doesn't have to be. The eternal chess master—Jesus Christ—can turn your situation around. He will make a way of escape for you if you will call upon Him. It gives Him great pleasure to spoil the enemy's evil plans. "For this purpose the Son of God was manifested, that He might destroy the works of the devil" (1 John 3:8).

Reflecting on Him

1. *Can you recall a time in your life when you felt betrayed by God?*

2. *Can you recall a time in your life when you were overwhelmed with feelings of gratitude toward God and a sense of being unworthy of His marvelous blessings?*

3. *How did your perception of God differ in these two experiences?*

4. *The latter part of the chapter relates how God provided Leah with a promise from His Word (Ps. 71:20–21). Whether you are a new or experienced Christian, God provides individual promises to each of us. What Scriptures come to mind when you think of the promises of God? Take a moment and jot down each one as completely as you can. Keep this list with you in your purse or wallet and whenever the enemy attempts to discredit God, take it out and reread His promises to you.*

THE THREE FACES
OF TEMPTATION

There is really only one temptation, and that temptation is to choose self-will over God's will. Although all temptation is rooted in this evil desire, it wears many faces. Most often it comes disguised as a need to prove our self-worth, or as a temptation to use God rather than serve Him, or as the lust for wealth and power. When Satan tempted Jesus in the wilderness, it was to these three areas that he appealed, for they encompass the full range of human experience.

THE THREE FACES
OF TEMPTATION

5

The Son of Man

Come with me into the wilderness west of the Jordan River. Here the terrain is jagged and warped, bleached nearly gray by a merciless sun, dotted here and there with gnarled and twisted trees. It is a desolate place, empty and foreboding, with barren hills jutting into a nearly white sky. To the south they drop twelve hundred feet to the lowest spot on the face of the earth, at the very edge of the Dead Sea. There the heat is unbearable, rising in simmering waves from the scorched landscape.

I cannot imagine spending forty days and nights alone in such a place without food or water, but that is exactly what Jesus did. Mark says, "And He was there in the wilderness forty days, tempted by Satan, and was with the wild beasts" (Mark 1:13).

Put yourself in Jesus' place if you can. Hardly had the spiritual and emotional high of His baptism waned before the Spirit drove Him into the wilderness, where He found Himself doing battle with the devil. Now there was no prophetic word from John the Baptist to bear witness to His mission, no adoring crowds to encourage Him, and no audible voice of the Father to affirm Him. Stripped of every human comfort, alone with the wild beasts, He waged war with the enemy of our souls. For forty days and nights He suffered every temptation imaginable, yet He did not break. Afterward, He was exhausted.

Never had He been more vulnerable. Physically, He was dehydrated, having fasted for nearly seven weeks. Starvation had slowed His bodily functions, leaving Him weak and susceptible to depression. His mental processes were numbed, and He was prone to suggestibility, making Him vulnerable to brainwashing and mind control. Starvation, sleep deprivation, and isolation had weakened His will, making Him especially susceptible to psychological manipulation. And, as any prisoner of war will attest, under such conditions honorable men have been known to break, confessing to spying or other things they did not do.

All of this Jesus voluntarily endured, and more, in order "that He might be a merciful and faithful High Priest in things pertaining to God. . . . For in that He Himself has suffered, being tempted, He is able to aid those who are tempted" (Heb. 2:17, 18).

Unfortunately, many of us have little or no appreciation for the things Jesus suffered while being tempted. Since He is the Son of God there is a tendency to dismiss His temptations as inconsequential, to assume that He didn't really have to struggle to resist evil as we do. But if that were the case He could not be truly "touched with the feeling of our infirmities" (Heb. 4:15 KJV), nor could He understand what we are going through when we are tempted (Heb. 2:18). If He did not truly struggle with temptation then His victory over the tempter's enticements is compromised, and His grounds for helping us in the hour of our temptation are suspect.

The source of our inability to allow the temptations of Jesus to be as real as our own is, at least in part, our unwillingness to believe that He was truly human. Although we pay lip service to the Incarnation, few of us ever consider its far-reaching ramifications. While liberal theologians struggle to accept the deity of Jesus, evangelical believers are hard-pressed to come to terms with His humanity. Yet both are equally true and of utmost importance. Jesus is both the Son of God and the Son of man!

Fully Human

The Scriptures are emphatically clear: Although Jesus was divine, He was also fully human. When He lived on this earth He was not God in a human disguise, rather He was very man of very man. "In all things He had to be made like His brethren" (Heb. 2:17).

Paul explains it this way: "His state was divine, yet he did not cling to his equality with God but *emptied himself* to assume the condition of a slave, and *became as men are;* and being as all men are, he was humbler yet, even to accepting death, death on a cross" (Phil. 2:6–8 Jerusalem Bible, emphasis mine).

Though Jesus was *in every way one with God,* He "emptied" Himself and became one of us. He did not empty Himself of His divine nature or essence. Rather, as the Phillips Modern English translation states, He "stripped himself of every advantage" (Phil. 2:7). He voluntarily relinquished every advantage of His divine nature in order to become a full-fledged human being. He was still very God of very God, but He freely chose to live life as a man in order to fulfill the righteous requirements of the Father's holy law.

Although I long understood His humanity from a theological perspective, I never allowed it to become "real" to me. All of that changed one afternoon, nearly twenty years ago, while reading Frederick Buechner's *Peculiar Treasures.* Suddenly I found myself weeping, so completely could I identify with Jesus as Buechner presented Him. The Jesus he wrote about was so exhausted by the demands of ministry that He fell asleep the minute He got into the boat (Mark 4:35–41). He must have been dead to the world because Mark says the storm didn't wake Him, not even when the waves started washing in over the sides of the boat. In the margin of my book I wrote in red pen, "Dear God He must have been tired!" Later when I read it to a friend, I broke down and wept again.

That experience stayed with me for several days, and I found myself puzzling over the apparent paradox of Mark 4. As a man, Jesus was so physically exhausted that He slept through a life-threatening storm, yet as the divine Son of God He commanded the winds and waves to cease, and they obeyed Him. Why, I wondered, didn't He use His divine power to rejuvenate Himself? Or for that matter, why didn't He use it to keep from getting tired in the first place?

Slowly it begin to dawn on me. Although Jesus was omnipotent He refused to exercise His divine power on His own behalf; He only used it for the benefit of others. For instance, He refused to turn stones into bread to feed Himself, but He multiplied the five loaves and two fish in order to feed the five thousand (Matt. 14:15–21). When it came to His earthly existence—His physical and spiritual needs—He voluntarily limited Himself to the resources that are available to all of us.

Throughout the Gospels there is this contrast between Jesus' deity and His humanity. We seldom see one without the other. As the Son of man, He is baptized by John in the Jordan River. As the Son of God, He baptizes others in the Holy Spirit. As the Son of man, He prays to the Father. As the Son of God, He hears the prayers of others and forgives their sins. As the Son of man, He weeps with Mary following the death of her brother. As the Son of God, He raises Lazarus from the dead. As the Son of man, He dies on the cross and is buried. As the Son of God, He conquers death, hell, and the grave!

Given the glory of His deity, it is not hard to see why we would be drawn to it at the expense of His humanity. Still it is to our detriment, for only as we grasp what it means for Jesus to be fully human can we truly appreciate what He has done for us. "In the beginning was the Word, and the Word was with God, and the Word was God. . . . And the Word became flesh and dwelt among us, and we beheld His glory, the glory as of the only begotten of the Father, full of grace and truth" (John 1:1, 14).

Think of it. The divine, eternal, preexistent Word became flesh not at the moment Mary gave birth in Bethlehem's shabby stable, but nine months earlier when the Holy Spirit came upon her and the power of the Highest overshadowed her. In that holy moment Mary conceived, and the eternal Word became a microscopic zygote clinging to the wall of her womb.

The eternal preexistent Creator, the One through whom all things were made and without whom nothing was made that was made (John 1:3), was now Himself the product of conception, albeit a supernatural one (Luke 1:35). Eternal God, the incomprehensible "I AM WHO I AM," had now become the most dependent, the most defenseless of all human beings—a fetus in the womb.

Jesus did not come into the world as a full-grown, fully mature man, but as a helpless baby with all the weaknesses and limitations of any other baby. Does a baby know how to walk when he is born? No. Does a baby know how to talk when he is born? Not hardly. Does a baby have memories, or an understanding of the world into which he has been born, or a cognitive understanding of God? Of course not. That being the case, does it not stand to reason that baby Jesus came into the world with these same limitations? If He was truly "made like his brothers in every way"

(Heb. 2:17 NIV), doesn't that mean He was born with no more understanding of self or the world around Him than any other newborn has at the moment of birth?

What does a newborn babe suckling at his mother's breast know about his calling, his ultimate purpose in life? Nothing at all. His worldview is limited to the sound of his mother's voice, the warmth of her arms, and the nourishment he takes at her breast. The knowledge that there is more to the world than this comes in bits and pieces over a period of weeks, months, and even years. The sense of his life's purpose is even slower coming into focus and often doesn't become clear until late adolescence or even early adulthood.

Was it not the same for Jesus? Did He not experience the developmental stages of growth common to every child? Isn't this what Luke the physician means when he writes, "The Child grew and became strong in spirit, filled with wisdom; and the grace of God was upon Him" (Luke 2:40)? A little later he says, "And Jesus increased in wisdom and stature, and in favor with God and men" (Luke 2:52).

Only in God can we find our true identity and value as persons. His every word—not our accomplishments—defines us.

By laying aside every advantage of His divine nature, did not Jesus the omniscient One voluntarily strip Himself of every memory of His eternal existence as very God of very God? Doesn't it seem logical that His earliest memories were a mosaic of Bethlehem, Egypt, and Nazareth? In eternity past He participated in the formulation of redemption's plan, but as a child it hardly seems likely that He had any conscious knowledge of it or the part He was destined to play; that would be revealed to Him by the Spirit as He grew older. As a child, if He thought about the future at all, He most likely dreamed of becoming a carpenter like His earthly father, Joseph.

Eventually Jesus would come to understand His unique relationship to both God and man, but it is unlikely that this knowledge was inherent to the Son of man. Since finding God's will for our lives and walking it out by faith is an area in which Satan tempts nearly all of us, it seems logical that Jesus had to be tempted on these same points as well. If He came into the world with an inherent knowledge of redemption's plan and His part in it, He could hardly be tempted in these areas. And if He wasn't tempted regarding God's plan for His life, then it cannot be said that He was tempted in all ways as we are. More likely, He came to understand His special destiny through the things His mother told Him, through the study of Scripture, and from the revelation of the Holy Spirit. Little by little He came to understand that while He was like other boys, He wasn't like them exactly. He was unique and God had a special plan for His life. By the time He was twelve years old, things were beginning to come into focus (Luke 2:49). But it wasn't until He returned from doing battle with the devil in the wilderness, at age thirty, that He fully understood His life's purpose. Then and only then did He announce His mission (Luke 4:14–21).

Fully Tempted

And because He was fully human, He was subject to the same passions as other men. He had the same needs and desires, the same drives that are common to all of us, except those urges and temptations that come from within as a result of our fallen nature. He developed naturally and participated in the full range of human experience. Most of all, He had the freedom of choice. Therefore the Scriptures declare, "We do not have a High Priest who cannot sympathize with our weaknesses, but was in all points tempted as we are, yet without sin" (Heb. 4:15).

As has already been stated (Chapter 2), there is really only one temptation, and that temptation is to choose self-will over God's will. Although all temptation is rooted in this evil desire, it wears many faces. Most often it comes disguised as a need to prove our self-worth, or as a temptation to use God rather than serve Him, or as the lust for wealth and power. When Satan tempted Jesus in the wilderness, it was to these three areas that he appealed, for they encompass the full range of human experience.

Satan did not approach Jesus with these three temptations until the Son of man was on the verge of collapsing. After forty days without food His body was well on its way to shutting down. Mentally and emotionally He was at a breaking point, having battled the hordes of hell, day and night, for nearly seven weeks. Just when

He thought His wilderness experience was over Satan returned with a vengeance. "And the devil said to Him, 'If You are the Son of God, command this stone to become bread'" (Luke 4:3).

Physically, Jesus was weak from hunger. Psychologically and spiritually, He was still coming to grips with what it meant to be the Savior of the world. Satan's approach appealed to both areas. And as David L. McKenna pointed out, "A legitimate appeal to a natural desire is the most subtle snare for sin."[1]

At first glance Satan's suggestion seemed innocent enough, even logical. By turning stones to bread Jesus could satisfy His physical hunger, while proving He truly was the Son of God. With a single miracle He could settle both issues, or so it seemed.

On closer examination, however, there was nothing innocent about the tempter's appeal. By casting doubt on the deity of Jesus he called the character of the Father into question—a tactic he has used from time immemorial. Immediately before entering the wilderness Jesus had been baptized by John in the Jordan River. Following His baptism God spoke from heaven in an audible voice, saying, "You are My beloved Son; in You I am well pleased"(Luke 3:22). Now Satan tempted Jesus to prove His sonship rather than trust the Father's Word, to validate Himself rather than find His identity in the Father's affirmation.

"But Jesus answered him, saying, 'It is written, "Man shall not live by bread alone, but by every word of God"'" (Luke 4:4). In other words, only in God can we find our true identity and value as persons. His every word—not our accomplishments—defines us. To attempt to prove our self-worth is an exercise in futility that leads to all kinds of temptations.

In the second temptation Satan again appealed to a legitimate need. As the Messiah, Jesus would be given power to rule the earth, and of His kingdom there would be no end. Now the enemy offered Him a shortcut: Jesus wouldn't have to suffer and die in order to be highly exalted, as God's plan required. "And the devil said to Him, 'All this authority I will give You, and their glory; for this has been delivered to me, and I give it to whomever I wish. Therefore, if You will worship before me, all will be Yours'" (Luke 4:6–7).

Was Jesus vulnerable to this temptation? Undoubtedly, for Satan attacks us only in those areas where we are susceptible. Knowing that Jesus came from an impoverished background—He was born in a manger, trained as a carpenter, and reared in a town that had a reputation for producing nothing good—this temptation surely had a powerful appeal to Him. It's quite likely that Satan bombarded Jesus' mind with a hundred ways He could use His power for good rather than evil. Yet Jesus did not succumb.

"And Jesus answered and said to him, 'Get behind Me, Satan! For it is written, "You shall worship the LORD your God, and Him only you shall serve"'" (Luke 4:8).

The third and final temptation was an attempt to get Jesus to use God rather than serve Him. "Then he brought Him to Jerusalem, set Him on the pinnacle of the temple, and said to Him, 'If You are the Son of God, throw Yourself down from here. For it is written: "He shall give His angels charge over you, / To keep you," and, "In their hands they shall bear you up, / Lest you dash your foot against a stone"'" (Luke 4:9–11).

Notice that this temptation was also carefully couched in legitimacy. What better way to launch His God-given ministry than with a spectacular display of supernatural power. Especially since a rabbinical tradition reads, "When the King Messiah reveals Himself, then He comes and stands on the roof of the Holy Place."[2]

At the corner of the temple where the royal porch and Solomon's porch met was a drop of 450 feet into the valley of the brook Kidron. It's not hard to imagine what an impression Jesus would have made had He chosen to launch His ministry in this way. With hundreds, perhaps thousands, watching from the temple courts below, including the most influential religious leaders of the day, He would have gained immediate credibility. With angels sweeping in from the four corners of the earth to catch Him just before He crashed to His death, who could have doubted His messianic claims?

But it was not God's way, and in rejecting it Jesus also rejected all the myriad ways in which the enemy tries to tempt us to use God rather than serve Him. "And Jesus answered and said to him, 'It has been said, "You shall not tempt the LORD your God"'" (Luke 4:12).

Of course this was not the first time Jesus had been tempted, nor was it the last. Since the Scriptures teach that He was "in all points tempted as we are" (Heb. 4:15), we can be sure that He experienced all of the temptations that are common to each stage of human development. As a young person He was undoubtedly tempted with the things that tempt all young people: peer pressure, self-doubt, sexual awakenings, selfishness, deceitfulness, disobedience, and temper, to name just a few. As an adult He continued to deal with temptation, only on a different level—one that was in keeping with His spiritual and emotional maturity. Now He was tempted with materialism and selfish ambition, with inappropriate relationships and ethical issues. There were times when disillusionment dogged His steps and He was tempted to despair, but through it all He remained faithful. Not once did He yield to temptation or fall prey to Satan's snare.

Fully Triumphant

The scriptural record is clear: Jesus was without sin! He triumphed over every temptation, defeated the devil at every turn. God the Father testified to His faithfulness: "This is My beloved Son, in whom I am well pleased" (Matt. 17:5). Peter, who knew Him intimately, having lived with Him for three years, said He "committed no sin, / Nor was deceit found in His mouth" (1 Peter 2:22). John the Beloved gives a similar testimony. He said, "In Him there is no sin" (1 John 3:5). Of Jesus the apostle Paul wrote that He "knew no sin" (2 Cor. 5:21).

Jesus was able to resist every temptation, not because He was divine, but because He was prepared.

Even Jesus' enemies acknowledged His sinlessness. Theirs was not testimony given willingly, but grudgingly, wrung from their lips by the sheer weight of irrefutable evidence. Judas, His betrayer, said, "I have sinned by betraying innocent blood" (Matt. 27:4). Pilate, the Roman governor who sought for a reason to condemn Him, finally acknowledged, "I find no fault in this Man" (Luke 23:4). Even the centurion in charge of Jesus' execution was forced to concede that He "was a righteous Man!" (Luke 23:47).

By remaining obedient to God in the face of every temptation, Jesus defeated Satan, thus making a way for all humankind to triumph over him as well. Through His faithful obedience the Son of man also completely fulfilled the righteous requirements of an altogether holy God. And by becoming "obedient to the point of death, even the death of the cross" (Phil. 2:8), He fully satisfied the just demands of almighty God, thus paying the penalty for the sins of every human being—past, present, and future.

Without His sinless life the sacrificial death of Jesus would have been in vain, satisfying the justice of God but not the righteous requirements of His holy law. By the same token, His sinless life, apart from His sacrificial death, would also have been in vain, satisfying the righteous requirements of God's holy law but not His justice. Only by becoming a man could Jesus resist temptation and faithfully fulfill the requirements of God's holy law. Only by dying as the innocent for the guilty could He satisfy the justice of God and make atonement for sin. Only through death could He "destroy him who had the power of death, that is, the devil, and release those who through fear of death were all their lifetime subject to bondage" (Heb. 2:14–15).

Because Jesus was fully human He became a compassionate High Priest, merciful and faithful (Heb. 2:17). Because "He Himself has suffered, being tempted, He is able to aid those who are tempted" (Heb. 2:18). And because He "was in all points tempted as we are, yet without sin" (Heb. 4:15), "He is also able to save to the uttermost those who come to God through Him, since He always lives to make intercession for them" (Heb. 7:25).

Having explored the meaning and the mystery of our Lord's humanity we now turn our attention to the specifics of His encounter with the devil. In the next three chapters we will see how He met and conquered temptation. From His experience we will gain insight into our own spiritual struggles and learn how to overcome the temptations that beset us. We will discover that Jesus was able to resist every temptation, not because He was divine, but *because He was prepared.* And we will come to realize that by practicing the spiritual disciplines that Jesus practiced—prayer, study, worship, and obedience—we, too, can be delivered from temptation.

Reflecting on Him

1. *Can you recall a time in your life when you experienced a significant spiritual victory or were part of an outstanding worship service? For most of us, an event like this is usually followed by an emotional letdown and a temptation to minimize its significance. How do your experiences mirror those of Jesus following His baptism?*

2. *To make it personal and real when the Bible states that Jesus ". . . was in all points tempted as we are, yet without sin," please complete a series of sentences that state the things that tempt you now or tempted you in your past. Then write a second sentence where you substitute Jesus' name for your own. For example, they might go something like this:*

   (Your temptation)—I am tempted to lose my temper and shout at others.

   (Jesus' temptation)—Jesus was tempted to lose His temper and shout at others.

   (Your temptation)—I am tempted to ignore the needs of my family when I am tired.

   (Jesus' temptation)—Jesus was tempted to ignore the needs of His family when he was tired.

   Write as many as you can. In your private time with God, it will benefit your comprehension of Jesus as the Son of man to be as embarrassingly specific as you can in acknowledging your temptations (for example, of a sexual nature, in being selfish, the desire to win at all costs, those feelings of hatred toward others, etc.). When you then fill in the name of Jesus with these same temptations it becomes clear that He can identify with each of us.

3. *The Scripture quoted in question two ends with the phrase, "yet without sin." What temptations in your life can you recall where this statement is true about you also? Can you see that it is through His presence in our daily lives that we, too, can be tempted "yet without sin"?*

4. *According to this chapter, what is the one critical strategy (available to each of us today) that Jesus used to successfully resist the temptations of the devil following His time in the wilderness?*

6

IN SEARCH OF
SIGNIFICANCE

Although Jesus was divine, He was also fully human when He lived among us—not carnal, but human. Having been supernaturally conceived (Luke 1:34–35) and born of a virgin (Matt. 1:18–25), He was not tainted by original sin. Within Him was no inherent sinful nature, no predisposition to do evil. Still, as a full-fledged participant in our humanity (Heb. 2:14–18) Jesus did battle with the same temptations that torment us (Heb. 4:15). Chief among them was the temptation to prove His value as a person by His accomplishments. It was the first of the three recorded temptations detailed in His wilderness encounter with the devil. Luke described it: "And in those days He ate nothing, and afterward, when they had ended, He was hungry. And the devil said to Him, '*If You are the Son of God,* command this stone to become bread'" (Luke 4:2–3, emphasis mine).

Let there be no mistake. This temptation was not about hunger, though Jesus was indeed hungry, nor was it about turning stones into bread. These were just the surface issues, the trappings. At its core this temptation challenged the very foundations of who Jesus was. It was designed to cast doubt on both His personhood and His mission. As such it tempted Him to *prove Himself,* to use His divine power for purely personal gain.

Although this was the first time this temptation was recorded in Scripture, it is not likely that it was the first time Jesus had had to deal with questions regarding His self-worth. As a boy growing up in Nazareth, He undoubtedly heard whispers regarding the legitimacy of His birth. It would be just like children to tell Him that Joseph wasn't His real father, repeating things they had heard their parents say. Childhood experiences of this nature wound the spirit, leaving festering pockets of self-doubt.

The Roots of Self-Doubt

The comedian Dick Gregory related a painful episode from his childhood that is a case in point. It occurred one Friday afternoon as the school day was drawing to a close. His teacher was asking each student how much his or her father would give to the community chest. It was an embarrassing time for Dick since he lived in a single-parent family, with no idea who his father was. As each child's name was called he seemed to withdraw within himself, sinking lower in his seat, dreading the moment when the teacher would call his name.

Suddenly he had an idea. He would buy himself a daddy. He had money in his pocket from shining shoes and selling papers, and whatever Helen Tucker (the richest kid in class) pledged for her daddy, he was going to top it. And he would hand the money right in. He wasn't going to wait until Monday to buy himself a daddy. No sir!

The teacher called Helen Tucker's name.

With a clear voice she answered, "My daddy said he'd give two dollars and fifty cents."

That made Dick feel pretty good. It wouldn't take too much to top that. He had almost three dollars in dimes and quarters in his pocket. He stuck his hand in his pocket and held on to the money, waiting for the teacher to call his name. But she closed her book after calling every child's name but his.

Standing up, Dick raised his hand.

"What is it now?" his teacher asked impatiently.

"You forgot me."

Turning toward the blackboard she said, "I don't have time to be playing with you, Richard."

Fighting back tears of rage and humiliation, Dick said, "My daddy said he'd . . ."

"Sit down, Richard, you're disturbing the class."

"My daddy said he'd give . . . fifteen dollars."

The teacher turned around and looked angry. "We are collecting this money for you and your kind, Richard Gregory. If your daddy can give fifteen dollars you have no business being on relief."

"I got it right now, I got it right now," Dick cried. "My daddy gave it to me to turn in today, my daddy said . . ."

"And furthermore," she said, looking right at him, "we know you don't have a daddy."[1]

Perhaps his teacher was being cruel, but more likely she was just insensitive, unaware of how desperately Dick needed to feel a part of the class. Whatever the reason, the damage was done. Her reckless words shamed him, and it was a long time before he got over his humiliation.

The psychological wounds most of us suffer are less severe than his; still, we are haunted with self-doubt. Your father teased you about having knobby knees or being overweight. You were repeatedly thumped on the head for eating with your mouth open. You were told time and again that you would never amount to anything. Soon you began to see yourself as unworthy, and no amount of success in later life could totally free you from the long shadow of inferiority.

And there was more: A beloved parent betrayed your innocence, and you blamed yourself. A trusted friend let you down, and you assumed responsibility. Rejection followed rejection, grinding your flagging self-esteem beneath the calloused heel of disappointment. Each painful experience simply reinforced the growing conviction that you were a person of little worth.

When you find yourself struggling with feelings of worthlessness, you may be tempted to think it is only the spiritually weak or emotionally wounded who battle with self-doubt, therefore you must be one or both. Of course such faulty reasoning only reinforces your self-deprecation, which in turn tempts you to try all the harder to prove you are a person of significance. It is a vicious cycle, one that will eventually rob life of its meaning and, if you cannot resolve it, perhaps even cause you to make shipwreck of your faith.

It is helpful to remember that you are not alone. To one degree or another every human being, including the Son of man, has had to deal with the issue of significance. How you answer the question regarding your value as a person will go a long way toward determining the quality of your life and your eternal destiny. If you base your significance on how others perceive you, you will be forced to live your entire life on tiptoe. Everything you do will be an attempt to measure up, to please someone else. If you perceive that your self-worth is based on personal achievement, you can never stop proving yourself. No matter what you accomplish, it will never be enough.

Is there another solution to this age-old question of self-worth? Yes, and it is found right here in our Lord's response to the devil in His first wilderness temptation: "It is written, 'Man shall not live by bread alone, but by every word of God'" (Luke 4:4). With these thoughts in mind, let's take a closer look at how Jesus dealt with this issue.

The First Temptation

Although the entire forty days and nights that Jesus spent in the wilderness were a time of doing battle with the devil (Luke 4:2), they were followed by three specific temptations, each carefully crafted to strike at a point where Jesus was most vulnerable. The first temptation (Luke 4:2–3) was a two-pronged attack appealing to both His physical hunger and His need to prove Himself: "And the devil said to Him, 'If you are the Son of God, command this stone to become bread'" (Luke 4:3).

This temptation really had little to do with physical hunger, though Jesus was indeed hungry. It was not about turning stones into bread; it went deeper than that. By calling the deity of Jesus into question, Satan struck at the foundations of our Lord's self-esteem. Would Jesus look to the Word of the Father—"You are My beloved Son"—for His validation, or would He try to prove His self-worth by turning stones into bread? Would He trust His identity to the Father, or would He trust in His own accomplishments? That's what this temptation was about!

Given the fact that Jesus is divine—very God of very God—it may be difficult for you to understand how Jesus could have doubts regarding His deity. That's understandable. It is only natural to assume that He was untroubled by such things. Because He possesses all the attributes of deity—being omnipotent, omnipresent, and omniscient—it is logical to believe He entered the world with an inherent knowledge of *who* He was and *what* His mission was. A careful study of the Word, however, may lead one to conclude that being divine did not make Him immune to temptations in these areas. It seems not only possible, but likely, that Jesus was tempted with self-doubt and questions regarding His identity, since these very issues are at the core of humanity's struggle. How else can we say He "was in all points tempted as we are, yet without sin" (Heb. 4:15)?

It is helpful for me to remember that being omnipotent did not prevent Jesus from experiencing the weaknesses of His physical body. Though He was divine, He required food and rest just like any human being. Nor did His being omnipresent release Him from the limits that time and space placed upon Him. As a man He could only be in one place at a time. In view of this, is it not logical to assume that the fact that He was omniscient did nothing to free Him from the limitations of His human mind?

If that is the case, we can assume that Jesus struggled to comprehend how He could be both the Son of man and the Son of God. When He emptied Himself of every advantage of His divine nature (Phil. 2:6–8), that likely included any conscious knowledge of His eternal existence as very God of very God. Nor is it likely that He retained any inherent understanding of His redemptive mission. It may well be that all He came to know about His unique relationship to God and man He learned from His parents, from His study of Scripture, and from the inner witness of the Holy Spirit. If this was the case, we can be sure it was a tenuous process and one fraught with inner turmoil—and a likely place for Satan to attack Him!

As a child He may have readily believed He was the Son of God. Spiritual truths are often taken at face value by the very young, especially if they are communicated by a loving parent. This would explain His seemingly impertinent response to Mary and Joseph when they found Him in the temple at age twelve: "Why did you seek Me? Did you not know that I must be about My Father's business?" (Luke 2:49). He may have thought that they should know what He was doing. After all, most likely they were the source of His knowledge regarding His birth (Luke 2:19, 51) and His special relationship to the Father.

However, things that are easy to believe at age twelve become increasingly difficult as we grow older. Life becomes more complex; things are not as simple as they once seemed. Though Jesus still believed He was the Son of God, He now spent countless hours in the synagogue, poring over the Scriptures in an attempt to find objective proof of His deity. As He worked in the carpenter shop, His mind wrestled with the far-reaching ramifications of His life mission. What exactly did it mean to be the Savior of the world? How would He accomplish this?

By the time He departed the carpenter shop to begin His ministry at age thirty, He had probably settled the issue in His heart, at least insofar as it could be. It was likely that He now had a clear vision of the big picture, although the details probably remained hidden. And still there may have been times when He wondered if He truly was the Only Begotten Son of God. It could hardly have been otherwise if He was truly made like us in every way (Heb. 2:14–18).

Knowing His inner struggles, the Father provided special confirmation. When John the Baptist saw Jesus approaching to be baptized he said, "Behold! The Lamb of God who takes away the sin of the world!" (John 1:29). How Jesus' heart must have leaped at those words, so reminiscent of the things Mary and Joseph had told Him as a child.

> And John bore witness, saying, "I saw the Spirit descending from heaven like a dove, and He remained upon Him. I did not know Him, but He who sent me to baptize with water said to me, 'Upon whom you see the Spirit descending, and remaining on Him, this is He who baptizes with the Holy Spirit.' And I have seen and testified that this is the Son of God." *(John 1:32–34)*

As meaningful as John's testimony was it could not compare with the subsequent confirmation of the Father. After Jesus was baptized, "a voice came from heaven which said, 'You are My beloved Son; in You I am well pleased'" (Luke 3:22). There would be other times when the Father repeated that confirmation (Matt. 17:5), but nothing could match the first time. It was the special revelation that Jesus needed to move forward with confidence.

In the first wilderness temptation, all of this was called into question. Everything that Jesus believed about Himself, everything that He was, was challenged by the enemy. "And the devil said to Him, 'If You are the Son of God, command this stone to become bread'" (Luke 4:3).

Though He was physically and emotionally wasted, Jesus did not fall prey to the enemy's trap. Instead of being baited into turning stones into bread He said, "It is written, 'Man shall not live by bread alone, but by every word of God'" (Luke 4:4). By refusing to be tempted into *proving* who He was He settled the issue once and for all. He would not use His divine power to benefit Himself, but only for the good of others. He would not build His identity on personal achievements, but only on the Word of the Father: "You are My beloved Son" (Luke 3:22). Personal achievements will pass away, but the Word of the Father is established forever (Ps. 119:89).

The account of this temptation is included in Scripture, not simply because it was so critical to the formation of our Lord's character, but also because it goes to the heart of our human condition. Most of us are born with self-doubts that are exacerbated by the emotional wounds we suffer while growing up. Consequently we question our value as persons. We question our value and our place in our family circle. We question our value to our spouse, to our friends, to our employer, to our church, and to our pastor. And most of all we doubt our value to God. As a result we spend much of our life trying to prove our worth.

Though I possess a reasonably healthy self-esteem, I still see self-doubt and the accompanying need to prove myself at work in my own life. I've written about it in my prayer journal for years. In my experience it wears many faces—the egomaniac who talks too much; the proud, presumptuous me; the pseudospiritual me; the critical, cutting me;—but at the core it is ever the same. I'm talking about that part of me that constantly questions my value as a person. That part of me that always feels a need to measure up, to prove myself, to show how important I am. It is my way of shouting to the world: Look at me. Notice me. Make me feel important.

Such behavior is generally counterproductive, alienating the very people whose affirmation we crave. Even if we experience a significant accomplishment that brings us the acclaim of others, the accompanying sense of well-being is fleeting. To our chagrin we discover that there is not enough applause in the world to silence our self-doubts for very long. Nor can we achieve enough success to finally still the troubling voices within.

To complicate matters, the enemy is always whispering his subtle suggestions: "If you are truly the important person you think you are, then turn these stones into bread." Of course he tailors each temptation to fit our individual situation. Do you struggle with fear? Perhaps he tempts you to take some foolish dare in order to prove your courage. Are you losing your girlish figure as you enter midlife? Maybe he tempts you to have an affair to prove to yourself that you still have "it." Or perhaps he tempts you to spend inordinate amounts of time and money trying to reverse the aging process and reclaim your youthful beauty. Have a couple of business deals gone south, calling your judgment into question? It is likely he will tempt you with the "big deal." The list goes on and on, for Satan has as many scenarios as there are people. And if we are not careful, we will find ourselves doing absolutely absurd things in a desperate attempt to prove ourselves.

We Are in Good Company

When you find yourself struggling with self-doubt you may be tempted to despair, to think you are beyond help, but you are not. Nearly everyone struggles with self-doubt to some degree, even those we consider spiritual giants. The fact that they also made significant contributions to the kingdom gives us hope. If God could use them, in spite of their feelings of unworthiness, then maybe He can use people like us as well.

Take, for instance, Dietrich Bonhoeffer, the German theologian and martyr. He was executed one week before the end of World War II after having spent months in prison. During his imprisonment he appeared to be the epitome of a man at peace with himself and God. Yet beneath his confident exterior he struggled with the same self-doubts that tempt us all.

One of his prison prayers, titled "Who Am I?", gives us a glimpse of his inner struggle:

> Who am I? They often tell me
> I stepped from my cell's confinement
> Calmly, cheerfully, firmly,
> Like a squire from his country-house.
> Who am I? They often tell me
> I used to speak to my wardens
> Freely and friendly and clearly,

As though it were mine to command.
Who am I? They also tell me
I bore the days of misfortune
Equably, smilingly, proudly,
Like one accustomed to win.

Am I then really all that which other men tell of?
Or am I only what I myself know of myself?
Restless and longing and sick, like a bird in a cage,
Struggling for breath, as though hands were
      compressing my throat,
Yearning for colors, for flowers, for the voices of birds,
Thirsting for words of kindness, for neighborliness,
Tossing in expectation of great events,
Powerlessly trembling for friends at an infinite distance,
Weary and empty at praying, at thinking, at making,
Faint, and ready to say farewell to it all?

Who am I? This or the other?
Am I one person today and tomorrow another?
Am I both at once? A hypocrite before others,
And before myself a contemptible woebegone weakling?
Or is something within me still like a beaten army,
Fleeing in disorder from victory already achieved?
Who am I? They mock me, these lonely questions
      of mine.
Whoever I am, Thou knowest, O God, I am Thine![2]

The Source of Our Significance

"Whoever I am, Thou knowest, O God, I am Thine!" That's
the secret isn't it. Not *who* we are, but *whose* we are. Bonhoeffer
was trying to tell us that his value as a person was not based on
the many books he wrote, or the prestigious positions he held, or
even in the martyr's death he would eventually die. His hope, his
salvation, his significance rested in one thing and one thing alone—
his relationship with the Father through Jesus Christ the Son.

Only God can heal the deep self-doubt that haunts the human
race. Only He can make us feel like persons of worth and dignity.
To that end He gives us "the Spirit of adoption by whom we cry
out, 'Abba, Father.' The Spirit Himself bears witness with our spirit

that we are children of God, and if children, then heirs—heirs of God and joint heirs with Christ" (Rom. 8:15–17).

If Jesus dared not turn stones into bread to prove His self-worth but trusted only in the Word of the Father, how dare we do otherwise (Luke 4:3–4). We must not turn inward in search of significance, for we will never find it within ourselves. Nor do we dare turn outward, hoping to find personal validation through our achievements. There simply is not enough success in all the world to satisfy the heart's hunger for significance. Men and women created in the image of God cannot live by bread alone.

> *"Whoever I am, Thou knowest, O God, I am Thine!" That's the secret isn't it. Not who we are, but whose we are.*

Our search for significance ends only when we look backward to the Cross and upward to the throne. Through the finished work of Jesus we have been transformed into persons of worth and dignity. "Behold what manner of love the Father has bestowed on us, that we should be called children of God!" (1 John 3:1). "Now, therefore, [we] are no longer strangers and foreigners, but fellow citizens with the saints and members of the household of God" (Eph. 2:19). We are people of significance because we are significant to God.

"Whoever I am, Thou knowest, O God, I am Thine!"

Reflecting on Him

1. *Describe a time in your life when you were tempted to act in a rash or foolish manner to prove your worth, your toughness, or your spiritual strength.*

2. *Reread 1 John 3:1 and Ephesians 2:19. In your own words, what does it mean to be "fellow citizens with the saints and members of the household of God"?*

7

THE LURE OF
MATERIALISM
AND POWER

Having failed in his previous attempt to seduce Jesus, Satan now took Him up on a high mountain and showed Him all the kingdoms of the world in a moment of time. How breathtaking the splendor of Rome, Greece, and the other kingdoms must have seemed to the Son of man, having been reared in the frontier town of Nazareth, a place known more for its crudeness than its culture. Among the Jews of His day there was a common saying: "Can anything good come out of Nazareth?" (John 1:46).

Like Satan's previous attempt, this temptation was ensconced in legitimacy. Being steeped in the Scriptures, Jesus knew that He was destined for the throne of David and that of the increase of His government there would be no end (Isa. 9:7). One day all the kingdoms of the world would become His (Rev. 11:15).

Now the enemy offered Him a shortcut. Jesus wouldn't have to suffer and die in order to be highly exalted, as God's plan required. "And the devil said to Him, 'All this authority I will give You, and their glory; for this has been delivered to me, and I give it to whomever I wish. Therefore, if You will worship before me, all will be Yours'" (Luke 4:6–7).

It is quite likely that Satan bombarded our Lord's mind with thoughts concerning all the good He could do as the supreme world ruler. By imperial decree He could have abolished slavery, making

71

it unnecessary for any person to ever be in bondage to another. Under His direction laws could have been established, making racism illegal. Women and minorities could have been granted equal rights. Wealth could have been redistributed so no one need ever know the pinch of poverty. He could have put an end to all war. Never again would the strong exploit the weak. Or so His thoughts may have tempted Him.

High Places

Had Satan approached Jesus straightforwardly, demanding that He bow down and worship him, it would have been no temptation at all. Instead he "led him up to a high place and showed him in an instant all the kingdoms of the world" (Luke 4:5 NIV). With that dazzling display of wealth and power Satan hoped to overwhelm the Son of man. He was giving Jesus a glimpse of what life could be like if He would play along. Then the devil said to Him, "If You will worship before me, all will be Yours" (Luke 4:7).

As you can readily see, a high place can be a dangerous place indeed. It exposes you to temptations you have never before had to deal with. You now move in circles where anything you want can be had for a price. Powerful people court you, take you into their confidence, put you in their debt. Now you are tempted to believe that you are different from other people, immune from the petty rules that govern their lives. There is no limit to how far you can go if you will simply turn a blind eye to the ethical compromises and questionable business deals.

You do not have to be enormously successful to experience temptations of this nature. Every level of success, no matter how modest, is a "high place" in its own right. Sooner or later we all find ourselves standing on a high mountain surveying the kingdoms of this world, while Satan makes his most beguiling pitch. If we will cut a deal with him, unlimited success will be ours. Let him drape that "success" in spiritual trappings, and the temptation is even harder to resist. Now we are not doing it just for ourselves, but for the good of the kingdom.

Well do I remember finding myself on what was to me a high place some years ago. A "Christian" marketing firm had approached me about forming a partnership with our *Straight from the Heart* radio ministry. I was immediately interested because the financial burden was a heavy one, and their plan would put us in a positive cash flow position. Though I felt uneasy in my spirit, I gave them tentative approval.

The agreement itself was simple enough. Each radio station that broadcast our daily, two-minute *Straight from the Heart* feature provided us with a sixty-second spot that we could use as we saw fit. The marketing firm wanted to utilize our sixty-second spot to advertise their 900 number. *Straight from the Heart* would receive a 10 percent commission on each 900 call generated. In addition one of the computer options offered to each caller would be an opportunity to hear the *Straight from the Heart* feature and order products from the ministry. Profits from the products sold would be divided equally between the marketing firm and the ministry. Each caller would also have the option of talking with a trained "counselor" or another caller of similar interests.

All of that sounded good from a financial perspective. There was little or no monetary risk to the ministry, yet the returns could be significant. I was more than a little troubled, however, at the thought of exploiting people's loneliness for profit. Since their 900 calls would be charged to their credit card I could envision scores of lonely people running up hundreds of dollars in charges. Charges they most likely could ill afford. An additional concern involved the telephone "counselors." I knew we were not talking about certified professionals. And helping people "connect" with a friend of similar interest seemed inherently risky to me. What did we really know about these people? Nothing other than what they told us.

On top of all of that there was the matter of the silent partner—the one who was going to provide all of the expensive equipment to make our plan a reality. When I asked the marketing firm whom we were dealing with, they hedged. I continued to press them until they finally disclosed that the company providing the telephone equipment was one of the pioneers in the use of 900 numbers. At the time, telephone sex—via 900 numbers—was the rage, and I knew immediately that we were talking about telephone pornographers.

Sensing my disapproval, the people from the marketing firm hastened to tell me that our only connection with the silent partner would be the use of their equipment. In reality, they explained, it was not any different from what the inspirational networks do when they share the same satellite with the Playboy network. I was not convinced, but I held my peace.

Why didn't I veto the deal right up front? Because I could see the kingdoms of the world spread out before me. Already we were heard on more than 150 stations daily. Once the revenue from this venture started pouring in we could enlarge our network. Soon we would be heard on two hundred stations, then three hundred stations, maybe even four hundred. Who knows, we might become as big as *Focus on the Family*. Think of the good we could do, the people we could help. All I had to do was "cut a deal with the devil."

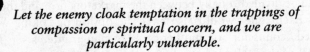

Let the enemy cloak temptation in the trappings of compassion or spiritual concern, and we are particularly vulnerable.

Two things saved me from myself. First God spoke to my heart while I was in prayer. So clear were His words that I recorded them in my journal. "Be careful whom you associate with lest you become entangled with their excesses and be brought down with them. Keep your own counsel and be careful with whom you speak. Choose character before riches and truthfulness above prosperity."

Though the Lord's message was painfully clear, still I might have yielded to temptation had it not been for my ministry board. An agreement of this type would require a resolution from them, which would necessitate a detailed proposal from me. As I considered it I simply could not see myself taking this kind of an offer to them. That I would even consider a deal with these kinds of unethical implications would be a disappointment to them. They thought better of me than that.

From that experience I learned an important lesson. If I cannot be completely up front about the details of what I am doing then I should not be doing it at all. No matter how great the potential good, the end never justifies the means.

Appealing to Our Innate Desires

On another level this second wilderness temptation forced Jesus to confront both His conscious desire to alleviate human suffering and His subconscious psychological needs. Possessing an extraordinary capacity for compassion, He was undoubtedly sensitive to any temptation that seemed to afford Him the opportunity to do good. Having been reared on the ragged edge of poverty, He may well have had a psychological need for security. Possibly having been looked down on by His childhood companions because of His station in life, He might have hungered for success and the recognition it brought. Such psychological needs are not evil, but human. And if this was the case, Jesus was simply being "tempted in every way, just as we are" (Heb. 4:15 NIV).

It is interesting, is it not, to consider how many successful entrepreneurs were reared in an environment of personal poverty. The same thing can be said of many of the most highly visible ministers and churchmen. One cannot help but wonder how much of their drive to succeed is rooted in a desperate desire to escape the humiliation and deprivation of their childhood. That is not necessarily a bad thing, but it can be a dangerous thing, leaving a person vulnerable to those temptations that play on his subconscious psychological need to transcend his past.

The Reverend Charles Blair, pastor of the six-thousand-member Calvary Temple in Denver, Colorado, is a case in point. In his book, *The Man Who Could Do No Wrong*, he candidly acknowledged the part his poverty-stricken childhood played in his success and in his subsequent failure. He said growing up during the Great Depression left him with a deep-seated self-doubt and a burning desire to succeed. He was determined that no one would ever look down on him again, nor would his children ever endure the bitter humiliation that characterized his childhood. Consequently he was ever conscious of his public image. He drove the right kind of car, wore the best suits, and fraternized with the right people.

This inordinate concern for his public image, coupled with his enormous success, made it nearly impossible for him to distinguish between the voice of God and the enemy's subtle appeal to his subconscious ego needs. As a result he undertook to build a Life Center for the handicapped and the aged when the ministry was in no position to do so. This brought on some ill-advised financial decisions that ultimately resulted in bankruptcy. Investors lodged complaints with the Securities and Exchange Commission, causing them to launch an investigation. Charges were filed, and Pastor Blair went to trial where a jury found him guilty of securities fraud.

Charles Blair is not a criminal except in the eyes of the court. He is simply a good man whose psychological needs made him especially susceptible to any temptation that appeared to be an opportunity to enhance his image while doing good for others. Knowing his psychological profile, Satan designed a temptation that would appeal to his deep-seated needs without appearing to be evil in any way. Once he succumbed to the temptation to build the Life Center one thing led to another. It should be noted, however, that the illegal sale of securities was done out of ignorance, not criminal intent. Even in the midst of the financial crisis Blair had no conscious knowledge of wrongdoing. There is absolutely no evidence to suggest that he intended to defraud anyone.

Be that as it may, the thing that makes this kind of temptation so persuasive is the fact that it appeals to us on several levels simultaneously. As we have already noted there is the lure of altruism—the potential good we can do. It is more mirage than reality, but it does serve to ennoble our desires. It is especially appealing to those of us who see ourselves as caring people. Let the enemy cloak temptation in the trappings of compassion or spiritual concern, and we are particularly vulnerable. Now add the fact that it also appeals to our subconscious psychological needs, and it is not hard to see why so many of us succumb.

Thankfully Jesus did not allow His psychological needs to blind Him to the intrigues of the evil one. Though the kingdoms of the world and all their glory were spread out before Him, Jesus refused to be taken in. Instead He resisted the devil, saying, "Get behind Me, Satan! For it is written, 'You shall worship the LORD your God, and Him only you shall serve'" (Luke 4:8). His victory here gave Him a firm foundation from which to resist every later attempt to make Him a king (John 6:15).

False Security

Another factor that makes this temptation so appealing is that it promises not only power and wealth but personal fulfillment as well. By implication Satan leads us to believe that if we can achieve enough success, or make enough money, or amass enough power then we will be happy. Unfortunately that just isn't true. According to the apostle Paul, "Those who desire to be rich fall into temptation and a snare, and into many foolish and harmful lusts which drown men in destruction and perdition. For the love of money is a root of all kinds of evil, for which some have strayed from the faith in their greediness, and pierced themselves through with many sorrows" (1 Tim. 6:9–10).

The famous Edgewater Beach Hotel in Chicago was the site of a 1923 meeting of some of the world's most powerful financiers. In attendance were Charles Schwab—the president of the largest independent steel company, Samuel Insull—the president of the largest utility company, Howard Hopson—the president of the largest gas company, Arthur Cutten—the greatest wheat speculator, Richard Whitney—the president of the New York Stock Exchange, Albert Fall—a member of the president's cabinet, Jesse Livermore—the greatest bear on Wall Street, Leon Fraser—the president of the Bank of International Settlement, and Ivar Kreuger—the head of the world's greatest monopoly. Collectively they controlled more wealth than there was in the United States Treasury.

> *Those who are serious about serving God rather than money know that the real test of allegiance is not how much a person gives, but how much he keeps.*

Yet, for all their financial expertise, theirs is not a pleasant story, for they each came to a bitter end. After living on borrowed money for the last five years of his life, Schwab died penniless. Insull, too, died destitute, a fugitive from justice and in a foreign country. Insanity claimed Hopson, while Cutten died abroad, insolvent. Both Richard Whitney and Albert Fall ended up in prison, while Livermore, Fraser, and Kreuger all committed suicide.[1]

Although the details of their disastrous demises vary from individual to individual, the similarities give us reason to pause and consider. They were addicted to wealth and the power it represented, and in the end this was their undoing. It is little wonder that Jesus repeatedly warned us to be on guard.

If the Gospel record is any indication, Jesus talked more about money than any other single subject during His earthly ministry. In the Gospels, an average of one out of every ten verses—288 in all—deals directly with the subject. Sixteen of our Lord's thirty-eight parables address the same issue. And every time the tone is the same—somber. "And He said to them, 'Take heed and beware of covetousness, for one's life does not consist in the abundance of the things he possesses'" (Luke 12:15).

Another time He said, "How hard it is for those who have riches to enter the kingdom of God! . . . It is easier for a camel to go through the eye of a needle than for a rich man to enter the kingdom of God" (Mark 10:23, 25).

Based on this wilderness temptation, Jesus declared: "No one can serve two masters; for either he will hate the one and love the other, or else he will be loyal to the one and despise the other. You cannot serve God and mammon" (Matt. 6:24).

There is only one way to deal with our human proclivity toward greedy materialism, only one way to overcome the temptation to trust in riches, and that is to give regularly and sacrificially. Therefore we are told to "command those who are rich in this present age not to be haughty, nor to trust in uncertain riches but in the living God, who gives us richly all things to enjoy. Let them do good, that they be rich in good works, ready to give, willing to share, storing up for themselves a good foundation for the time to come, that they may lay hold on eternal life" (1 Tim. 6:17–19).

Those who are serious about serving God rather than money know that the real test of allegiance is not how much a person gives, but how much he keeps. As C. S. Lewis said, "If our charities do not at all pinch or hamper us, I should say they are too small. There ought to be things we should like to do and cannot do because our charitable expenditure excludes them."[2]

Making High Places Holy Places

The final dimension of this temptation is rooted in Satan's ability to blur the distinction between *high places* and *holy places*. He wants us to believe that every high place is a holy place. That the applause of the world can be equated with the approval of the Father. That the adulation of others is equal to the Lord's "Well done, good and faithful servant" (Matt. 25:21).

That is what this second temptation is all about—the danger of thinking that worldly success is the same as spiritual success. In truth they are not remotely alike. Worldly success focuses on externals—marrying the right person, sending your children to the right schools, holding the right positions and titles, making the right salary, amassing enough net worth. Spiritual success focuses on internals—character, integrity, purity of heart, faithfulness, compassion.

In his biography of Dr. James Dobson, Rolf Zettersten includes a glimpse of the temptations that have come Dobson's way. Among the things he has had to contend with have been offers from presidents to serve in high places and opportunities to parlay his ministry into personal fame and fortune.

Following a guest appearance on the *Larry King Show* in early 1983, Dr. Dobson was invited to meet with the president of the Mutual Broadcasting Network—the largest system of commercial stations in the country. On the basis of the response Dobson had generated on the *Larry King Show,* Mutual's president wanted to discuss the possibility of a new radio series focusing on the family. It would be produced by the Mutual Broadcasting Company and aired throughout its vast network.

After accepting the invitation to meet, Dr. Dobson and his leadership team flew to Washington, D.C. The meeting took place in Mutual Broadcasting's corporate offices—a "high place" if ever there was one for a radio minister. Remember, in 1983, Dr. Dobson's *Focus on the Family* was on approximately 150 stations. That was "small potatoes" compared to the huge Mutual Network.

Intrigued by the possibility of creating a special program that would potentially reach millions of unchurched people, Dr. Dobson listened as Mutual's president laid out his proposal. He suggested that Dr. Dobson cancel his current program on Christian Radio, in order to devote himself to a new daily, secular series, including broadcasts on Sundays. The implication was that by doing so he could become a major personality on American radio.

After listening to the promising proposition Dr. Dobson politely declined the offer on the spot. He later explained his reasoning: "I believe that God has called me first to strengthen the Christian home. We may have the opportunity some day to reach a broader audience but it will never be at the expense of that primary ministry to Christians."[3]

There were at least two other reasons he declined the offer, which could have made him a wealthy man. First, he would have been required to broadcast four hours on Sunday, which is a family time and a church day for him. And second, commercial sponsorship would have prohibited Dr. Dobson from talking specifically about his faith. This was out of the question.

Zettersten went on to write:

> During my association with Dr. Dobson, I have witnessed other situations where the secular media have enticed him with the prospects of speaking to a national audience. That is simply not a major objective for him. He routinely turns down guest appearances on *Nightline* with Ted Koppel, *Crossfire*, and other programs. . . . The producers of these shows can't understand Dr. Dobson's independence. Most people dream about the kind of instant notoriety they offer. Some actively seek it but until he feels the Lord directing him otherwise Dobson is content to convey his thoughts to the Christian community.[4]

What we have here is a twentieth-century version of the kind of temptations Jesus faced when the devil took Him to a high mountain and showed Him all the kingdoms of the world. No one can doubt that the enemy has made a play for Dobson's soul. He has tempted him with wealth and fame, not to mention political power. And all under the guise of "doing good."

It is hardly surprising. There are no new temptations. Only the same old temptations wearing new disguises. Look beneath their distinctly modern veneers, and you will find the same three faces—a hunger for significance, the lure of materialism and power, and the temptation to use God rather than serve Him. These three temptations appeal to all of us at our most vulnerable points, and they represent Satan's best chance to lead us astray.

Jesus was able to resist Satan's most determined efforts because He had a clear understanding of His call. He was not called to be an earthly king, for His kingdom was not of this world (John 18:36). He "did not come to be served, but to serve, and to give His life a ransom for many" (Matt. 20:28). His will, His dreams and ambitions, His hopes and desires, were fully submitted to the Father's will. And because His mind and Spirit were totally immersed in the Father's plan, He was able to resist any and all temptation. When Jesus said, "You shall worship the LORD your God, and Him only you shall serve" (Luke 4:8), He wasn't simply quoting Scripture. Pleasing God and doing His will were the consuming passions of Jesus' life, and they enabled Him to resist the most beguiling temptations the enemy could throw at Him.

Shortly after I became the senior pastor of Christian Chapel, God spoke to my heart concerning the mission of the church. After consultation with the elders, I formulated a vision statement expressing the things God had impressed upon my heart. We called it "Christian Chapel's Fourfold Vision." It included: (1) a commitment to world missions; (2) a commitment to preach and teach the Word of God; (3) a commitment to Spirit-directed worship; and (4) a commitment to biblical relationships.

In the years that followed, many ministry opportunities came our way. Almost all of them were "good" things, worthy things, but only a few of them were "God" things. Early on we learned that one of Satan's most effective tactics was to involve us in things God had not called us to do. After a few painful experiences we began using our fourfold vision as the criteria for determining whether a ministry opportunity was from God or not. If it enhanced our ability to accomplish our God-given vision, we adopted it. If it did not, we rejected it, no matter how attractive it might seem.

The key to resisting temptations, especially those that come disguised as ministry opportunities, is to have a clear understanding of your call. Those who have remained faithful over the course of a lifetime have refused to allow anything to compromise their calling. Take Billy Graham for instance. Although he has had audiences with numerous world leaders and been the personal friend of presidents of both parties, he has steadfastly refused to become involved in politics. God did not call him to be a politician or a reformer, but an evangelist, and to that calling he has remained true.

Although most of us will never consort with presidents and world leaders, we will, nonetheless, have to contend with the tempter. He will make a play for our soul in ways that are particularly appealing to us. It may come in a moment of crisis when it seems our world is caving in around us, or it may come at the height of success, but rest assured it will come. In that hour only those who have a clear understanding of their call and an uncompromising commitment to the One who called them will be able to stand. All others will be led astray.

Reflecting on Him

1. Do you think of your career or life accomplishments in terms of "titles, positions, or awards" or in terms of "the influence" you can have on others?

2. How would you define power and authority? Complete a Scripture search regarding the concepts of power and authority, and then compare God's definition to yours.

3. What personal "holy places" do you believe that God has in store for you and your family?

8

THE LURE OF FANATICISM

Having stripped Himself of His glory, and being found in the likeness of a man, Jesus must have seemed an easy prey. Surely He would be no match for the subtlety of the evil one. And if He did turn out to be more astute than anticipated, then He could be overwhelmed with a mind-numbing display of the wealth and glory of this world's kingdoms. Few men could resist the lure of such power and certainly not this unsophisticated carpenter with His backward ways, or so the devil may have thought.

But he was wrong! Satan completely underestimated the Son of man. Not only did Jesus rebuff his cleverly crafted temptations, but He did so with an authority that left no doubt as to who was the victor. Yet, the devil was not finished. Having failed to entrap Jesus with either an appeal to prove Himself or with the lure of power, Satan now turned his attention to the most insidious temptation of all—the lure of fanaticism.

Then he brought Him [Jesus] to Jerusalem, set Him on the pinnacle of the temple, and said to Him, "If You are the Son of God, throw Yourself down from here. For it is written:
'He shall give His angels charge over you, To keep you,' and, 'In their hands they shall bear you up, Lest you dash your foot against a stone.'" *(Luke 4:9–11)*

Had the Son of man accepted the devil's challenge and leaped from the pinnacle of the temple, He most likely would have plunged to His death. Such an act would have been sheer presumption—a misguided attempt to force God's hand. Those who walk by faith take risks, to be sure, but they do so as an act of obedience in response to a divine initiative. God speaks, and they obey. Conversely, those who succumb to fanaticism seize the initiative. They presume upon the grace of God, going beyond what He has decreed in an attempt to bend Him to their will. Often they mistakenly assume that God will not let them fail lest His reputation be damaged. They may appear to prosper for a while, but in the end their misguided zeal will prove to be their undoing.

Ascetics and Cults

Fanaticism is not a new temptation. The evil one has been using it for centuries. Failing to entice a man to do evil, he then tempts him to take good to an extreme. It has been effective, too, for what is heresy but truth taken to an excess? And what is fanaticism but devotion taken to ridiculous lengths?

Although the Scriptures repeatedly warn of the dangers of fanaticism (1 Tim. 4:1–3), there are those who continue to be led astray. The extremes to which the devout have been known to go may differ from century to century, but whatever form fanaticism takes, the loss to the kingdom of God is always significant.

Consider the example of the ascetics.[1] Rather than pouring their devotion into the preaching of the gospel or acts of charity, they devoted themselves to the denial of their flesh. Besarion, a monk who lived during the fourth century, slept standing or sitting up for forty years rather than yield to his body's need for comfortable rest. St. Maron lived for eleven years in a hollowed-out tree trunk, and St. Ascepsimas was so weighted down with chains that he could not walk upright. He had to crawl around on hands and knees.

Two of the most celebrated ascetics were Simeon the Stylite of Syria and Daniel the Stylite of Constantinople. Together they lived a total of seventy years on different pillars. Simeon spent thirty-seven years on various pillars, each one loftier and narrower than the last. His final pillar towered sixty-six feet into the air. For thirty-three years Daniel lived on a single pillar, and it is reported that he was nearly blown off numerous times by the storms that swept in from Thrace.

One of the most tragic accounts of this kind of fanaticism involves Agnes de Rochier, who at the age of eighteen decided to become what was then called a recluse. As such she would spend the rest of her life enclosed in a narrow cell built within the wall of the church. On October 5, 1403, the Bishop of Paris, attended by the chaplains and the canons of Notre Dame, entered the cell and celebrated a pontifical Mass. They then departed the cell, the bishop sprinkling the opening with holy water. After he finished, workmen closed the opening using stones and mortar. They left only a small loophole, through which Agnes could hear the offices of the church and receive the scraps of food given to her by the charitable. For the next eighty years she did not leave her living tomb, finally escaping through death at the age of ninety-eight.

No one can question the sincere devotion of these misguided souls, but it seems a tragic waste. Had their passion for God been channeled into fulfilling the Great Commission or in loving service to others, there is no telling what eternal good they may have done. As it is their fanatical devotion serves only to bring attention to themselves.

Although asceticism is no longer in vogue, the lure of fanaticism has not diminished. Taken to its ultimate conclusion it often produces bizarre cults like Heaven's Gate. Blending a concoction of distorted Christianity, New Age "spirituality," and Star Trek science fiction, it led followers to believe that by killing themselves they could shed their "containers" and move to a "higher level." According to their beliefs, they expected to rendezvous with a UFO that was supposedly trailing behind the Hale-Bopp comet. Consequently thirty-nine members packed their suitcases for what they believed would be an intergalactic trip, videotaped farewells, and took their own lives. On March 26, 1997, police found their bodies inside a hilltop mansion in Rancho Santa Fe, California. As incredible as it may seem, ex-members, interviewed after the suicides, expressed confidence that the departed members were on a spacecraft in the heavens.

The Appeal of Fanaticism

How, you may be wondering, do sincere believers go astray? The truth is that succumbing to the lure of fanaticism is a little like eating an elephant—you do it one small piece at a time. Few people ever swallow the whole elephant, but even half an elephant, or a few mouthfuls for that matter, can be quite a load. Once the purity of doctrinal truth is compromised it is only a matter of time until it produces a corresponding aberrant behavior. Or to use the words of the apostle Paul, "A little leaven leavens the whole lump" (Gal. 5:9).

Of course when Satan tempts us with fanaticism it does not appear to be fanaticism at all. Consider the final wilderness temptation of Jesus for instance. After transporting Him to the pinnacle of the temple, the devil then drew upon both cultural expectations and the Scriptures in an attempt to lead Jesus astray. Quoting from Psalm 91:11–12 Satan said, "If You are the Son of God, throw Yourself down from here. For it is written: 'He shall give His angels charge over you, / To keep you,' and, 'In their hands they shall bear you up, / Lest you dash your foot against a stone'" (Luke 4:9–11).

According to Norval Geldenhuys in his commentary on the gospel of Luke:

> It should be noted that the rabbis identified the person addressed by God in Psalm xci with the Messiah. The Midrash, known as *Pesiqta Rabbati* (162a), records a traditional belief that Messiah would manifest himself standing on the roof of the temple. The part of the temple indicated in the temptation narrative may have been the part overlooking the "Royal Colonnade"—which Josephus (*Antiquities*, XV, II, 5) describes as looking down a precipitous descent into the Kidron valley, the height being so great as to make the spectator dizzy.[2]

Obviously Jesus was familiar with the Scriptures that Satan quoted. And it is quite likely that He had also heard the traditional belief regarding the Messiah's revealing Himself from the pinnacle of the temple. Needless to say this temptation was well conceived. On the surface it appears to be both scriptural and logical, but on a deeper level it is simply the same old temptation to choose self over God, to do it "my" way rather than God's way. At its core, fanaticism always tempts a person to use God rather than serve Him.

The thing that makes this temptation so deadly is that it comes cloaked in a spiritual guise. It is not about satisfying our physical or psychological hungers, at least not directly. On the surface it appears to have nothing to do with the kingdoms of this world or wealth or power. Instead it appeals to the genuinely spiritual part of us that wants to be used of God and wants to live a life of radical dependence upon Him.

While no one has ever been tempted to the full extent of what Jesus experienced in His wilderness battle with the devil, those who are called to do great things for God are exposed to a form of what He encountered. Once they rebuff the tempter's initial offerings— i.e., the lust of the flesh or the pride of life—he then tempts them to take their faith to an extreme. Of course, once they succumb to fanaticism they leave themselves open to all manner of temptation.

John Alexander Dowie,[3] the controversial nineteenth-century apostle of healing and founder of Zion, Illinois, is a classic example. By all accounts he was a brilliant man, incisive and articulate, but his most outstanding characteristic was his passionate devotion to Jesus Christ. While serving as the pastor of the Congregational Church at Newton, a suburb of Sydney, Australia, he found himself confronted by a plague of sickness and death. More than forty members of his small congregation perished in a few short weeks, and there was no end in sight. The general population was similarly affected and nearly paralyzed with fear.

In desperation Dowie searched the Scriptures and spent hours in prayer, finally concluding that sickness and disease were the works of the devil. Having just reached that conclusion he was called to the bedside of a young girl who was dying. Acting on his newfound knowledge, he prayed for her, and she was miraculously healed. As a result his healing ministry was launched.

In 1888 Dowie came to America and began healing crusades in California. Eventually he moved his ministry to Chicago, Illinois, where he founded the great Zion Tabernacle. His remarkable healing ministry continued, and soon the six-thousand-seat auditorium was filled for every service. With a passion for evangelism he sectioned off the districts of the city and trained and sent out teams called "The Seventies" (Luke 10:1). Soon there was hardly a person in the great city of Chicago who had not heard the gospel message.

As is often the case, his success also proved to be his undoing. At the height of his popularity he decided to found a holy city, a place where the inhabitants would live by the decrees of God rather than the mere laws of men. Secretly he hired proprietors to survey land forty miles north of Chicago as a potential site, eventually buying sixty-six hundred acres on Lake Michigan. The architectural plans for the city of Zion were unveiled at the New Year's Eve Watch Night service on January 1, 1900. Through the Zion Land Investment Association, subdivisions were allotted and home-building began. Homebuilders were not allowed to buy the land upon which their houses were built. Instead they leased it for a period of eleven hundred years. The terms of the lease strictly forbade the possession or use of tobacco, liquor, or pork anywhere within the limits of the city.

Having deemed himself the General Overseer of Zion, Dowie was soon spending nearly all of his time running the city. Taking counsel from no one, he now removed all restraints that could have prevented him from being led astray. Soon he was proclaiming himself to be Elijah the prophet (Mal. 4:5–6), saying, "A voice seemed to say, 'Elijah must come, and who but you is doing the work of Elijah?'"

We will never consistently overcome temptation until pleasing the Father becomes the consuming passion of our life.

By now he had all but forsaken the preaching of the gospel, so taken up was his time with running the city of Zion and with his grandiose plans for establishing other Zions in close proximity to all of the major cities in America. In his declining years he grew more and more eccentric. Having denounced his last name, he began referring to himself as the First Apostle of the renewed, end-time church. While his followers fell upon hard financial times, he lived like a king, hosting lavish parties and taking a world tour.

Near the end of his ministry, Dowie granted an interview to Dr. Buckly, the editor of the denominational newspaper for the Methodist church. Buckly wrote that Dowie was "in the moonlit border land of insanity where large movements of limited duration have sometimes originated. . . . If he believes it or not, he is but another imposter."[4]

What happened? How could such a gifted man who accomplished so much for God get so far off track? One can only assume that Dowie had a temptation experience, or a series of temptation experiences, not unlike the one Jesus experienced when Satan took Him to the pinnacle of the temple. The lure of fanaticism was apparently more than he could resist. Doubtless he rejected any second thoughts he might have had, justifying his ambition by interpreting it as a vision for the kingdom, a divine call for his life—God's will; and herein lies part of the deception. Dowie was committed to the kingdom, he did care about reaching the world with the gospel, but it was all tangled up with his own ego needs.

In that he is not unique. As disconcerting as it may be, ambition and obedience will probably always share the seat of power in the believer's life. It's not ideal, but it is, I think, a realistic appraisal of our situation. Our salvation does not come in totally divorcing ourselves from personal ambition, that's virtually impossible, but in recognizing it for what it is and honestly dealing with it. The real trouble starts when we experience success, when we find ourselves on the pinnacle of the temple, and interpret our high standing as divine approval for all of our dreams and visions. When that happens, there's little or nothing left to restrain our ambitious ego. Without a moment's hesitation we leap from the pinnacle of the temple, fully expecting God to bless all that we do in "His" name.

Spiritual leaders who experience significant success find themselves in a kind of double bind. Not only are they in a "high place," but they are in a "holy place" as well—a high, holy place to be completely accurate. And as Richard Foster notes:

> Power can be an extremely destructive thing in any context, but in the service of religion it is downright diabolical. Religious power can destroy in a way that no other power can. . . . Those who are a law unto themselves and at the same time take on a mantle of piety are particularly corruptible. When we are convinced that what we are doing is identical with the kingdom of God, anyone who opposes us must be wrong. When we are convinced that we always use our power to good ends, we believe we can never do wrong. But when this mentality possesses us, we are taking the power of God and using it to our own ends.[5]

The first casualty of religious power gone awry is almost always the possessor of that power. Richard Dortch, second in command at PTL in 1987 when that scandal broke, concluded:

> A television camera can change a preacher quicker than anything else. . . . It turns good men into potentates. . . . It's so easy to get

swept away by popularity: Everybody loves you, cars are waiting for you, and you go to the head of the line. That's the devastation of the camera. It has made us less than what God has wanted us to become.[6]

The lure of fanaticism is never easy to resist because it seems so logical, at least to the one being tempted. When Satan suggested that Jesus leap from the pinnacle of the temple, it must have seemed an ideal way to launch His ministry. Knowing men as He did (John 2:24–25), Jesus knew they were always looking for a supernatural sign. By leaping from the heights of the temple without perishing, He would gain immediate credibility in their eyes; but it was not God's way. And had He yielded to Satan's suggestion to throw Himself from the pinnacle of the temple, it is not hard to imagine that He would have come down from the cross when the religious leaders taunted Him, saying, "If You are the Son of God, come down from the cross . . . and we will believe" (Matt. 27:40–42). Once a person begins to do things *his* way rather than *God's* way it is a difficult habit to break.

Instead, Jesus

> humbled Himself and became obedient to the point of death, even the death of the cross. Therefore God also has highly exalted Him and given Him the name which is above every name, that at the name of Jesus every knee should bow, of those in heaven, and of those on earth, and of those under the earth, and that every tongue should confess that Jesus Christ is Lord, to the glory of God the Father. *(Phil. 2:8–11)*

Overcoming Temptation

How is it that Jesus triumphed over temptation under the most adverse circumstances, while we often fail even under the best of conditions? Desire, I am sure, plays no little part. Everything within Jesus recoiled at the thought of displeasing the Father, while we often have no real aversion to sin. As one man told me, "I never had any real trouble with temptation until midlife. Until then I simply yielded to it."

In truth, we will never consistently overcome temptation until pleasing the Father becomes the consuming passion of our life.

Of course desire alone is not enough, for as Paul said, "I have the desire to do what is good, but I cannot carry it out" (Rom. 7:18 NIV). To our desire we must add spiritual disciplines—especially the discipline of the Word. Jesus overcame every temptation the enemy threw at Him by defending Himself with the holy Scriptures. They were His first and last defense. Each time the enemy approached Him, He said, "It is written. . . ." So immersed was He in the Scriptures, so at one with the Word, that truth literally flowed out of His innermost being. No matter whether the enemy came in like a roaring lion (1 Peter 5:8) or disguised himself as an angel of light (2 Cor. 11:14), he was no match for the Son of man.

If we are truly serious about overcoming temptation we, too, will become students of the Scriptures. We will read God's Word in order to be wise. We will practice it in order to be holy. We will "study to shew [ourselves] approved unto God, a workman that needeth not to be ashamed, rightly dividing the word of truth" (2 Tim. 2:15 KJV). We will memorize the Word, hiding it in our hearts against the hour of temptation (Ps. 119:11). It will become bread for our soul and nourishment for our spirit. We will meditate upon it day and night, and by its sanctifying power our minds will be renewed.

When the enemy comes against us, as he surely will, the Word becomes the sword with which we defend ourselves. Following in the footsteps of our Master, we defend ourselves, saying, "It is written, 'Man shall not live by bread alone, but by *every word of God*'" (Luke 4:4, emphasis mine). And because we have followed the Lord's example, we now experience His victory!

Reflecting on Him

1. *Someone once said, "We should accept no dogma without careful examination for it might be incorrect, and we should discard no dogma without careful examination for it might be true." How can personal dogmatism make one susceptible to fanaticism?*

2. *Using a study Bible or common concordance, make a list of Scriptures that address humility and pride. Now review the Beatitudes found in the fifth chapter of Matthew. What do you believe is God's prevention plan for avoiding fanaticism?*

9

THE PERILS OF POWER

Who could ever forget the pictures of former President Richard Nixon leaving the White House in disgrace following his resignation? Though it has been nearly twenty-five years since that fateful day, I can still see it in my mind as clearly as if it happened only yesterday. Determinedly he climbs the stairs to board *Air Force One* for his final flight. Reaching the top stair he turns and faces the press corp for the last time. Forcing a tired smile, he waves briefly, then ducks through the door a beaten man.

For all of his accomplishments as president—initiating the Strategic Arms Limitation Talks (SALT) with the Soviet Union in 1969; normalizing relationships with China in 1972; and the negotiation of a cease-fire in Vietnam in 1973—Richard Nixon will be forever remembered for Watergate. Instead of being esteemed by historians as a great president, he will go down in history as the only U.S. president ever forced to resign from office.

After achieving so much, President Nixon was brought to his knees, not by a political opponent, but by the blatant abuse of power. Thinking he was above the law, he participated in illegal activities that resulted in the House Judiciary Committee's recommending that he be impeached on three charges: obstruction of justice, abuse of presidential powers, and trying to impede the impeachment process by defying committee subpoenas. Whether Nixon was involved in the decision to break into the Democratic National Committee headquarters at the Watergate office building remains unclear. That he was an active participant in the cover-up from the very beginning is indisputable. With House impeachment inevitable and Senate conviction probable, Richard Nixon resigned on August 9, 1974.

Pondering his last fateful days twenty-three years later, I cannot help but grieve for him and all the other men and women who have succumbed to the perils of power. They include not only presidents but kings and emperors, as well as business tycoons, entertainment moguls, professional athletes, ministers, and regular people like you and me. Like Humpty Dumpty, they all had a great fall, and neither the king's horses nor the king's men could put them back together again—but Jesus can.

This Thing Called Power

Contrary to a common misconception, power is not inherently evil. It is morally neutral—it can be utilized for the good of all or abused for selfish purposes. Without power it is impossible to do good, yet the person who possesses it must ever be on guard lest he allow it to corrupt him. The more power a person has, the greater the risk. History bears ample witness to power's seductiveness and the destructive abuses that inevitably follow.

That being the case, it is small wonder that the issue of power was at the heart of our Lord's three wilderness temptations. Although Satan presented each temptation in a distinctly different manner, the core issue was the same: the abuse of power for selfish reasons. In the first encounter, Jesus was tempted to use His power for purely personal reasons: to satisfy His hunger and prove His worth. In the second, He was enticed with political power. Satan tempted Him to establish a political kingdom rather than a spiritual one. In the third, He was tempted to abuse His spiritual power—to use it for self-aggrandizement rather than for the glory of God. The devil tempted Jesus to use God for His own purposes rather than being used by God.

Thankfully Jesus resisted every temptation, and in doing so He showed us how power can be redeemed and used for God's holy purposes. Having been faithful in His administration of the Father's power on earth, He was now made the supreme authority of both heaven and earth. As He was about to ascend into heaven He told His disciples, "All authority has been given to Me in heaven and on earth" (Matt. 28:18).

In His wilderness temptations Jesus showed us what to do in order to overcome the perils of power. To learn what *not to do* I would like to consider a case study of one who was ruined by power. The biblical examples are numerous: Lucifer, son of the morning (Isa. 14:12–15); Samson the judge (Judg. 16:21); Nebuchadnezzar, king of the neo-Babylonian Empire (Dan. 4:33); and King Herod (Acts 12:21–23), to name just a few. Any one of them would provide a fascinating case study, but none can benefit us as much as Saul, the first king of Israel.

The Rise and Fall of King Saul

When I think of the perils of power, when I think of a man ruined by success, the first person who comes to mind is King Saul. The last weeks and months of his reign were a hellish odyssey through the barren wastes of spiritual torment. He was harassed by an evil spirit (1 Sam. 16:14), sought the divination of a witch (28:6–24), and fell upon his own sword after seeing his armies routed by the Philistines (31:1–6)—hardly the end we would expect for the man chosen by God to be Israel's first king.

When we first met Saul on the pages of holy Scripture, he was a winsome man, physically attractive, standing "a head taller than any of the others" (1 Sam. 9:2 NIV), yet gifted with the grace of humility. To use the language of the Scriptures, he was a man who was "little in [his] own eyes" (15:17).

When Samuel the prophet informed him that he had been chosen by God to be king, he protested, "Am I not a Benjamite, of the smallest of the tribes of Israel, and my family the least of all the families of the tribe of Benjamin? Why then do you speak like this to me?" (9:21). Even after Samuel anointed him king, Saul remained unaffected, and on the day of his coronation he could not be found, for he was "hidden among the equipment" (10:22).

How different this young man was from the power-hungry despot who ruled Israel for forty years. What, I ask you, changed this gifted and humble man into a paranoid powermonger, given to jealousy and murderous rages? The answer in a word is *power*. Well it has been said, "Power corrupts, and absolute power corrupts absolutely." History is filled with a long line of Sauls. Fine men, brilliant men, even godly men, who were corrupted by the deceitfulness of power.

Saul's degeneration took place over a period of years and was first the work of independence, then pride and disobedience. Initially he made himself accountable to Samuel. He sought Samuel's counsel and obeyed his instructions. His first rallying cry to the nation of Israel was: "This is what will be done to the oxen of anyone who does not follow Saul and Samuel" (1 Sam. 11:7 NIV).

As time progressed, however, Saul was increasingly tempted toward irresponsible independence. Perhaps he was influenced by the counsel of others, who suggested that, as king, it did not become him to seek the advice of the old prophet. "In the early days of your administration," they may have told him, "you needed his input, but now you are far more knowledgeable about the affairs of state than he is."

Or maybe Saul's change of heart was totally his own. Perhaps the prophet's counsel had begun to grate on him, causing him to chafe under its restraints. *What right does that doddering old codger have to interfere in the affairs of the king of Israel?* he may have fumed to himself. Whatever the case, it's not likely that Saul made a conscious decision to end his relationship with Samuel, but over the course of time it became easier and easier to ignore him. Now Saul began to take matters into his own hands, even disobeying the direct counsel of the prophet on occasion, as he did when he usurped the ministry of the priests (13:8–9).

When Samuel confronted him, Saul attempted to justify his behavior by saying that the circumstances were pressing and extraordinary measures were necessary: "Therefore I felt compelled, and offered a burnt offering" (13:12), he explained to Samuel.

Is there anyone who cannot identify with Saul's predicament? Probably not, for who among us hasn't been tempted to take matters into our own hands when life presses in upon us? Maybe it is a wayward son or daughter, or a troubled marriage, or a stubborn business deal. We've prayed and maybe even fasted; still, God has not intervened. Impatiently we take matters into our own hands, wielding whatever power we have in a reckless and irresponsible manner, causing no little damage. Like Saul, *we felt compelled* to do something even if it was wrong.

"You have done foolishly," Samuel replied. "You have not kept the commandment of the LORD your God, which He commanded you. For now the LORD would have established your kingdom over

Israel forever. But now your kingdom shall not continue. The LORD has sought for Himself a man after His own heart, and the LORD has commanded him to be commander over His people, because you have not kept what the LORD commanded you" (13:13–14).

It is interesting to note that Saul never acknowledged his disobedience in any way. In his mind, he had simply done the expedient thing. Disobedient yes, but expedient. A kind of "the ends justify the means" type of reasoning. Saul may have been thinking, *Samuel is old. He belongs to another generation. He does not understand the demands of kingship. As a leader I have to seize control, take responsibility, and make decisions.*

What we are talking about here is the world's way of doing things versus God's way. In the world's economy it is the movers and shakers who get things done. They take the bull by the horns and make things happen. In the economy of the kingdom, the Word of God is supreme, and we move only in God's timing. We do only what He directs us to do, and we do it only in His way. There is never a situation in which we can justify bending the rules in order to get the job done. Those who yield to the temptation to go their own way court destruction, for it is only a small step from foolish independence to sinful disobedience as Saul was soon to learn.

This time the Lord commanded Saul to utterly destroy the Amalekites. "Now go and attack Amalek, and utterly destroy all that they have, and do not spare them. But kill both man and woman, infant and nursing child, ox and sheep, camel and donkey" (15:3). And again Saul disobeyed, only this time it was not born of foolishness, but rebellion. To the king's way of thinking it seemed a waste to slaughter all of that prize livestock. And why kill King Agag when he could be used for propaganda purposes?

When confronted with his sinful disobedience, Saul once again refused to accept responsibility. This time he blamed the people: "For the people spared the best of the sheep and the oxen, to sacrifice to the LORD your God; and the rest we have utterly destroyed" (15:15). This is just more of the "blame game" we talked about in Chapter 2. As far as King Saul was concerned, it was never his fault. And because he never owned his sinful mistakes, he was never able to receive God's forgiveness or overcome his failures.

Then Samuel said to Saul, "Why did you swoop down on the spoil, and do evil in the sight of the LORD?" (15:19).

Again Saul hedged, attempting to justify his own disobedience and cloak his sinful self-interests with "spiritual" rationalization:

> "But I have obeyed the voice of the LORD, and gone on the mission on which the LORD sent me, and brought back Agag king of Amalek; I have utterly destroyed the Amalekites. But the people took of the plunder, sheep and oxen, the best of the things which should have been utterly destroyed, to sacrifice to the LORD your God in Gilgal." So Samuel said:
> "Has the LORD as great delight in burnt offerings and sacrifices,
> As in obeying the voice of the LORD?
> Behold, *to obey is better than sacrifice*,
> And to heed than the fat of rams.
> For rebellion is as the sin of witchcraft,
> And stubbornness is as iniquity and idolatry.
> Because you have rejected the word of the LORD,
> He also has rejected you from being king."
> *(1 Sam. 15:20–23, emphasis mine)*

Finally Saul acknowledged his sin; that is, he confessed it—*but he did not repent*. And without repentance confession is often self-serving—nothing more than a means of invoking sympathy and a way of relieving guilt. True repentance includes not only godly sorrow but a genuine change of heart—both sadly lacking in Saul. Even now he was more worried about his image, how he was going to look in the eyes of his people, than he was in pleasing the Lord.

"Then he said, 'I have sinned; yet honor me now, please, before the elders of my people and before Israel, and return with me, that I may worship the LORD your God'" (15:30). That is, "Don't let my sin become public knowledge. Too many people will be hurt." Tragic, isn't it, how Saul was more concerned about his public image than he was about the sin and rebellion that reigned within. His only concern, it seemed, was the possible impact his sin might have on the kingdom, never realizing that the kingdom was already gone.

Even after Samuel died, his words lived on, ringing in Saul's ears, "The LORD has torn the kingdom of Israel from you today, and has given it to a neighbor of yours, who is better than you" (15:28). Those words haunted Saul, drove him mad, and made him suspicious of every man and protective of his domain.

Consequently, his last years were a reign of terror fueled by fear and suspicion.

Although Saul remained in power for several years, he was king in name only. The anointing was gone. The Spirit of the Lord had departed from him. Nothing could save his kingdom now. "He who is the Glory of Israel does not lie or change his mind; for he is not a man, that he should change his mind" (15:29 NIV). Confession and repentance could have saved Saul's soul, but his kingdom was gone forever. Unfortunately he lived out his years in tragic defiance and died by his own hand, having lost both his kingdom and his soul.

The Perils of Power

This is more than just a Bible story, more than just a bit of ancient history: It's a word from God to each of us in this present age. Paul wrote, "These things happened to them as examples and were written down as warnings for us" (1 Cor. 10:11 NIV). With that thought in mind, let us examine our own lives lest, like King Saul, we succumb to temptation and the abuse of power destroys us.

Of course the enemy would like us to think that this is one temptation we don't have to worry about. After all, we are not elected officials or business tycoons, not televangelists or senior pastors of megachurches. Don't kid yourself. Those in high places may wield more power than we do, but every one of us has a certain amount of power, and you can be sure the enemy will tempt us to abuse it. I know. I've been there.

Some years ago God gave a ministerial colleague a vision for me. In his vision I was on a raft with two of my elders. A large, green serpent came out of the water and fastened itself onto my leg and began pulling me into the river. The elders attacked it with their oars, but to little avail. My colleague was watching helplessly from the shore. Finally, he left and returned almost immediately with a lion, which plunged into the water and attacked the green serpent. They fought furiously, in and out of the water, before the lion finally killed the serpent.

The next morning he began sharing his vision with me. The moment he began speaking it seemed a sword pierced my heart. The conviction of the Spirit was so great that I was in physical pain. Instantly I knew that green serpent represented the *spirit of power,* and it had fastened itself upon me. It was attempting to destroy me.

Every time I went to prayer for the next six or seven weeks, God would reveal another area in which I had abused power. These were not painless revelations of insipid facts. No! Each time I literally gasped with pain. I wept in repentance before the Lord. I begged Him to change me, to create in me a new heart, one of humility and service. One day it was the painful memory of a terrible thing I had said to Brenda, in anger, years before. Although I had apologized, I had not realized until now how deeply I had wounded her. There in prayer, in the presence of God, it seemed her pain became mine, and with the pain came a terrible shame. Another day it was a mortal wound I had inflicted on the spirit of a young man named Terry who was a member in one of the first churches I had served as pastor. Then there was the day the Lord revealed the hidden depths of my critical spirit, especially toward other ministers, and how I had used the power of my influence to discredit them. Day after day, week after week, it went on, this terrible soul-searching, this awesome battle between the Lion of the tribe of Judah and that awful serpent called power.

This is the kind of abuse of power ordinary people like us have to contend with. Because we are liked and respected, we have a certain amount of power over others. As parents we can bless or curse our children. If we use our power to affirm them they will be blessed; conversely if we demean them they will be cursed. The same thing is true in our marital relationships. We can use our power to build each other up or to tear each other down. As the Bible says, "Death and life are in the power of the tongue" (Prov. 18:21).

As painful as that experience was, I will always be grateful that God did not allow the abuse of power to go unchecked in my life. Had He not brought me to my knees when He did, there is no telling what havoc I may have wrought. Nor is the battle over. As long as we have power we will be tempted to abuse it. Alone we are no match for it, but together with the Lion of the tribe of Judah we shall overcome. With God's help we can make power our servant rather than our master.

The Ultimate Danger

Power itself is not inherently evil, but it is dangerous. And the most dangerous power of all is that which cloaks itself in the guise of religion. The spiritual leader who wants to keep his own ambition and lust for power in check must be willing to submit his plans and visions to the judgment of a council of godly advisers. Spiritual guidance, whether it comes in the form of an inner witness or through a personal vision, is simply too subjective to be left to a person's own judgment.

According to Richard Foster,

> Nothing is more dangerous than leaders accountable to no one. . . . If we look at the abuses of power in the Church today, very often we will see that behind them is someone who has decided that he or she has a direct pipeline to God and therefore does not need the counsel and correction of the community.[1]

This is the kind of thing that Jim Bakker writes about in his book *I Was Wrong*, when he talks about the "work" of the Lord becoming more important than the Lord Himself. At the height of the PTL expansion there was no time for personal spiritual disciplines, no time for staff devotions, no time for family life, no time for anything except daily television programs and the construction of hotels, theme parks, and halfway houses. Had anyone suggested to Jim that he was being disobedient he would have been indignant. Couldn't they see he was busy with the Lord's work? The only thing was that the Lord was no longer in it.

Had Jim Bakker realized what was happening in the early to mid-1980s he might have been spared the tragedies that befell him. As it turned out he was forced to resign from PTL in disgrace. He was convicted of criminal charges—twenty-four in all—and sentenced to forty-five years in prison. While incarcerated in the federal prison in Rochester, Minnesota, his wife divorced him and married his best friend.

Yet all was not lost. Even as the Lord was with Joseph during his time in the king's prison (Gen. 39:20–23), so was He with Jim Bakker. Although the five years Jim spent in Rochester Federal Prison were the most difficult of his entire life, God used them to conform him to the image of His dear Son (Rom. 8:29). Jim writes,

> In prison, I came to the end of Jim Bakker. God was teaching me that I must "die" daily. . . . I truly believe that one of the reasons God allowed me to go to prison was to learn this principle.[2]

I had accepted Jesus as my Savior and with my lips I had called Him "Lord," but in my heart and lifestyle, I now realized that He was not the Lord of my life; I was. . . . Although I was committed to following Jesus, I wanted to do it my way rather than His; I had given my life to Him, but I was still in control of it. As a result, although I knew and used the correct words and terminology, Jesus was not in fact Lord of my total life. Unwittingly, I had attempted to compartmentalize my relationship with Him, giving Him control of certain parts of me, yet not surrendering to His absolute Lordship. To put it another way, I wanted Jesus to be in my life, to be the engine, the power in my life, to be the motivator and the enabler who supplied the resources to do great things for God on earth and eventually take me to heaven, but I wanted to keep my hand on the controls.[3]

Who among us cannot identify with him? The potential for the abuse of power is present in every one of us. Frequently, it is held in check, not by true humility, but only by a lack of opportunity. Reading Bakker's book I found myself shuddering at the thought of the things I might have done had I been in his position. Like Jim, I had often reserved a part of my heart for myself. The only reason it had not destroyed me was because I lacked the "power" to act on it.

When Jesus came He introduced us to a new kind of power—a selfless power married to a holy love.

As I thought about these things I recalled a recurring dream from my earlier years. Before I get into it, let me tell you that many dream analysts believe that every person in our dreams represents a part of our personality. They also believe that our dreams are messages to ourselves even when they involve other people. I don't think that is always the case, but where my dream is concerned it seems to make sense.

In my dream, Brenda (my wife) was emotionally involved with another man. While the other man's identity varied from dream to dream, the theme never changed. He was always a public figure, rich and powerful. In the dream I tried to reason with Brenda, tried to tell her she was throwing away a beautiful relationship for a cheap thrill, but I couldn't reach her. She seemed oblivious to both my pain and my pleas. "It's nothing," she insisted. "Just something to do." Yet she could not be persuaded to give up the relationship. "I'm not doing anything," she explained irritably. "We're just friends."

Then I would awake feeling sick and angry. Although this went on for almost sixteen years, I tried to tell myself that it was only a dream, nothing to be concerned about. Still, I dreamed it again and again, at least once a month, sometimes as often as twice a week. Well do I remember the last time I dreamed it nearly fifteen years ago. Upon awaking I went into the bathroom. Leaning my head against the wall, I cried, "Lord, what does this mean?"

Instantly He answered me. Not with an audible voice, but with such clarity that I could not doubt its reality. He said, in a voice audible only to my spirit, "That dream is not about Brenda. It's about you and Me, and you're breaking *My* heart."

At once I knew what He meant. Although I had been actively involved in the ministry all my adult years, in my heart of hearts, I had nurtured a secret fantasy. I dreamed of being rich and powerful—a criminal lawyer perhaps, or a politician. A novelist or an actor. I had never pursued those dreams, but I wasn't willing to give them up either—that is, until that morning in 1982.

For the first time I understood what they meant, what they were doing to my relationship with the Lord. In truth, I was an unfaithful wife, reserving a part of my heart for someone, or something, other than Him. "Forgive me, O Lord," I prayed. "I renounce everything but You. I love You, and You alone, with all of my heart."

There, in the predawn darkness in that tiny bathroom, with my tear-dampened face pressed against the rough, textured wall, I made my peace with God, the lover of my soul. I walked from there a new man, never to dream that dream again so long as God was my heart's only desire.

I've only dreamed that dream one time since, and it was as the direct result of a "ministry" opportunity that appealed to my ego. For several years I had hosted a live ninety-minute call-in radio broadcast on Sunday nights. It had proved to be an effective vehicle for ministry, and the station manager asked me to host a daily program as well. After much discussion, I reluctantly agreed. When I shared it with the radio staff, they were apprehensive, but deferred to my judgment.

That very night I dreamed "the dream" again, only this time Brenda was emotionally involved with a minister who had a national ministry. He was not identified in my dream, but somehow I knew how successful and powerful he was. When I awoke, I knew instantly what God was telling me. This radio opportunity was not part of His plan for my life. Once again I was tempted with wealth and power, only this time it was in the form of a "ministry"! Needless to say, I immediately called the station manager and told him that I couldn't accept his offer; God would not permit it.

Herein lies the subtlety of power for the spiritual leader—often it comes disguised as ministry, an opportunity to do something important for God. I shudder to think what might have happened if it had not been for the apprehension of my staff, the faithfulness of a friend to speak the truth in love, and that God-given dream.

A New Kind of Power

When Jesus came He introduced us to a new kind of power—a selfless power married to a holy love. He voluntarily abdicated His divine rights in order to show us how to use power redemptively. In the Incarnation He left the throne room of heaven to live among men, and in His earthly ministry he renounced His rights in order to accept the higher calling of a servant. Notice that He did not give up His responsibility as a leader—just His rights and privileges. He said of Himself, "The Son of Man did not come to be served, but to serve" (Matt. 20:28).

How different is the model of the Master who took a towel and a basin of water and washed the disciples' feet. "Do nothing out of selfish ambition or vain conceit," wrote the apostle Paul. "Your attitude should be the same as that of Christ Jesus:

> Who being in very nature God,
>> did not consider equality with God
>>> something to be grasped,
>> but made himself nothing,
>>> taking the very nature of a servant,
>>> being made in human likeness.
> And being found in appearance as a man,
>> he humbled himself

and became obedient to death—
even death on a cross! *(Phil. 2:3, 5–8 NIV)*

Based on the example of Jesus, who made Himself nothing, humbled Himself, and became obedient, we can only conclude that discipline and self-denial are the only ways to control our lust for power. We must voluntarily limit our lifestyles in order to keep the "old man" in check. Indulge him just a little, and he will demand more and more. "Inordinate passions" according to Richard Foster, "are like spoiled children and need to be disciplined, and not indulged."[4]

As we have already noted, the potential for the abuse of power is present in every one of us. If we are given a little power, let the world beware! Alone, none of us is a match for its beguiling temptations, but together in mutual accountability, with God's help, we can overcome. Loving and humble service, in a room where nobody sees and nobody knows, is what transforms power into redemptive ministry. Only in serving others are we saved from our selfish selves and enabled to resist the temptation inherent in power.

Reflecting on Him

1. *In your own words, how can success in one's career lead to becoming more dependent on self and less reliant on God?*

2. *Can you identify an area in your life where you, like King Saul, rationalized a half-obedience to God's direction? What were the consequences or outcomes?*

3. *What have you done this past year to serve others? This past month? This past week?*

4. *What will you do, beginning today, to serve others?*

10

THE DISCIPLINES
OF JESUS

Recently I was discussing the manuscript for this book with a friend when the subject of our Lord's temptations came up. My friend's brow furrowed, and he looked at me with intense eyes. "Do you think," he asked, "that Jesus really struggled with temptation as we do? Or do you suppose that it was no big thing to Him?"

Tossing the ball back into his court, I countered, "What do you think?"

"I guess I've never really taken His temptations seriously. I mean, He was the Son of God and all. I just sort of assumed resisting temptation was second nature to Him.

"I will tell you this," he continued. "Overcoming temptation isn't easy for me. I'm kind of like the guy who said he could resist anything but temptation."

He laughed uneasily, fearing he might have revealed more about himself than he intended. When I didn't react, he continued in a more somber tone. "I'm a committed Christian and I love God, I really do, but if I'm gut-level honest with myself I have to admit that more often than not I don't want to resist temptation. I enjoy playing with fire, I just don't like getting burned."

Our conversation drifted to other things as afternoon turned into dusk. Finally it was time for us to go, and we made our way toward the cashier to pay for our coffee. Waiting in line my friend said, "About this temptation thing . . . If Jesus really did struggle with temptation as I do, then I would sure like to know His secret. I mean, how did He live His whole life without sinning?"

That's the question isn't it? How could Jesus be tempted in every way as we are and yet never succumb? How could He resist every temptation and live a perfectly sinless life?

Like my friend, many of us have a tendency to assume that He was victorious in temptation simply because He was divine. In fact nothing could be further from the truth. As Dr. David L. McKenna points out,

> He [Jesus] had to exercise self-discipline over his human nature in order to remain free from sin. No special gift was conferred upon him because he was the Son of God or because he was filled with the Holy Spirit at baptism. Jesus entered the temptation with the same resources that are available to every common man or woman who seeks to do the will of God.[1]

After a thorough study of the Gospels, I am convinced that the source of Jesus' strength lay in the spiritual disciplines He practiced: prayer, study of the Scriptures, public worship, and obedience to the Father's will. Through the consistent practice of these disciplines He was able to bring every thought, every desire, and every action into submission. If Jesus had to practice these disciplines in order to overcome temptation, how can we think for a minute that we can do any less?

The Discipline of Prayer

The whole of our Lord's life was permeated with prayer. He prayed publicly and in private. While others slept, He arose in the predawn darkness to seek the Father's face (Mark 1:35). Long after most people had retired for the night, He could be found on His knees praying. Often He slipped away into the mountains to pray (Mark 6:46), and if not into the mountains then to Gethsemane, as was His custom (Luke 22:39).

Every significant event in His ministry, from His baptism (Luke 3:21) to His death on the cross (Luke 23:34), was characterized by prayer. When it came time to choose the Twelve, He spent all night in prayer (Luke 6:12). When He was transfigured and the "appearance of His face was altered, and His robe became white and glistening" (Luke 9:29), Luke reports that He was praying. And in

Gethsemane He prayed so earnestly that "His sweat became like great drops of blood falling down to the ground" (Luke 22:44).

For Jesus, prayer was a way of life. It was not a duty but an opportunity. Prayer was to His Spirit what breath was to His physical body. In prayer Jesus experienced fellowship with the Father who nourished His soul. He received guidance to direct Him in His life's work and anointing to accomplish His ministry. It was the single most important discipline of His earthly existence and the source of His strength.

As His popularity grew, prayer became increasingly critical if He was to resist temptation and fulfill the Father's purpose. Now He was pressed on every side by the ever expanding demands of public ministry. He was tempted to yield to the expectations of the multitudes, rather than do the Father's will. Continually He was caught in the tension between those who wanted to make Him a king and those who sought His death. He was isolated by His call. It seemed that no one understood His true mission, not even those closest to Him. Of necessity He more and more "withdrew to lonely places and prayed" (Luke 5:16 NIV), for only in fellowship with the Father could He find the focus He needed and sought. Only through prayer was He able to renew His physical and emotional energy so He could remain effective in public ministry. And most important of all, only in the solitude of secret prayer could He strengthen Himself in God to overcome temptation.

We have often heard that prayer changes things, and it does. But more important, prayer changes us! This is the power of true prayer. It does for us what it did for Jesus: It brings our thoughts and feelings into perfect accord with the Father's desires. It restores our soul, reshapes us into God's image. It enlarges our vision and enables us to think God's thoughts after Him. It puts all of life into perspective and brings eternity into focus. This is true even when we are not consciously praying for these things, even when we do not realize it is happening. And it is this inner transformation that enables us to overcome temptation.

Prayer ushers us into the presence of God in a special way, and it is impossible to spend time in God's presence without being changed. This transformation will likely be so gradual that we will be aware of it only in retrospect, if at all. Still, over the course of a lifetime, prayer will do its refining work until at last we are conformed to the image of our Lord.

Sometimes though, the change may be so profound as to seem almost instantaneous. We may not be aware of it ourselves, but to those who know us it will be obvious. That's what happened to Moses on Mount Sinai. When he returned from spending forty days and forty nights in the presence of God, his face radiated with the glory of the Lord. Although he was totally unaware of it, Aaron and all the Israelites could see it clearly (Ex. 34:28–35).

In regard to ourselves we are not talking about a physical change, but a transformation of character. As we consciously spend time with God, we are being changed from the inside out. Or in the words of one country preacher, "God is changing our want to's." By the power of His Spirit God is writing His laws on our minds and in our hearts (Heb. 8:10). And as we continue to behold His glory we "are being transformed into the same image from glory to glory, just as by the Spirit of the Lord" (2 Cor. 3:18).

Because Jesus made prayer a priority, His life was God-centered rather than self-centered. His passion was to "do the will of Him who sent [Him] and to finish His work" (John 4:34). This was evident in all He did. The words Jesus spoke were the Father's words (John 12:49). Of His ministry He testified, "The Son can do nothing of Himself, but what He sees the Father do; for whatever He does, the Son also does in like manner" (John 5:19). His was a purpose-driven life, and though it did not make Him immune from temptation, it did minimize its impact. And because He was God-centered rather than self-centered, He was able to overcome every temptation.

The Discipline of Scripture

To the subjective discipline of prayer Jesus added the objective discipline of Scripture. By New Testament times synagogues were numerous and played a number of roles in Jewish community life, including the teaching of children. It was here that Jesus most likely learned to read and became acquainted with the Scriptures. That He was a student of the Scriptures we know, not by direct reference, but by inference. While the Gospels give a detailed overview of Jesus' prayer life, they are silent regarding His study habits. That He was a student of the Word, however, is evident throughout the Gospels. By the age of twelve He was so versed in the Scriptures that He was able to astound the teachers in the temple for three days. Luke said, "All who heard Him were astonished at His understanding and answers" (Luke 2:47).

Following His resurrection He spent an entire day expounding the Scriptures to two despairing disciples as they journeyed from Jerusalem to Emmaus.

> Then He said to them, "O foolish ones, and slow of heart to believe in all that the prophets have spoken! Ought not the Christ to have suffered these things and to enter into His glory?" And beginning at Moses and all the Prophets, He expounded to them in all the Scriptures the things concerning Himself. *(Luke 24:25–27)*

On numerous occasions Jesus quoted from the Psalms and the Prophets, especially Isaiah (Matt. 15:7–9). His teachings were laced with references from the Law and the Prophets. He alluded to the judgment of Sodom and Gomorrah (Matt. 10:15), referred to the days of Noah (Luke 17:26), spoke of the sign of Jonah the prophet (Matt. 12:39–41), and used the example of David eating the show-bread (Matt. 12:1–8). No one could teach this way unless his mind was steeped in the holy Scriptures. We can only conclude that as the product of a devout Jewish home, Jesus memorized the Scriptures from earliest childhood. Undoubtedly it was a discipline that He continued throughout His life. Like the psalmist He could say, "Your word I have hidden in my heart, / That I might not sin against You" (Ps. 119:11).

His ability to expound the Scriptures was legendary. Again and again He amazed the multitudes with His knowledge of the Law and His wisdom. "So all bore witness to Him, and marveled at the gracious words which proceeded out of His mouth" (Luke 4:22). "And they were astonished at His teaching, for His word was with authority" (Luke 4:32). It was obvious to all who heard Him that He had firsthand knowledge of the things about which He spoke.

Even more important is what the lifelong study of the Scriptures did for Jesus personally. By living in the Word, Jesus fortified His soul against the attack of the enemy. And when temptations came He was *prepared*. Without fail He defended Himself with the Word. Each time Satan tempted Him, He said, "It is written . . ." (Luke 4:4) and then quoted the rebuttal. Had He relied upon His own resources of logic or willpower He undoubtedly would have failed. "Humanity, however strong or good is never a match for evil. Only the Word of God has the authority to resist the power of Satan."[2]

While preaching in Puerto Rico some years ago I met a wonderful Christian lady who was known simply as "Black Evie." As a young person she had moved with her parents from San Juan to Spanish Harlem, where her life went from bad to worse. Soon she became addicted to drugs and was forced to resort to prostitution in order to support her habit.

For years she lived a nightmare existence in a world where nothing mattered except her next fix. Her companions were pimps and prostitutes and drug addicts like herself. She liked nothing better than tripping out with her "friends." Not infrequently she was stoned out of her head, sometimes for two or three days at a time. Following one such episode she returned to reality only to discover that her only child—a baby girl not yet a year old—was dead. Try as she might she could not reconstruct the weekend in her mind. She had absolutely no idea how or why her child had died.

Following a police investigation, she was charged with murder. However, before she could be brought to trial she suffered a complete mental collapse. Eventually she was placed in a state hospital for the criminally insane where she remained in a catatonic state.

Somehow a local pastor learned of her situation and felt compelled of the Lord to visit her. His first attempts were soundly rebuffed by the hospital administration, but he refused to give up. Eventually his persistence paid off, and he was granted permission to visit her for thirty minutes each day.

When he walked into her room the first time he hardly knew what to do. Evie sat in a chair, zombielike, staring at nothing with unseeing eyes. She did not return his greeting or in any way acknowledge his presence. In desperation he opened his Bible and began to read the Scriptures to her.

Though it was a depressing experience, he returned the next day, and the day after that, and every day thereafter for six long months. Not once during all of that time did Evie's condition change. She continued to stare through him as if he weren't there. And if she heard the Scriptures he so faithfully read to her, she never acknowledged it in any way.

One day early in the seventh month, he noticed a tear glistening on Evie's cheek as he finished his reading. That's all—just a single tear—but it set his heart to racing. The wall had been breached. The Word of God had penetrated her heart. Though she was locked in a dungeon of darkness, the light of the Lord had found her. The healing Word that the pastor had planted and so faithfully tended had germinated. Like a blade of grass forcing its way through a crack in a concrete sidewalk, it now pushed its way to the surface of her life.

Within a week Evie was fully restored to her right mind and she received Jesus Christ as her Savior. Eventually the charges against her were dropped, though no explanation was given, and she was released into the custody of a Christian rehabilitation ministry. After completing their two-year program she became the director of their center in San Juan, Puerto Rico.

I share Evie's testimony to illustrate the transforming power of God's Word. Although medication and psychiatric treatment had proved powerless to heal her tormented mind, the Word of God made her whole. Even when she could not grasp the meaning of the words, the Word was doing its redemptive work. "He sent His word and healed them, / And delivered them from their destructions" (Ps. 107:20).

If the Word of God could heal and restore Evie's burned-out mind, imagine what it can do for us. As we read it daily, meditate upon it, and memorize it we, too, will be changed. According to Romans we are "transformed by the renewing of [our] mind" (Rom. 12:2), and it is the Word of God that does that. And it is this inward transformation that gives us, not only the *will* to overcome temptation, but the *power* to do so as well.

The Discipline of Public Worship

To the disciplines of prayer and Scripture Jesus also added the discipline of public worship. Returning to Nazareth following His wilderness encounter with the devil, He went into the synagogue on the Sabbath day "as His custom was" (Luke 4:16).

Now why, I ask you, would Jesus find it necessary to practice the discipline of public worship? What possible benefit could He, who had known intimately the power of eternal worship, now glean from such a pedestrian experience? Surely the shabby service in a village synagogue could not compare with the splendor of heaven's throne room, where seraphim worshiped Him day and night, crying, "Holy, holy, holy, / Lord God Almighty, / Who was and is and is to come!" (Rev. 4:8). Nor could the simple liturgy of a first-century Galilean congregation compare with the order of worship in heaven's sanctuary where God Himself is enthroned. In heaven there are lightning and thunder, living creatures full of eyes, and twenty-four elders who fall on their faces and cast their crowns before the throne. They worship Him who lives forever and ever, saying, "You are worthy, O Lord, / To receive glory and honor and power" (Rev. 4:11).

Nor is there a village choir anywhere that can compare with that celestial choir, which is composed of many angels, the living creatures, the elders, and those whom the Lamb has redeemed out of every tribe and tongue and people and nation. The number of them is "ten thousand times ten thousand, and thousands of thousands" (Rev. 5:11). When they lift their voices, all eternity echoes with the sound of their praise. "Blessing and honor and glory and power / Be to Him who sits on the throne, / And to the Lamb, forever and ever!" (Rev. 5:13).

His faithful obedience in the little things enabled
Him to be obedient in all things.

On a more pedestrian level, what could Jesus experience in the synagogue that He had not already experienced alone with God in private prayer or as He pored over the Scriptures? What could a lay reader or a visiting rabbi possibly tell Him about God that He didn't already know?

The answer to these questions is readily obvious—nothing! Still, the more I think about it, the more convinced I am that these are not the right questions. Public worship isn't about getting, but about giving. In public worship we offer ourselves, not only to God in worship, but to each other in Spirit-directed ministry. Here we not only love God with all our heart, mind, soul, and strength, but also our neighbor as ourself (Matt. 22:37–39).

Jesus went to the synagogue on the Sabbath day because that was where needy people went in search of love and healing. And the synagogue is where He performed some of His most wonderful miracles: healing a man with a withered hand (Matt. 12:9–13), casting out an unclean spirit (Mark 1:21–26), and healing a woman who had been crippled for eighteen years (Luke 13:10–13).

In public worship we lose our independence and become inter-
dependent. God becomes "our" Father instead of "my" Father. In
corporate worship the great truths of Scripture and the spiritual
life are fleshed out. Here, in relationship with one another, we learn
to serve, to forgive, to share, and to love.

Fred Craddock, professor of preaching at Emory University,
relates an experience from his early ministry that is a case in point.
At the time he was single and serving a small mission congregation
in the Appalachians. It was the custom in that church to have a
baptismal service on Easter evening. Since they baptized by immer-
sion, the baptismal service was conducted in Watts Bar Lake at sun-
down.

Following the baptismal service the little congregation would
gather around a bonfire and eat supper together. When the meal
was over one of the elders, a man named Glen Hickey, introduced
the new members. He gave their names, where they lived, and their
work.

The rest of the congregation then formed a circle around the new
members, and one by one each person in the circle gave his or her
name and said: "My name is _____, if you ever need somebody to do washing and ironing." "My name is _____, if you
ever need anybody to chop wood." "My name is _____, if
you ever need anybody to baby-sit." "My name is _____, if
you ever need anybody to repair your house for you." "My name
is _____, if you ever need anybody to sit with the sick." "My
name is _____, if you ever need a car to go to town."

When everyone had introduced themselves and offered their
services, then they had a square dance. Finally Percy Miller, with
thumbs in his bibbed overalls, would stand up and say, "It's time
to go," and everybody would leave.

The first time Pastor Craddock conducted one of those services,
he and Percy Miller were the last to leave. After everyone else was
gone they stood in the dark watching the fire die. "Craddock,"
Miller mused, "folks don't ever get any closer than this."

When I heard him tell that story he ended it by saying, "In that
little community, they have a name for that. I've heard it in other
communities, too. In that community, their name for that is *church*.
They call that church."[3]

What, you may be wondering, does all of that have to do with
overcoming temptation? More than you might suppose, although

it relates to temptation indirectly rather than directly. Remember that there is really only one temptation—the temptation to choose my will over God's will. Therefore any discipline that requires me to choose God over self or others over self—as public worship does—prepares me for the moment of temptation. Having learned to choose God and others over self in the spiritual environment of worship, I am now better prepared to make that same choice in the hour of temptation.

The Discipline of Obedience

To the disciplines of prayer, Scripture, and public worship Jesus added the discipline of obedience. While each discipline was vitally important to His spiritual life, none went to the heart of temptation in quite the same way as the discipline of obedience. Through the discipline of obedience Jesus dealt directly with the roots of temptation by bringing His human will into submission to the will of God.

Obedience was a learned behavior even for Jesus, and He learned to be obedient to the Father by being obedient to His earthly parents. Following the episode in the temple when Jesus was twelve years old, He returned to Nazareth with His parents "and was obedient to them" (Luke 2:51 NIV). Consequently He "increased in wisdom and stature, and in favor with God and men" (Luke 2:52).

Obedience did not come naturally to Jesus' human nature. "Though He was a Son, yet *He learned obedience* by the things which He suffered" (Heb. 5:8, emphasis mine). Little by little He mastered the discipline of obedience—first as a child, then as an adolescent, and finally as an adult. His faithful obedience in the little things enabled Him to be obedient in all things.

The key to overcoming temptation is the way we live our lives before temptation strikes.

While there were undoubtedly many turning points throughout His life, points at which a single act of disobedience could have derailed redemption's plan, no experience was more critical than that which He underwent in Gethsemane the night He was betrayed. There His human will drew back in revulsion from the

116

plan of God. It was not the Roman cross He feared, nor the shame of being crucified with criminals, but separation from His heavenly Father. As inconceivable as it may seem, if He surrendered to the will of the Father, He would suffer the one thing He could not bear—His rejection! It was the price He must pay in order to redeem Adam's lost race, but His soul recoiled in horror at the thought.

Three times He was tempted to resist the purposes of the Father. Three times He cried out, "O My Father, if it is possible, let this cup pass from Me" (Matt. 26:39). In the end, however, the disciplines of a lifetime prevailed. In obedience He surrendered to the will of the Father, praying, "O My Father, if this cup cannot pass away from Me unless I drink it, Your will be done" (Matt. 26:42).

In resisting the temptation to choose His will over God's will Jesus was able to fulfill the Father's purpose.

> He humbled Himself and became obedient to the point of death, even the death of the cross. Therefore God also has highly exalted Him and given Him the name which is above every name, that at the name of Jesus every knee should bow, of those in heaven, and of those on earth, and of those under the earth, and that every tongue should confess that Jesus Christ is Lord, to the glory of God the Father. *(Phil. 2:8–11)*

Like us, Jesus had to work to bring His humanity in line with the eternal purpose of God. He had to exercise spiritual discipline to live by the commandments rather than by the self-centered needs of His human nature. But because He did, He was able to overcome every temptation and endure the Cross, thus becoming "the author and finisher of our faith" (Heb. 12:2).

The spiritual disciplines that Jesus practiced did not in and of themselves enable Him to overcome temptation and live a sinless life. God the Father provided the power that enabled Jesus to overcome. The disciplines were merely the vehicle through which that power was transferred from the Father to the Son.

As we seek to be like Christ, the disciplines of prayer, Scripture, public worship, and obedience will become increasingly important to us. At this point we will likely encounter a new temptation. Now we will be tempted to look to the disciplines as the source of our strength. They are not the source, and in fact they have value only as a way of drawing us closer to God. The living Christ is our strength. The disciplines are merely the means whereby we tap into His inexhaustible resources.

The key to overcoming temptation is the way we live our lives before temptation strikes. If we wait until the enemy has us cornered before we attempt to draw upon the strength of Christ, we will likely fail. Instead we must daily draw upon His strength so we can confront temptation from a position of spiritual strength rather than one of weakness. Even then we will likely require an infusion of spiritual power in order to overcome, but at least we will know where to find His help, having made it a practice to go to Him daily. This is the value of the disciplines.

Reflecting on Him

1. *Make a careful inventory of how often you have practiced the four spiritual disciplines in your life over the past two weeks to establish a baseline of your present level of activity. What is a realistic expectation for improving in each area?*

2. *How often do you spend time in prayer, and by how much do you wish to increase your prayer time?*

3. *What portion of God's Word do you wish to improve your knowledge of—the Gospels, the New Testament church, the lives of the apostles, etc.*

4. *Do you need to improve your attendance at regular church services—Sunday morning, Sunday school, Sunday evening, or midweek services?*

5. *Jot down all of the ways you have been obedient to God, then take a moment and celebrate this with a word of thanksgiving to God. In what areas of your life could you become more obedient?*

THE SEVEN STAGES
OF TEMPTATION

When sincere believers succumb to temptation, it is seldom a sudden thing. Rather it is the culmination of a series of seemingly innocent compromises that ultimately result in a tragic fall. The evidence of this is found repeatedly in both contemporary Christendom and throughout the Scriptures.

No case study reveals it more clearly, however, than does Peter's denial of Jesus. It was the final act in a seven-part drama that began with overconfidence and ended with bitter regret. Along the way there were prayerlessness, misguided zeal, distancing, and fellowship with the world.

These seven stages are not unique to Peter. They can be found, in one form or another, in almost every sinful failure. The task before us then is to identify the early stages in temptation's downward spiral. If we can recognize them and respond accordingly, we will significantly increase our chances of escaping the tempter's snare. Failing here, we condemn ourselves to repeated failure.

11

THE DREAM

Some years ago a colleague invited me to conduct a leadership retreat for the church where he was serving as senior pastor. The night before I was scheduled to leave for the retreat, God came to me in a dream with a message for my friend. Although this was not something that had ever happened to me before, I did not question its validity, so real was the sense of the Lord's presence.

The next day Bill picked me up at the airport, and we headed across the mountains toward the retreat center. For the better part of an hour we made casual conversation, catching up on what was going on with our families and the congregations we served. Finally, I took a deep breath and said, "Bill, there is something we need to talk about."

Glancing my way he said, "Fire away."

"Last night God came to me in a dream with a message for you."

It seemed his grip tightened on the steering wheel, but I might have imagined it. When I hesitated, he gave me a quick look before saying, "Well, what was it?"

"Bill," I said, "God told me to tell you not to have anything to do with Ruth."

This time his knuckles turned white, so tightly did he grip the steering wheel. For what seemed a long time neither of us spoke, the only sounds being the hum of the tires on the blacktop and the rush of the wind past the windows. Finally I asked, "Who is Ruth?"

"Ruth is part of our pastoral staff," he replied. "She is the director of our counseling center. Her husband is one of my closest friends."

He offered no further explanation, and I decided to let the matter drop. It was not a comfortable situation, and having delivered the message, I was only too happy to move on to more pleasant topics. In retrospect, I realize I should have pressed the issue. I should have asked Bill what was going on, but I didn't.

Although Bill and I maintained a long-distance relationship, talking by telephone every few weeks, we never spoke of that incident again. To my way of thinking he was a most unlikely candidate for infidelity. From all appearances he loved his wife of more than twenty years, his children, and his ministry. I simply could not imagine that he would do anything to jeopardize all of that.

Tragedy Strikes

Then one Monday, nearly four years later, I felt compelled to telephone Bill. At the time I did not recognize it as the prompting of the Holy Spirit, though I now believe it was. His wife answered the telephone, and as soon as she recognized my voice she began sobbing uncontrollably. When she finally composed herself she said, "Bill wants a divorce. He is having an affair with Ruth."

After comforting her as best I could, I asked to speak to Bill. As soon as he said hello, I asked him what was going on. In an embarrassed but determined tone, he told me that he had found something with Ruth that he had never had with Janet, and he was not willing to give it up.

"Please listen to me, Bill," I pleaded. "This is not the kind of decision you want to make without getting professional help. Brenda and I have enough frequent flyer miles to provide you and Janet free tickets to anywhere in the continental United States. Please let us fly both of you to EMERGE Ministry,[1] where you can receive the help you need."

Promising to think about it, Bill ended our conversation and I hung up the telephone feeling sick. Sitting at my desk I pondered the situation. There was a time when I believed only bad people did such things, but that time was long past. Now I knew better. Over the years I had witnessed the tragic failures of numerous friends and colleagues, good people every one, yet they had not been able to resist temptation.

Three days later Bill and I talked again. He declined my offer to fly to EMERGE Ministry. As far as he was concerned there wasn't anything a counselor could say that would make him change his mind. He simply could not imagine spending the rest of his life without Ruth.

I tried to reason with him, telling him that as serious as adultery was, divorce was far more serious. I begged him not to betray the trust of his children, not to throw away twenty-five years of marriage. It was no use. He was determined to do things his way regardless of who got hurt.

Finally I asked, "Bill, what about the dream God gave me? What about His warning telling you to have nothing to do with Ruth?"

For what seemed a long time he didn't say anything. Then in a voice that sounded terribly tired he said, "It was already too late."

"What do you mean?" I demanded. "Were you already having an affair with her?"

"No," he replied, "but we had already formed an emotional bond between us."

That was the last time we talked. Though I tried to call him several times, he did not return my calls. Finally I stopped calling. Try as I might, though, I could not get his final words out of my mind. Nor could I help wondering how many good people go awry in the same way—never realizing until it is too late that once that emotional bond is formed, it is nearly impossible to break, making the actual act of physical adultery almost inevitable.

Sickness Strikes

Following their separate divorces, Bill and Ruth were married; though, how they could think that marriage would make their terrible wrongs right is beyond me. As fate would have it, they were not to know the happiness they envisioned. Shortly after their wedding, Bill underwent a routine physical examination. During the process the doctors discovered that he had cancer. Neither radical surgery nor radiation treatment was completely successful, and six months later the cancer reappeared. After another round of radiation therapy, the cancerous tumor was gone, but subsequent blood tests indicated that cancer was still alive somewhere in his system.

The doctors informed him that it would probably take three to five years for the cancer to fully manifest itself. "By that time," they encouraged him, "there should be a cure."

"And if there isn't?" Bill asked.

"In that case," the doctor replied soberly, "you probably have somewhere between three and seven years to live."

I am not suggesting that Bill was stricken with cancer because he was involved in an adulterous affair with Ruth. Life is simply not that cut-and-dried. It cannot be reduced to a mathematical equation. Not every adulterer gets cancer, nor is it only adulterers who are stricken with the disease. Faithful husbands and wives by the hundreds do battle with cancer every week.

Once that emotional bond is formed, it is nearly impossible to break, making the actual act of physical adultery almost inevitable.

Beyond the simple explanation that sickness and death are a result of humanity's fallen state, God has not given us insight into the why of every individual situation. Jesus shed some light on the issue in Luke 13 when He referred to some Galileans who were put to death by Pilate and to another eighteen who died when a tower in Siloam fell on them. He asked, "Do you suppose that these Galileans were worse sinners than all other Galileans, because they suffered such things? I tell you, no" (Luke 13:2–3).

Jesus did not tell us why these particular individuals died while others equally sinful were allowed to live, but He did make it clear that their deaths had nothing to do with the degree of their sinfulness.

A Severe Mercy

In light of that I can say with confidence that God did not strike Bill with cancer. I am equally confident that God will redeem the situation; He will use Bill's illness as an instrument of discipline to bring him to repentance. It is not judgment that motivates God, but mercy. Not anger, but love.

Hebrews 12 declares:

> The Lord disciplines those he loves,
> And he punishes everyone he accepts as a son. . . .
> Our fathers disciplined us for a little while as they thought best;
> but God disciplines us for our good, that we may share in his holi-
> ness. No discipline seems pleasant at the time, but painful. Later on,
> however, it produces a harvest of righteousness and peace for those
> who have been trained by it. *(Heb. 12:6, 10–11 NIV)*

I'm convinced that God loves Bill and Ruth too much to allow
them to experience any lasting contentment except in relationship
with Him. Even in this dark hour of sickness He seeks only their
eternal good. All He desires is that they turn to Him with all their
hearts. And when they do they will surely hear Him say:

> All which I took from thee I did but take,
>   Not for thy harms,
> But just that thou might'st seek it in My arms.
>   All which thy child's mistake
> Fancies as lost, I have stored for thee at home:
>   Rise, clasp My hand, and come![2]

Reflecting on Him

1. *Can you recall a time in your life when you ignored warnings
   and fell prey to temptation?*

2. *As you reflect on this occasion, what have you learned that
   you would like to pass on to newer Christians so that they
   might be more apt to hear warnings from God?*

12

OVERCONFIDENCE

When sincere believers like Bill and Ruth succumb to temptation, it is seldom a sudden thing. Rather it is the culmination of a series of seemingly innocent compromises that ultimately result in a tragic fall. The evidence of this is found repeatedly in both contemporary Christendom and throughout the Scriptures.

No case study reveals it more clearly, however, than does Peter's denial of Jesus. It was the final act in a seven-part drama that began with overconfidence and ended with bitter regret. Along the way there was prayerlessness, misguided zeal, distancing, and fellowship with the world.

These seven stages are not unique to Peter. They can be found, in one form or another, in almost every sinful failure. The task before us then is to identify the early stages in temptation's downward spiral. If we can recognize them and respond accordingly, we will significantly increase our chances of escaping the tempter's snare. Failing here, we condemn ourselves to repeated failure.

A Case Study in Denial

With these thoughts in mind let us turn our attention to Peter's situation. I call it a case study in denial. Mark wrote:

> "You will all fall away," Jesus told them, "for it is written:
> 'I will strike the shepherd, and the sheep will be scattered.'
> But after I have risen, I will go ahead of you into Galilee."

Peter declared, "Even if all fall away, I will not."

"I tell you the truth," Jesus answered, "today—yes, tonight—before the rooster crows twice you yourself will disown me three times."

But Peter insisted emphatically, "Even if I have to die with you, I will never disown you." And all the others said the same. *(Mark 14:27–31 NIV)*

The first step in Peter's journey toward denial was overconfidence. In spite of Jesus' repeated warnings, Peter refused to consider the possibility of personal failure. As far as he was concerned there was absolutely no way that he would deny his Lord. The others might all forsake Jesus, but he would remain faithful even at the risk of death. Or so he thought.

> *An unguarded strength is a double weakness.*
> *—Oswald Chambers*

Unfortunately Peter's bold words proved to be just that—words. When his moment of truth came, he caved in. Confronted by a servant girl in Caiaphas's courtyard, he emphatically denied any knowledge of Jesus, not once but three times. And in the distance a rooster crowed.

Some years ago Gordon MacDonald, author of *Ordering Your Private World*, gave the commencement address at a college. Before the ceremony began, he sat with a member of the school's board in the president's office. As they were all getting acquainted the man suddenly turned to MacDonald and asked, "If Satan were to blow you out of the water, how do you think he would do it?"

After thinking about it for a moment, MacDonald replied, "I'm not sure I know. All sorts of ways, I suppose; but I know there's one way he wouldn't get me. He'd never get me in the area of my personal relationships. That's one place where I have no doubt that I'm as strong as you can get."[1]

Unfortunately, MacDonald's bold assurance turned out to be just words, and some years later his world blew apart. Of that tragic experience he writes: "A chain of seemingly innocent choices became destructive, and it was my fault. Choice by choice by choice, each easier to make, each becoming gradually darker. And then my world broke—in the very area I had predicted I was safe."[2]

Like Peter, he failed in an area where he was absolutely sure he could not fail. The enemy tripped him up, not at his weakest point, but at the point of his perceived strength. Coincidence? I don't think so, for history is filled with men and women who have succumbed to temptation in areas where they seemed immune to failure.

Unguarded Strengths

Is there a lesson for us here? Undoubtedly. For as Oswald Chambers reminded us, an "unguarded strength is [a] double weakness."[3] If I understand Chambers correctly, he was saying that we may well be most vulnerable in the very areas where we think we are least vulnerable.

Return with me to the case of Pastor Charles Blair (Chapter 7). In many ways he was a man ahead of his time. While most ministers were still locked in a 1950s mind-set, Blair was forging ahead. He was an innovator, always looking for new and more effective ways to reach the unchurched with the Gospel. As such he was one of the first ministers to found an independent, nondenominational church. He was also a pioneer in the utilization of television as a vehicle of outreach. Through his weekly broadcast of Calvary Temple's Sunday morning service he reached tens of thousands of unreached men and women with the Gospel.

Unfortunately, the very strengths that enabled him to do great things for God also made him vulnerable to temptation. In August 1976 a jury found him guilty of seventeen counts of fraudulent and otherwise prohibited sale of securities in connection with the church's ill-fated geriatric center. He was fined $12,750 and placed on five years' probation. He was allowed to remain the senior pastor of Calvary Temple, and under his leadership the church was able to repay the investors according to a plan approved by the bankruptcy court.

As I reflect on that incident, these many years later, I cannot help wondering how it could happen. From all reports Charles Blair is a man of integrity. There is no evidence that he, or his family, benefited in any way from the illegal sale of securities. Nor is there anything to suggest that he intended to defraud those who invested. All of which simply makes this scenario more troubling. This is not the story of an evil man reaping the wages of his sin, but the tragic account of a good man whose vision exceeded his judgment.

In his book, *The Man Who Could Do No Wrong*, he candidly confesses his mistakes: (1) According to Blair, prior successes caused him to believe that anything he attempted for God would succeed. (2) He trusted others to oversee the financial affairs of the ministry and never became knowledgeable enough to give proper oversight in that area. (3) He was overly busy with the multitude of demands made by an expanding, multifaceted ministry. (4) He ignored the concerns expressed by his wife, Betty—never really praying through the Life Center project with her until they were one in heart and mind. He says, "I never really submitted my dream until we reached the place were we could say, 'It seemed good to the Holy Spirit and to us' (Acts 15:28) to proceed."[4]

Although God has promised to provide a way of escape each time we are tempted, it is our responsibility to seek for it as soon as the tempter whispers his beguiling suggestions.

By his own admission he ignored all the warning signs, dismissing them as obstacles to be overcome by faith. And because it seemed a good thing to build a geriatric center to care for the elderly he trusted his own wisdom rather than seeking the counsel of God through prayer and the advice of godly men. In a word, he was overconfident! His unguarded strength became a double weakness.

No One Is Immune

Undoubtedly overconfidence also played a major role in the tragedy in which Bill and Ruth found themselves. Surely they recognized the warning signs, having counseled others regarding these very pitfalls. They must have reasoned that although their relationship was risky they could handle it. After all, they were both spiritually mature. And who can doubt that Satan used the very gifts God had entrusted to them for their destruction?

Among the strengths that made them effective in ministry were their *genuine concern for people* and their *gift for empathetic listening*. In the end these qualities also proved to be their undoing.

At some point their concern for each other became more than pastoral, more than mere friendship. And at that point they undoubtedly found themselves meeting emotional needs for each other that could be met legitimately only by their spouses. Although they hadn't yet done anything sexually inappropriate they were, nonetheless, guilty of emotional adultery. And because they did not take immediate steps to rectify the situation, it was only a matter of time until they found themselves entangled in a full-blown affair. Like so many others, their unguarded strengths became double weaknesses.

The way of escape is broad and easy to find in the initial moments of temptation, but if we delay, it becomes increasingly difficult to find.

Throughout history, men and women of God have fallen prey to the enemy. Not infrequently overconfidence has played a critical role. That should come as no surprise, for the Scriptures are filled with repeated warnings. Proverbs 11:2 declares, "When pride [overconfidence] comes, then comes shame." Proverbs 16:18 says, "Pride goes before destruction, / And a haughty spirit before a fall." No passage, however, states it more clearly than 1 Corinthians 10:12: "Therefore let him who thinks he stands take heed lest he fall."

The Road Not Taken

How differently things might have turned out for Peter if, instead of proclaiming his undying loyalty, he had fallen to his knees in prayer. We can only imagine what holy thing might have been wrought in him had he prayed, "Lord, have mercy upon me. Save me from myself. What do You know about me that I don't know about myself? What do You see in my heart that I can't see? Change me, Oh Lord. Make me into the man I ought to be."

How differently things might have turned out for Bill and Ruth if only he had pulled the car to the side of the road and bared his soul to me. If only he had said, "Richard, you don't know how many times I have reached for the telephone to call you, but I couldn't. I wanted to, but I just couldn't. Thank God you had that dream. With you I don't have to pretend. Now I can share my struggles and find the help I so desperately need."

Unfortunately, what's done is done. No matter how much we would like to, we cannot undo the past. We can, however, learn from it. We can determine that, by the grace of God, we will not think more highly of ourselves than we should. Instead let us continually commit ourselves to the faithfulness of God, for it is written: "God is faithful, who will not allow you to be tempted beyond what you are able, but with the temptation will also make the way of escape, that you may be able to bear it" (1 Cor. 10:13).

Although God has promised to provide a way of escape each time we are tempted, it is our responsibility to seek for it as soon as the tempter whispers his beguiling suggestions. Experience has taught me that the way of escape is broad and easy to find in the initial moments of temptation, but if we delay, it becomes increasingly difficult to find. Or as Thomas à Kempis pointed out, "The only time to stop temptation is at the first point of recognition. If one begins to argue and engage in a hand-to-hand combat, temptation almost always wins the day."[5]

Reflecting on Him

1. *In what area of your Christian walk do you feel most secure? Take time to immediately ask for God's grace in this area of your life and commit it anew to Him.*

2. *What have you been taking for granted about your relationship with God?*

13

PRAYERLESSNESS

Overconfidence leads to prayerlessness as surely as summer follows spring. It could not be otherwise, for when a person feels self-sufficient, prayer is totally foreign to him. He may mumble a few perfunctory words out of force of habit, but that hardly constitutes prayer. If he is honest with himself, he has to admit that as far as he is concerned prayer may be nice, but it is not necessary. He can manage just fine by himself, thank you.

Months may go by, even years, but eventually he will be brought face-to-face with the barrenness of his soul. It may take a family tragedy—death or divorce. Or it may be nothing more than unemployment or a major financial reversal. Still, when it comes, whatever form it takes, he will suddenly discover that his inner resources are sadly lacking.

Such was the case for the eleven disciples, especially Peter. Following His grim prediction that they all would desert Him (Matt. 26:31–35), Jesus led them to Gethsemane, a garden located on the Mount of Olives. It was a favorite retreat of His, a place where He went often to be alone with the Father. But on that fateful night it afforded Him no comfort, for His soul was "exceedingly sorrowful, even to death"(Matt. 26:38).

Taking Peter, James, and John, Jesus led them apart from the others. Turning to them, He looked into their eyes with a sobering intensity. "Stay here and watch with Me," He said before going deeper into the garden (Matt. 26:38). Alone now, He fell facedown on the ground in prayer.

After Jesus disappeared into the darkness, Peter and the two brothers looked at each other. They didn't say anything; they just looked. Having never seen Jesus like this, they were at a loss for words. Finally they each found a place to pray, but their efforts were short-lived. Having never mastered the discipline of intercessory prayer, their attempts at it were awkward at best.

After a period of intense travail, in which Jesus pleaded with the Father that the cup might be taken from Him (Matt. 26:39), He returned to the three. Finding them asleep He cried, "What? Could you not watch with Me one hour?" (Matt. 26:40).

Temptation, in whatever form it comes, always appeals to our self-life.

According to Mark the disconcerted disciples were speechless: "They did not know what to answer Him" (Mark 14:40). The Master's need had laid bare the barrenness of their souls. Now they stood revealed for what they were: good men, but largely empty on the inside. Though they had spent three years in the Lord's company, they were not prepared for the temptations that now pressed in upon them.

Under different circumstances Jesus might have rebuked them for their negligence, but not tonight. Now their grieving silence touched something deep in His heart and He said, "Watch and pray that you may not enter into temptation; the spirit indeed is willing, but the flesh is weak" (Mark 14:38 RSV).

The Flesh Is Weak

"The spirit indeed is willing, but the flesh is weak" (Mark 14:38). These words of Jesus strike at the very core of our being, laying bare the thoughts and intents of our hearts. A part of us— our spirit—hungers for prayer; but another part of us—the flesh— rebels. If the truth be known, most of us love to talk about prayer. We love sermons on prayer and books about prayer, as well as testimonies of answered prayer. We just can't discipline ourselves to pray, at least not with any real consistency. Our spirit is willing, but our flesh is weak.

And because we have not practiced the discipline of prayer with any consistency, we find ourselves falling into temptation and the snare of the enemy. This is especially true if one is battling a sinful habit or a stronghold in his or her life.

Overcoming Strongholds

For years I struggled with what the wise man refers to as "reckless words" (Prov. 12:18 NIV). In public I managed to keep my remarks under control for the most part, but with my family I could be a terror. That's not to say that I was not affectionate or affirming, but only that my kind words could turn cutting and cruel in an instant. Let the almighty "I" (Chapter 2) not get his way, and I would rage like a spoiled child. This went on for years, and I was mostly blind to the pain I inflicted. Finally Brenda could take no more. "I can't live like this," she sobbed. "When Leah graduates, I am going to divorce you."

For the first time in my life, I began to realize the damage wrought by my reckless words. As the wise man said, they pierced like a sword, ripping and tearing. Having finally been brought face-to-face with Brenda's hurt and pain, I determined to change. However, much to my dismay, I discovered that the sinful habits of a lifetime are not overcome by sheer willpower. Try as I might, I could not reform myself.

In desperation I turned to the Lord. Day after day I prayed, "'Set a guard, O LORD, over my mouth; / Keep watch over the door of my lips' [Ps. 141:3]. Let me speak no unkind word, 'but only what is helpful for building others up according to their needs, that it may benefit those who listen'" (Eph. 4:29 NIV).

"Go deeper, Lord," I prayed. "Change my heart, 'For out of the abundance of the heart the mouth speaks' [Matt. 12:34]. 'Create in me a clean heart, O God, / And renew a steadfast spirit within me'" (Ps. 51:10).

In the early stages of the battle I found it necessary to pray, not just once a day, but several times a day. As I was faithful in prayer God was able to do His redemptive work in me. Little by little my behavior changed, until, finally, reckless words were the exception rather than the rule.

Then I faced a new temptation—overconfidence. Thinking I could handle things on my own, I stopped praying with such faithful intensity. Things were all right for a day or two, then I found myself slipping back. Soon my words became biting and bitter again.

I should have learned from that first relapse, but of course I didn't. In fact, I've had several relapses over the years, each one following a period of overconfidence, accompanied by prayerlessness, when I was sure I had the thing whipped. Belatedly, I am realizing that I will never be totally free of this hurtful tendency, that I can live in victory only as long as I guard my heart in prayer. Failing to pray, I will fall into temptation and failure, as surely as water freezes at thirty-two degrees Fahrenheit.

In truth, prayer is an unspoken declaration of our utter dependence upon God. Every time we pray we are renouncing fleshly pride and self-sufficiency. It is our way of acknowledging that we cannot be the persons He has called us to be apart from the ongoing work of His Holy Spirit in our lives. Given our strong bent toward self-will, it may well be necessary to surrender our recalcitrant selves to Him many times every day for the rest of our lives.

The Self-Life

Temptation, in whatever form it comes, always appeals to our *self-life*. By virtue of our fallen nature we tend to see ourselves as the center of the universe. This is true whether we are egomaniacs or victims of a tragically poor self-image. Either way, the world revolves around us. The self-conscious person is sure every eye is on him; every slight, real or imagined, is personal. For his part, the egomaniac seeks the center stage. As far as he is concerned, no one's needs or desires are as important as his own. People then fall into two categories: fans or enemies.

In the heat of temptation we can think only of ourselves, only of the moment. The deceiver tells us to take control of our lives, to do it our way. "Rules were made for others," he says. "You are smart enough to know what is best for you. Seize the moment. Don't be intimidated by what others say."

He tells us to think only of ourselves, regardless of the consequences our actions may have. Once we buy into his way of thinking there is almost no sinful choice that we cannot justify. Our "needs" take precedence over everything else—marriage vows, children, even God's law.

When confronted by the wife he had betrayed, one unfaithful husband naively explained his sinful actions saying, "I was attracted to her." Nothing more, just that, as if his whims, his desires, were all that mattered.

After filing for a divorce (for which there were no scriptural grounds) a disgruntled wife told her husband, "I know this is painful for you, and I'm sorry, really I am, but I've got to think of myself. At this point in my life I have to think of my own needs."

In the moment of temptation it is as if we are looking at life through a telephoto lens. The object of our selfish desire is magnified until it fills the entire frame of our existence. It is the only thing in focus, everything else is blurred.

Eternal Perspective

No wonder Jesus urged us to "watch and pray, lest you enter into temptation" (Matt. 26:41). Only prayer can put "this moment" of temptation into eternal perspective. Only prayer can enable us to see the big picture. Yes, we are free to pursue our sinful desires if we so choose, but we do not live in a vacuum. There will be consequences—in this life and in the next.

Prayer neutralizes the tempting lies of the enemy by refocusing our attention on God. In the secrecy of the imagination, where self is king, the beguiling suggestions of the deceiver are mesmerizing, even hypnotic. But when we enter the presence of God, we see them for the tawdry things they really are.

In prayer we see God, high and lifted up, and His glory fills our being. Like the prophet of old we cry, "Woe is me, for I am undone! / Because I am a man of unclean lips, . . . For my eyes have seen the King, / The LORD of hosts" (Isa. 6:5).

In His presence we see ourselves as He sees us, and that can be terribly disconcerting, for nothing is hidden from Him. Yet for all of our flawed humanity He does not condemn us, nor does He reject us. Rather He touches our lives with His sanctifying power, and we are changed.

Leslie Dunkin shares an experience from her childhood that illustrates how prayer counteracts temptation. She writes, "My father used to put a bit of meat or biscuit on the floor near a dog we had and say, 'No!' and the dog knew he must not touch it. But he never looked at the meat. He seemed to feel that if he did so, the temptation to disobey would be too great, so he looked steadily at my father's face."[1]

Prayer is like that. It turns our attention away from temptation and toward the face of God. Now we see all things clearly. God is the center of the universe. He is in heaven. We are on earth. It is His kingdom, His glory, and His power that we seek and not our own.

Reflecting on Him

1. *What do you imagine Jesus' life would have been like had He prayed less?*

2. *How different do you think your life could be if you would identify one key behavior you would like to change and submit it to God daily?*

14

MISGUIDED ZEAL

Return with me once again to Gethsemane. By now the hour was late, and in the shadowy darkness beneath the olive trees, the Son of man groaned in agony, then grew still. After a long while He spoke again in a choked voice, but with firm resolve: "Not My will, but Yours, be done" (Luke 22:42). At last He pushed himself up from the ground. His garments were soiled, damp with sweat and dew. The last hours had been harrowing, and they had taken a frightful toll. Even in the darkness, the price He had paid was visible in His face.

Returning to the disciples for the third time, He found them asleep again. Quickly He aroused them. His hour was at hand and through the trees the flickering light of several torches was clearly visible. Turning to the groggy disciples He said, "Here comes my betrayer!" (Mark 14:42 NIV).

Human zeal tempts us to attempt things God has not called us to do.

Hardly were the words out of His mouth before Judas entered the clearing, leading a contingent of armed temple guards. Without hesitation he came to Jesus and greeted Him with a kiss. Before he could step away, Jesus gripped him by the shoulders and looked deep into his eyes.

"Judas," He asked in a voice all could hear, "are you betraying the Son of Man with a kiss?" (Luke 22:48).

139

Jerking free of Jesus' grip, Judas stepped aside and instantly Jesus was surrounded by the guards. Drawing his sword, Peter struck the man nearest him, cutting off his right ear (John 18:10).

Human Zeal

With this daring but rash act, Peter moved into the third stage in his descent toward denial—that of *misguided zeal.* That prayerlessness leads to misguided zeal should come as no surprise. When a man loves Jesus but cannot discipline himself to pray, he often becomes overactive in the work of the Lord. Attempting, as it were, to compensate for his poor showing in prayer by his busyness. Unfortunately, frantic activity is generally counterproductive in the work of the Lord.

More often than not, misguided zeal causes a man to attempt to do more than God has called him to do, making frustration and failure inevitable. Little wonder the landscape of contemporary Christendom is littered with partially completed medical centers, abandoned theme parks, crumbling television empires, and sprawling church complexes now in foreclosure. These all stand in mute testimony to the ever present dangers of human zeal. Well it has been said, "We have met the enemy, and the enemy is us."

A classic example of this kind of well-intended but misguided zeal is found in 2 Samuel 7. King David had established his throne in Jerusalem and was finally free from conflict with his enemies. One day he said to Nathan the prophet, "'See now, I dwell in a house of cedar, but the ark of God dwells inside tent curtains.' Then Nathan said to the king, 'Go, do all that is in your heart, for the LORD is with you'" (2 Sam. 7:2–3). I cannot read that without thinking how human it is to assume that God will bless every "good" thing we desire to do.

Unfortunately neither David nor Nathan had sought the counsel of the Lord. Apparently they did not think it was necessary. Building a temple seemed the logical thing to do, a good thing, but "good" things are not necessarily "God" things as they were soon to discover. And herein lies a great danger to the man or woman of God—human zeal tempts us to attempt things God has not called us to do.

Still, if we are sensitive to the Holy Spirit, the Lord will correct us before we get in over our heads. That is what He did for David.

According to 2 Samuel 7:4, the word of the Lord came to Nathan the prophet that same night directing him to tell David not to build the temple. Following this divine revelation, Nathan faced that moment dreaded by all counselors and advisers to powerful men: He must stand in opposition to the leader's plan. Complicating everything was the fact that he initially supported David's desire to build a house for the Lord.

Had Nathan been more self-serving and less obedient, he might have ignored the word of the Lord and let David go ahead with his plans. By the same token, had David been more "zealous" he might have rejected Nathan's counsel. Strong leaders, like David, are usually determined men who get things done when others cannot. The downside of that is that they are often headstrong, making them especially susceptible to misguided zeal—a fact not lost on the tempter. Frequently they take a dim view of anyone who opposes their plans. Thankfully, David did not. Consequently, he was spared the painful humiliation that has befallen so many spiritual leaders who refused to heed the counsel of godly friends and advisers.

Proving Our Zeal

Excellent outline!!

How, you may be wondering, can you differentiate between godly zeal and human zeal? How can you know if the thing that is motivating you comes from God or from self?

First, you can practice a ruthless self-honesty, admitting daily that you have to deal with your own ambition and that you are not spiritually qualified to make important decisions without the counsel of godly advisers.

Second, you can refuse to accept your zeal at face value. Over the years I've developed the practice of asking myself some hard questions in this regard:

1. Have I Fully Surrendered This Desire to the Lord?

Knowing how headstrong I can be, I've developed a habit of daily laying all of my hopes, dreams, ambitions, and desires at the foot of the Cross. I give them to God while praying, "Lord Jesus, I give You permission to change my desires, to superimpose Your will on mine. Now guide me through my surrendered desires and fulfill Your purposes in my life."

When I have an especially strong desire, it is doubly important to surrender it to the Lord. If my desire persists after I have unconditionally surrendered it then I tentatively assume it is part of God's plan for my life and move to the next question.

2. Is This Truly God's Plan or Just My Own Ambition?

This is a tough question, one that forces me to prayerfully search my heart. With the help of the Holy Spirit I examine the roots of my desire to determine its origin. I measure it against the overall vision God has for my life to determine if it will help me to fulfill my call. If it does not, then it surely isn't from God and must be dismissed as nothing more than human ambition. If it seems to be in keeping with my call, I again move to the next question.

3. Am I Waiting for the Lord to "Open the Door" or Am I Impatiently Forcing Things to Happen?

Frequently I am tempted to make things happen, to take matters into my own hands. When I do, things seldom work out as I planned. More often than not I am victimized by my own bullheadedness. When God opens the door, on the other hand, things seem to "fall" into place. There may still be challenges, but there is a natural flow, a forward progression in all we do when God is directing it.

4. Am I Sure That I Am Moving in God's Timing?

Timing is every bit as important as direction when pursuing the purposes of God. Remember, "To everything there is a season, / A time for every purpose under heaven" (Eccl. 3:1).

Experience has taught me that strong leaders are seldom slow to act. Therefore, they are often tempted to move ahead of God's timing. Rarely does God have to prod them, but He often has to hold them back, making patience a critical quality in spiritual leadership.

It's not only men who have to deal with misguided zeal. Some of the most zealous people in all of history have been wives and mothers—especially when it comes to the careers of their husbands and children. Take the case of Salome, the mother of James and John, for instance. She asked Jesus to grant her sons a special place of honor in His kingdom, creating no little animosity among the rest of the disciples (Matt. 20:20–24).

5. Am I Resorting to "Human" Methods in an Attempt to Accomplish God's Plan?

The Bible is filled with countless examples of men and women who succumbed to the temptation to take matters into their own hands. Two who immediately come to mind are Abram and Sarai. When Abram informed Sarai that God had promised them a son—though he was nearly ninety, and she was barren and well past the age of childbearing—she immediately set about to "make" it happen. "So Sarai said to Abram, 'See now, the LORD has restrained me from bearing children. Please, go in to my maid; perhaps I shall obtain children by her.' And Abram heeded the voice of Sarai" (Gen. 16:2).

Sarai's plan was "successful," and nine months later Hagar gave birth to a son whom Abram named Ishmael. Some years later Sarai became pregnant and gave birth to a son, exactly as God had promised. Soon the camp was rife with jealousy, and Sarah demanded that Abraham cast out the bondwoman and her son. Then Abraham found himself forced to choose between his sons— a position no man should ever be in—and all because he resorted to human methods in a misguided attempt to fulfill the plan of God. The principle inherent in this account should be obvious. Although our human methods may succeed, they will inevitably create more problems than they solve. You simply cannot build a spiritual work by resorting to carnal methods. Those who attempt to do so may appear to succeed for a time, but in the end their efforts will prove futile.

6. Am I Attempting This Because God Has "Called" Me to Do It or Because I Am Driven to Succeed?

To truthfully answer this question I must take a hard look at myself. I must honestly examine both my motivations and my goals, for it is the only way I can determine whether I am called or driven. I often find it helpful to remember that a driven person is consumed with his own needs and desires, while a called person is committed to the Father. A driven person is ambitious; a called person is obedient. A driven person is competitive, always measuring his accomplishments against those of his colleagues. A called person, on the other hand, is faithful, only measuring his accomplishments against the vision God has given him. A driven individual is ever conscious of the symbols of power—title, office size and location, and salary. The called person focuses on the inner issues of character and integrity. While each of us probably has some of both characteristics, it is important to determine which one dominates in our lives. In so doing we will discover whether we are called or driven.

Even if I am able to satisfactorily answer these questions, I still cannot fully trust my own conclusions, for as Jeremiah said, "The heart is deceitful above all things, / . . . Who can know it?" (Jer. 17:9). Determining the will of God in matters relating to vision and zeal is never easy and almost always requires the counsel of a spiritual friend or adviser. I must submit my vision, my zeal, to the scrutiny of godly advisers, and only when it passes muster with them can I move ahead with confidence. If I refuse to make myself accountable, I open the door to the enemy and leave myself vulnerable to temptation.

The Consequences of Misguided Zeal

Zeal is a wonderful thing when it is inspired by the Lord (John 2:17), but when it is birthed by the flesh it becomes the instrument of the devil, producing many of the darkest stains on church history. Consider the French Wars of Religion, which culminated in the Saint Bartholomew's Day Massacre on August 24, 1572, when it is estimated that tens of thousands of protestants were slaughtered. Then there were the Salem witch trials, a miscarriage of justice if ever there was one. Before it was over nineteen so-called witches were hanged and one was stoned to death—all in the name of religion. In modern times we have seen the tragic end of those who followed cultist leaders like Jim Jones and David Koresh.

Misguided zeal undermines the work of the Lord in any number of ways. Frequently it produces unrealistic expectations, which in turn lead to devastating disappointment. When you have the *wrong people* doing the *wrong things* for the *wrong reasons*, you end up with an aberration, a monument to a man rather than a work that glorifies God. Let that man succumb to the excesses his zeal encourages, and no little damage is done to the body of Christ.

Another common consequence of zeal is burnout. When a person is doing all that the Lord has *called* him to do and no more, his labor of love will be renewing. Physically he may grow tired by the end of the day, but emotionally and spiritually he is renewed.

In fact this is one criterion a person can use to determine whether he is motivated by godly zeal or human zeal. If he is truly doing the work of the Lord, in God's timing and in God's way, he will be refreshed in his spirit and strengthened in his body (Matt. 11:29–30). But when he allows misguided zeal to make him hyperactive in the work of the Lord, he soon grows weary in well-doing. He is not just physically tired, but bone weary, exhausted from the inside out—the kind of tiredness that cannot be relieved by a good night's rest or even a two-week vacation.

Godly Zeal

Yet when a man is truly called by the Lord to a given task it seems as if there is almost no limit to what he can accomplish. For instance no man could do all that John Wesley did, but by the grace of God. It is said that

he averaged more than three sermons a day for fifty-four years preaching all-told more than 44,000 times. In doing this he traveled by horseback and carriage more than 200,000 miles, or about 5,000 miles a year.

His published words include a four-volume commentary on the whole Bible, a dictionary of the English language, a five-volume work on natural philosophy, a four-volume work on church history; histories of England and Rome; grammars on the Hebrew, Latin, Greek, French and English languages; three works on medicine, six volumes of church music; seven volumes of sermons and controversial papers. He also edited a library of fifty volumes known as "The Christian Library."

He was greatly devoted to pastoral work. Later, he had the care of "all the churches" upon him. He arose at 4:00 A.M., and worked solidly through to 10:00 P.M., allowing brief periods for meals. In the midst of all this work he declared, "I have more hours of private retirement than any man in England."

At age 83, he was piqued to discover that he could not write more than 15 hours a day without hurting his eyes; and at the age of 86 he was ashamed to admit that he could not preach more than twice a day. In his 86th year, he preached in almost every shire in England and Wales, and often rode thirty to fifty miles a day.[1]

Both Martin Luther and John Calvin kept schedules not unlike Wesley's. Like him they were uniquely called and gifted of God.

Luther preached almost daily; he lectured constantly as a professor; he was burdened with the care of all the churches; his correspondence, even those now extant, fills many volumes; he was perpetually harassed with controversies, and was one of the most voluminous writers of his day.

The same, and even more, may be said of Calvin. While in Strasburg, he preached or lectured every day. In Geneva, he was pastor, professor, and almost magistrate. He lectured every other day; on alternate weeks, he preached daily; he was overwhelmed with letters from all parts of Europe, and was the author of works numerous and bulky, that any man of our day would think more than enough to occupy his whole undivided time: and all this, too, in the midst of perpetual infirmity of the flesh.[2]

These spiritual giants managed all of this because they were doing only what the Lord had assigned them. By working only in partnership with Jesus they discovered that His yoke was easy and His burden light. It could not be otherwise or else their zeal would have consumed them, crushing their spirits and ruining their ministries. By limiting our assignments, God is not trying to keep us *from* doing things, rather it is His way of keeping us *involved* for the long haul.

Disillusionment

Misguided zeal may motivate a man in the short term, but it cannot sustain him over the long haul. Indeed when his self-motivated efforts are not rewarded, he soon grows disillusioned, even bitter. Perhaps this is what happened to Peter. Surely he expected to be commended for his daring act in attacking those who came to arrest Jesus, but instead, he was rebuked.

Nor is this the first time his misguided zeal had gotten him into trouble. Earlier, at Caesarea Philippi, when Jesus initially revealed that He was destined to die in Jerusalem, Peter took Him aside and rebuked Him. "Far be it from You, Lord; this shall not happen to You!" (Matt. 16:22).

Turning to him Jesus said, "Get behind Me, Satan! You are an offense to Me, for you are not mindful of the things of God, but the things of men" (Matt. 16:23).

It is not hard to imagine how a stinging rebuke like that might crush a person's spirit. Let it happen several times—as it did to

Peter—and the most confident among us might well be tempted with disillusionment. Feeling misunderstood and unappreciated, following his daring, albeit ill-advised, defense of Jesus, Peter found himself drawing back, not just physically but emotionally as well. With a little encouragement from the enemy he withdrew into himself to nurse his wounded spirit. He still followed Jesus, but only at a distance, making further failure nearly inevitable. Soon he would warm his hands at the fire of the enemy, then he would deny his Lord, and finally he would go out into the night and weep bitterly. All because he tried to do in the strength of his flesh what he failed to do in prayer.

Reflecting on Him

1. *In what area of your Christian walk are you overinvested in the outcome of the effort rather than focused on the process of your calling?*

2. *Are you more interested in doing things or growing people?*

3. *Can you think of someone (a friend or associate) who has become disillusioned owing to misguided zeal in their service to God? If so, please make time to spend with them and encourage them in the Lord to prevent them from distancing themselves from God.*

15

DISTANCING

Following Peter's sudden and unexpected attack, the temple guards who had come to arrest Jesus fell back in confusion. But instead of seizing the moment to make His escape, Jesus rebuked Peter, saying, "Put your sword in its place. . . . Do you think that I cannot now pray to My Father, and He will provide Me with more than twelve legions of angels? How then could the Scriptures be fulfilled, that it must happen thus?" (Matt. 26:52–54).

Turning to the wounded man whose name was Malchus (John 18:10), Jesus "touched his ear and healed him" (Luke 22:51).

In short order the guards regained their composure and placed Jesus under arrest. After binding His hands they led Him away to be tried by the Sanhedrin. According to Matthew, "all the disciples forsook Him and fled" (Matt. 26:56). Everyone, that is, except Peter, who "followed Him at a distance" (Matt. 26:58).

Disillusionment

It is common to assume that it was cowardice that caused Peter to distance himself from Jesus, especially in light of his shameful denial in Caiaphas's courtyard later that same night. I'm not so sure. Undoubtedly he was afraid, anyone in their right mind would have been under those circumstances, but if fear was his overriding emotion, why didn't he escape with the rest of the disciples?

To my way of thinking it was disillusionment more than fear that caused Peter to follow at a distance. It must have seemed to him that no matter what he tried to do, it was wrong. When he protested the thought of Jesus' suffering and dying at the hands of elders and chief priests he was soundly rebuked (Matt. 16:23). At the transfiguration of Jesus he suggested, "Master, it is good for us to be here; and let us make three tabernacles: one for You, one for Moses, and one for Elijah" (Luke 9:33). This time Jesus did not even dignify his suggestion with a response. And when Peter objected to Jesus' washing his feet, sure that the Master should not wash the disciples' feet, he was rebuked yet again. "If I do not wash you," Jesus said, "you have no part with Me" (John 13:8). And then when he risked his life to save Jesus in Gethsemane, he was told to put his sword away (Matt. 26:52).

No wonder he was disillusioned! Things had not worked out the way he had anticipated, nor had Jesus lived up to his expectations. Instead of saving Himself and those who followed Him, Jesus had meekly submitted to the religious leaders, crushing whatever hopes Peter still had.

Most of us can probably identify with him, at least to a point. When our best efforts go unrewarded it is easy to become discouraged. When things don't work out the way we planned it is easy to question God. It may seem He has let us down. He hasn't, but it may seem that way.

Recently a discouraged minister confided in me. His eldest child had become sexually active, resulting in an illegitimate pregnancy. To make matters worse his second child was rebellious and running with a bad crowd, causing him and his wife no little grief. With deep sadness he said, "Things weren't supposed to turn out this way."

Another pastor and his wife recently suffered their second miscarriage in a five-month period. When I called to comfort them, they were grieving but brave—hoping more than believing. "God is faithful," they said. "He will not forsake us in the hour of our grief." Still, beneath their brave assurances I could sense their deep hurt and the painful questions it birthed.

When our daughter was going through a tragic divorce, I found myself not so much angry with God but deeply disappointed. Her terrible pain and sense of betrayal ripped at my heart. I knew God was not responsible, but surely He could have prevented it. More than once I wrestled with the question of why He didn't answer her prayers and ours to restore her marriage. Intellectually I knew that God would not violate a person's free will, but on an emotional level I felt He had let us down.

Life wasn't supposed to turn out this way. We had served the Lord faithfully, and so had Leah. Her marriage was supposed to be storybook perfect. There were supposed to be grandchildren and three-generation family holidays, not divorce proceedings. As our pain deepened we were tempted to withdraw, to lick our wounds in private.

Character Assassination

In times like that the tempter usually approaches us on one of two levels, and sometimes both. On one level he attacks the character of God. He tempts us to doubt God's faithfulness and to question His goodness. At first his slanderous suggestions fall on deaf ears, but as the unrelenting pain wears on us, we become more vulnerable. As one man told me following a personal tragedy, "I still love God, but I don't trust Him as I once did."

David Wilkerson, the founder of Teen Challenge and author of *The Cross and the Switchblade,* had an experience early in his ministry like that. As he was arriving at a church for a scheduled speaking engagement, an ambulance was driving away with lights flashing and sirens screaming. Turning to a bystander David asked, "What happened?"

Prayer and Christian fellowship are absolutely mandatory if we hope to remain faithful to the Lord and escape the snare of the enemy.

"The way I understand it," the neighbor told him, "the pastor was running late for a funeral. He jumped into his car and backed over his daughter who was playing in the driveway behind the car. Apparently he didn't see her."

Hurrying to the hospital to be with the pastor and his wife, David was accosted with a dreadful thought: *God must be punishing that pastor for some terrible sin.* Later, standing beside the grieving parents as they maintained their bedside vigil, he couldn't help noticing the tire tracks on the little girl's broken body. Silently he began to pray: *God, I'll do anything You ask me to do, only spare my wife and children.*

In the weeks that followed, his relationship with the Lord underwent a profound change. Gone was the joy, the love and intimacy; they were replaced by a grudging fear. Like the man in Jesus' parable of the talents (Matt. 25:14–30), David was now convinced that God was a "hard man"—merciless and exacting, quick to punish and slow to forgive. He continued to fulfill his ministerial duties, but there was no joy in them. As far as he was concerned, God could not be trusted.

Had God not moved in a sovereign way to deliver David Wilkerson from his warped thinking, chances are we would never have heard of him. There would most likely be no Teen Challenge, no *Cross and the Switchblade,* and no Times Square Church. People who see God as a "hard man" seldom accomplish great things for the kingdom. Instead they live in fear, burying their God-given talents.

No doubt the tempter was bombarding Peter's mind with just these kinds of thoughts as he watched Jesus being led away: *Maybe He is not the Messiah as I thought. Maybe He is just a man, His miracles notwithstanding. Maybe He is not who He claims to be. Maybe I have made a huge mistake.*

The second way the enemy comes at us is through an attack on our spiritual character, especially when we are dealing with disappointment and self-doubt. With insidious cruelty he reminds us of every sinful failure in our past. He tells us that we are not worthy of God's mercy, that we have outsinned His grace.

Many a man and woman has succumbed to Satan's relentless attack. Overwhelmed with feelings of worthlessness and failure, they distance themselves from the community of believers and anything else that might remind them of the Lord. Little by little they are dying on the inside. Only one thing can save them, yet they cannot find it within themselves to seek reconciliation with either the Lord or His people.

Restoring the Wounded One

In times like that it is up to the people of God to restore the wounded one. "Brethren, if a man is overtaken in any trespass, you who are spiritual restore such a one in a spirit of gentleness, considering yourself lest you also be tempted" (Gal. 6:1).

I'm reminded of the story of a Scottish shepherd who was absent from the house of the Lord three Sundays in a row. Following the third Sunday, his pastor determined to call upon him. The day he chose to go was cold and damp. Finding the shepherd in his hut at the side of the road, the pastor knocked at the door. The shepherd invited him in, and the two men sat before the fire in silence. Neither man spoke a word, but after a while the pastor picked up a pair of tongs, took a burning coal from the fire, and placed it on the hearth. In a matter of minutes the coal grew cold and black. Taking up the tongs, the pastor replaced the coal in the fire. In a matter of seconds it was burning brightly again. Still without saying a word the pastor excused himself and returned to his study. The following Sunday, and each Sunday thereafter, the shepherd was back in his place with the people of God.

Though the pastor did not speak a word that shepherd got the message. Alone we perish. Alone our faith grows cold and dark. But in the company of the redeemed we thrive. In the company of the redeemed our faith is renewed, our strength is restored, and we are made whole again.

Conclusion

In an interview with H. B. London Jr. and Neil Wiseman, Gordon MacDonald discussed the dangers of distancing ourselves from familiar people and places. He said,

> One of the greatest restraints to sin is a kind of fixed community like a neighborhood, village, small town, or even a church where people know you well. This is a place where you are committed to the norms and behavior patterns of this group of people day-by-day. . . . The moment there are no restraints, even passive restraints, a person may be in a vulnerable condition—open to a destructive response to an alluring temptation.[1]

Imagine how differently Peter might have responded in Caiaphas's courtyard had he been surrounded by the other disciples. Their expectations and their faith in him likely would have provided the courage he could not find in himself. Strengthened by their presence he most likely would have boldly declared his allegiance to Jesus, regardless of the personal risks.

Unfortunately such speculation is just that—speculation. The truth is Peter *did* distance himself from Jesus. He did warm himself at the fires of the enemy, and he did deny Jesus three times. Still, his tragic experience is not without redeeming value. From his mistakes we learn that prayer and Christian fellowship are absolutely mandatory if we hope to remain faithful to the Lord and escape the snare of the enemy.

Reflecting on Him

1. *Make a careful examination of your relationship with God to be sure that you are not allowing a past experience to cause you to begin losing your trust of Him.*

2. *In your own words, please describe what it means when the Scripture says that God "forgets" your sins.*

3. *What actions can you take to guarantee that your Christian brothers and sisters feel warm and accepted no matter their past and/or present failures?*

16

FELLOWSHIP WITH
THE WORLD

Peter never intended to deny Jesus.
You can be sure it was the farthest thing from his mind as he followed Jesus into the courtyard of Caiaphas the high priest. Perhaps
he still harbored some wild hope of rescuing Him. Or maybe he
simply could not bear the thought of deserting Him in the hour of
His need. Whatever the reason, his purpose in being there had
absolutely nothing to do with denying Jesus, of that I am sure.

How then did he end up doing just that? Not once, but three
times, and with a curse? A good question and one that deserves
our careful consideration.

Loneliness

Peter's tragic failure was not an isolated act; it was the culmination of a series of decisions, each building on the other until
denial was almost inevitable. Let me set the stage for you: It was
late, and Peter was not only physically exhausted, but emotionally
wrung out as well. He was cold and lonely.

Upon entering the courtyard Peter saw a collection of temple
guards and servants gathered around a fire. He hesitated for just a
moment, then he crossed the courtyard to join them. Perhaps he
used the cold as an excuse, or maybe he told himself that it was
information he sought, but in his heart of hearts he knew better.
Companionship was what he wanted, and though he was not likely

to find it in the company of those who warmed themselves at the fire, at least he would not be alone.

By nature he was a gregarious man. In the company of others he was confident and outgoing. He fed upon their presence, drawing his strength from their attention and approval. Alone he seemed to shrink within himself. The self-doubt his boisterous personality belied returned with a vengeance. Like many of us, he no doubt heard inner voices that told him that if others knew the truth about him they would know what a phony he was. As a consequence he could never rest. He needed constant reassurance from the people around him to still those nagging voices within. Tonight he was especially insecure. Not only had Jesus been arrested, but before He was taken away He looked Peter in the eye and said, "I tell you the truth, today—yes, tonight—before the rooster crows twice you yourself will disown me three times" (Mark 14:30 NIV). Of course Peter denied it emphatically. "Even if I have to die with you," he said, "I will never disown you" (Mark 14:31 NIV).

Still, squatting in the shadows on the far side of the fire, he could not help but wonder who the real Peter was. Was he the daring man who risked his life to defend Jesus in Gethsemane, or was he a coward destined to deny his Lord? Was drawing his sword an act of bravery or just another desperate attempt to be something he was not? These and a host of other tormenting questions drove him to seek solace in the company of strangers.

Peter's need for companionship at this critical hour should not be viewed as a weakness or a character defect. Like the body's need for food, which is expressed through hunger, the soul expresses its need for relationship through feelings of loneliness. In truth, companionship is to the soul what breath is to the body; without it we cannot truly experience life.

In his novel *Of Mice and Men*, John Steinbeck has a poignant exchange in which a crippled black man named Crooks laments his loneliness:

"A guy needs somebody . . ." Crooks said gently, "Maybe you can see now. You got George. You know he goin' to come back. S'pose you didn't have nobody. S'pose you couldn't go into the bunk house and play rummy 'cause you was black. How'd you like that? S'pose you had to sit out here an' read books. Sure you could play horseshoes till it got dark, but then you got to read books. Books ain't no good. A guy needs somebody—to be near him." He whined,

"A guy goes nuts if he ain't got nobody. Don't make no difference who the guy is, long's he's with you. I tell ya," he cried, "I tell ya, a guy gets too lonely an' he gets sick."[1]

And Crooks was right. If a person gets too lonely, he gets sick. But he was sadly mistaken to think that all a person needs is any physical presence. During times of inordinate stress a person is especially vulnerable to outside influence, and if he falls into the wrong company he will surely come to no good. Consider, for instance, what happened to Olympic ice-skater Tonya Harding.

Bad Company

In March 1994 Tonya Harding pled guilty in a plea bargain agreement to felony charges of helping to cover up the attack on figure skater Nancy Kerrigan. At the time of her plea she steadfastly maintained that she had no prior knowledge of the attack—a point strongly contested by her ex-husband, Jeff Gillooly, who was the mastermind behind the scheme to eliminate Kerrigan from the U.S. Figure Skating Championships. According to Gillooly, Tonya knew about it from the start. As part of her plea bargain, Harding was fined $100,000 and given three years' probation. The court also ordered her to undergo psychiatric examination, provide five hundred hours of community service, and donate $50,000 to the Special Olympics. Subsequently she was banned from all amateur ice-skating competition.

When a person keeps company with the world, it is only a matter of time until he is tempted to deny his Savior.

The incident that sparked the charges against Harding occurred on January 6, 1994. Following a workout at the U. S. Figure Skating Championships in Detroit, Michigan, Nancy Kerrigan was brutally attacked. Her assailant struck her in the knees with a metal baton. Although Kerrigan's injuries were not career threatening, they were serious enough to force her to withdraw from the U.S. Figure Skating Championships. Her withdrawal opened the door for Harding, who went on to win the championship and qualify for the Winter Olympics in Norway.

Because Harding and Kerrigan were bitter rivals, Tonya was an immediate suspect. Although she claimed no knowledge of the attack, few doubted her culpability, especially after authorities arrested her ex-husband, Jeff Gillooly, and two cronies. Harding and Gillooly had divorced in August of 1993, but they were reconciled and living together at the time of the attack. The other two men arrested were Shawn Eric Eckhardt, a bodyguard, who it turns out was the actual assailant, and Derrick Brian Smith, who drove the getaway car.

What happened? How could someone who seemed to have the world at her fingertips do something so stupid? Undoubtedly there is more here than meets the eye, but of one thing we can be certain—Tonya Harding fell in with the wrong crowd. In no way does that absolve her of the responsibility for her part in what happened. It may, however, shed some light on it.

Although Tonya came from a deprived background—both emotionally and economically—she was well on her way to transcending it when she met Jeff Gillooly, a controlling eighteen-year-old with a violent temper. Only fifteen years old at the time, she dropped out of high school shortly thereafter, and three years later she married him against the wishes of both her parents and her coach. Thus began a codependent relationship characterized by nightmarish episodes of physical abuse, separation, restraining orders, divorce, and reconciliation. Given these facts it is not hard to see the negative influence Gillooly had on Harding. One can only wonder how different her life might have turned out had she chosen her companions more carefully.

In truth, few things in life are more important than a person's choice of friends. They will influence our values, help shape our character, and determine to no little degree what we make of ourselves. If we choose our friends wisely they will prove an invaluable asset. By the same token, the wrong friends can cause us more grief than we could ever imagine.

Peter's downfall was facilitated, at least in part, by his failure to be more discriminating in the company he kept. Instead of remaining with John, who arranged for him to be allowed into the courtyard (John 18:15–18), Peter drifted over to stand with those who had gathered around the fire. "Blessed is the man," wrote the psalmist, "Who walks not in the counsel of the ungodly, / Nor stands in the path of sinners, / Nor sits in the seat of the scornful" (Ps. 1:1).

For a man who was surely taught the Scriptures from childhood, Peter displayed a shocking disregard for their clear precepts, at least he did on the night Jesus was betrayed. By seeking the company of those who considered themselves the enemies of Jesus he hastened his own shameful demise.

Denial

Hardly had he joined those gathered around the fire before a servant girl recognized him. Looking closely at him she said, "This man was also with Him [Jesus]" (Luke 22:56).

Of course Peter denied it vehemently. "Woman, I do not know Him" (22:57).

Turning his face away from the firelight, he hunkered down in the shadows, mumbling to himself. "I was a fool to come here," he may have muttered, "but I dare not try to leave now lest it appear I am a follower of His."

The person who would remain true to his commitment must keep the world at arm's length.

For a while it appeared that they had forgotten him and he began to relax a little. Around him the conversation swirled, but he paid it no mind. He was concerned with other things—like what he was going to do now. His whole life had been wrapped up in Jesus. Now he had *nothing*—no friends, no future, no dreams.

His melancholy thoughts were interrupted when another temple guard pushed his way into the circle around the fire. Standing directly across from Peter, he studied him intently. Under his breath Peter cursed himself for the risk he had taken. And for what? The warmth of the fire and some human companionship. Mustering his courage he determined to bluff his way through.

Moving around the fire, until he was standing beside Peter, the guard looked at him closely and said, "You also are one of them" (22:58).

"Man, I am not!" Peter replied through gritted teeth (22:58).

Shortly, a servant of the high priest noticed Peter and crossed the courtyard to speak to him. "Didn't I see you in the olive grove with Jesus?" he asked. Before Peter could respond, the servant continued, "Yes. I'm sure of it. You are the wild man who cut off my cousin's ear."

Angrily Peter began to call down curses on himself (Mark 14:71). Swearing, he said, "Man, I do not know what you are saying!" (Luke 22:60).

In the distance a rooster crowed and its call hung over the courtyard. Just then Jesus turned and looked straight at Peter. For a moment Peter met His eyes, then he looked away, shamefaced and sorrowful. Then the words of Jesus returned to haunt him. "Before the rooster crows, you will deny Me three times" (22:61). Stumbling across the courtyard, Peter disappeared into the dark where he wept bitterly (22:62).

Conclusion

When a person keeps company with the world, it is only a matter of time until he is tempted to deny his Savior. Generally it will not be so clear-cut a denial as Peter's, but on occasion it may be. Usually we will be tempted to deny Jesus by simply remaining quiet. Instead of giving a clear witness, we remain silent. Instead of speaking in defense of justice and truth, we say nothing. Rather than risk being identified as one of those "born-again" Christians, we pretend to go along with the crowd. While we may attempt to explain our actions as expediency, in our hearts we know that we have denied our Lord.

The person who would remain true to his commitment must keep the world at arm's length. For as John writes,

> Do not love the world or the things in the world. If anyone loves the world, the love of the Father is not in him. For all that is in the world—the lust of the flesh, the lust of the eyes, and the pride of life—is not of the Father but is of the world. And the world is passing away, and the lust of it; but he who does the will of God abides forever. *(1 John 2:15–17)*

Reflecting on Him

1. *Why do you suppose that God created us with such an innate need for the companionship of others?*

2. *Does this in any way reflect on the nature of God?*

3. *How does the story of Peter demonstrate the principle of Scripture when it states, "Be ye in the world but not of the world," and how should today's Christian live his or her life in a way that is true to this warning?*

17

DENIAL

Driving through the predawn darkness on rain-slicked streets, my body ached with fatigue. I was in the middle of a whirlwind book tour, and the demanding travel and interview schedules were taking their toll. Turning into the airport I found the "Rental Car Return" sign and followed the arrows to the designated parking slots. Belatedly I realized that I had forgotten to refuel the car. Glancing at the odometer I saw that I had driven only a few miles. The fuel gauge was still reading full, so I thought I would probably be all right. Besides it was too late to do anything about it.

At that early hour the airport was nearly deserted, and I was the only customer at the car rental counter. Perfunctorily the attendant checked me in, and then asked, "Did you fill the car with gas?"

Without a moment's hesitation I responded, "The fuel gauge is on full."

---

*I must acknowledge that there is within me a
nearly unbelievable capacity for sin.*

Instantly the Holy Spirit convicted me, for though I had told the exact truth, I had not been truthful. Instead I had used the truth to deceive, and that was dishonesty of the most serious kind. Through my shame I heard the attendant speaking to me. "Do you have a receipt for the gasoline?" she asked.

"No."

Once more I used the truth to deceive. It was wrong, and I knew it was, but having started down this slippery slope I couldn't seem to find a way back. Now one lie led to another.

The attendant must have sensed I was not being truthful because she pressed me. "What," she asked, "was the name of the gasoline station where you refueled the car?"

This time I did not even pretend to tell the truth. "I don't remember," I mumbled as I turned away and walked toward the concourse. I could feel her eyes boring into me, but I didn't look back.

Caught Again

At the gate I checked in before finding a seat in the far corner of the waiting area. Routine airport activity went on around me, but I was mostly oblivious to it. Like a broken record, the words of 2 Samuel 24:10 kept repeating themselves in my mind: "And David's heart condemned him. . . . So David said to the LORD, 'I have sinned greatly . . . but now, I pray, O LORD, take away the iniquity of Your servant, for I have done very foolishly.'"

Apart from the righteousness of Jesus Christ I have absolutely no moral or spiritual goodness.

Again and again I replayed the shameful scene in my mind. The absolute absurdity of it left me reeling. It was so pointless. All I had to do was tell the attendant that I didn't have time to refuel the car. What would it have cost? Surely less than five dollars for a couple of gallons of gasoline. And the money wasn't coming out of my pocket anyway. The publisher was covering all of my expenses.

What possible reason could I have had for being dishonest? With little or nothing to gain why did I have to lie? What did this whole experience say about me as a person, as a man of God? Those were the questions that haunted me as I boarded my flight.

Flying at 35,000 feet over the Midwest, I was still tormented by my shameful deed. Hard as it was to admit, I had to acknowledge that I was not the man I thought I was. With painful clarity I found myself identifying with an experience related by Augustine in his *Confessions*. It was the story of a youthful escapade in which he and some friends stole pears from a neighbor's tree. "We took great loads of fruit from it" he wrote, "not for our own eating but rather to throw it to the pigs."[1]

The thing that made this act so loathsome to Augustine was the fact that it served no purpose other than as an expression of his sinful self. More than any other single act, it revealed his true depravity. "The fruit I gathered," he wrote, "I threw away, devouring in it only iniquity. There was no other reason, but foul was the evil *and I loved it.*"[2]

I take no pleasure in my iniquity, but like Augustine I must acknowledge that there is within me a nearly unbelievable capacity for sin. And just when I think I have conquered it, I fail again. As I examine my repeated failures I discover they have only one thing in common. It is nothing so obvious as physical safety, personal popularity, or even financial gain. Had those factors been my undoing I might better understand my actions. Instead I find myself face-to-face with a shocking truth: Apart from the righteousness of Jesus Christ I have absolutely no moral or spiritual goodness. Left to my own devices I will choose to sin, and deny my Lord, even when there is absolutely nothing to gain.

"Left to my own devices"—that's the key isn't it?

History and personal experience have shown self-confidence is no match for the evil within or the tempter without.

Whether we are talking about Simon Peter in Caiaphas's courtyard or Richard Exley at a car rental counter, the root of our sinful failure is the same—self-sufficiency. If we trust our own instincts or rely on our own courage, we will fail. Our only hope is to throw ourselves upon Jesus, who is the source of our strength. His grace is sufficient, and His strength is made perfect in our weakness (2 Cor. 12:9).

Taking a Stand

After reviewing my personal spiritual history, I am tempted to conclude that I was a more courageous Christian as a youth than I am now at midlife. Several incidents come to mind that illustrate my point, but none are more graphic than what happened one Saturday afternoon in Texas City, Texas.

I was a member of the eighth-grade basketball team, and we were playing an out-of-town tournament. After winning our first two games, we had Saturday afternoon open before playing for the tournament championship that evening. Coach Johnson decided that a movie was the best way to keep us boys out of trouble until game time. The team greeted his announcement with loud cheers, but I did not join in. For me it was a moment of truth. Would I remain true to my spiritual convictions or would I give in to peer pressure?

To fully appreciate my predicament, you must remember that I was reared in an extremely legalistic church. Not only were cigarettes and liquor considered deadly sins, but so were dancing and going to movies. To my way of thinking, stepping inside a movie theater was tantamount to denying Christ.

All the way across town to the theater I was in mortal agony. Attending the movie with the team was not an option, but I dreaded the ridicule and rejection that I was sure would follow my stand. At last the bus turned into the parking lot and came to a stop. Around me the team was talking noisily and pushing toward the front of the bus.

I hung back, hoping for a chance to talk to Coach Johnson privately, but it was not to be. Ordering everyone back to their seats, Coach gave us some last-minute instructions. Finally he asked if there were any questions. Reluctantly, I raised my hand.

Nodding my direction he said, "What is it, Exley?"

Now every eye was on me and I swallowed hard past the fear that had formed a fist-sized lump in my throat. In a voice that was hardly more than a whisper I said, "Coach, it is against my religion to go to movies."

"What did you say?" he demanded. "Speak up so I can hear you."

Clearing my throat I blurted out, "I'm not going to any movie. It's against my religion."

Instantly the bus erupted with excited chatter as my teammates bombarded me with questions and comments: "You've got to be kidding me." "What kind of church do you go to anyway?" "What's wrong with going to a movie?"

Embarrassment painted my face a bright red, but I didn't back down. Finally the coach ordered the rest of the team off the bus. When they were gone he made his way to the seat in front of where I was sitting. Putting his arm on the back of the seat he looked at me without speaking.

"Exley," he asked at last, "if I let you stay on the bus will you give me your word that you won't set one foot off of it?"

Without a moment's hesitation I said, "Yes, sir!"

"We're going to be gone about two hours," he said. "That's a long time with nothing to do."

"I'll be fine, sir," I told him. "You can trust me."

I dare not open my heart to the smallest temptation, for once the door is open it is almost impossible to get it closed again.

He gave me one final look before making his way down the aisle and stepping outside where the rest of the team waited impatiently. I watched until they turned the corner and disappeared from sight, then I settled down to await their return.

The Secret of Success

How, you may be wondering, could a timid fourteen-year-old boy remain true to his convictions, while the man he became, a minister and a writer, caved in at the car rental counter? What did that teenage boy have that his middle-aged counterpart lacked?

The idealism of youth played a part to be sure, but the difference goes deeper than that. As a young man, I had no confidence in myself. I knew that my only hope was in Jesus. If I ever hoped to overcome temptation and live a victorious life I knew that I would have to depend wholly on Him. That afternoon on the bus I prayed desperately for the courage to do what was right. Without His help I knew I would succumb to peer pressure. In addition, the young man I was was convinced of sin's seductive power. I had no doubt that I would be a goner if I ever opened my life to the smallest compromise. Consequently I studiously avoided the very appearance of evil (1 Thess. 5:22). As a middle-aged man I was more confident of my own powers. I was a man of the world. I had been around. I could take care of myself, or so I thought.

We've come full circle haven't we? Peter's journey down the slippery slope toward denial began right here. He, too, was sure of himself, confident in his own commitment and courage. But as both history and personal experience have shown, self-confidence is no match for the evil within or the tempter without.

As I ponder these things my mind returns to the words of Jesus. "I tell you the truth, unless you change and become like little children, you will never enter the kingdom of heaven" (Matt. 18:3 NIV). After my shameful experience at the car rental counter those words take on a new significance. As a child I abhorred sin, but I had no confidence in myself or my ability to resist temptation. My only hope was to trust in the Lord Jesus with all my might and to resist every temptation, be it large or small. God honored my child-like faith and delivered me from evil.

As a midlife male I must return to the faith of my childhood. Like that fourteen-year-old boy I must take a stand against all evil. It is my only hope. I dare not open my heart to the smallest temptation, for once the door is open it is almost impossible to get it closed again. And I must not stand in my own strength, or I will surely fail. Like a child I must put my whole trust in Jesus, for only He knows how to deliver the godly out of temptation (2 Peter 2:9).

Reflecting on Him

1. *Have you experienced a similar episode in your life where it was easier to take a stand for God when you were a young Christian than after you had know the Lord for a number of years?*

2. *What can you do in your life to guard against the complacency toward God that comes of routine that leads to self-deception and denial?*

3. *How do you presently view the power of sin? Are you afraid of it? Or do you treat it with disdain?*

18

BITTER REGRET

More than a year passed before I finally heard from my friend Bill. Brenda and I stayed in touch with Janet, his former wife, and she kept us apprised of his circumstances. Through her we learned of his illness and the subsequent surgeries and radiation therapy. From her reports it seemed apparent that Bill was depressed, still I was not prepared for the emptiness I heard in his voice when I answered the telephone.

We made small talk for the better part of half an hour, then out of the blue he said, "Richard, it's not worth it. Don't let anyone try to tell you otherwise. How I could have made the decisions I did is beyond me. I must have been temporarily insane."

He paused for a moment, giving me a chance to speak, but I couldn't think of anything to say. Finally he continued in a voice that sounded terribly old and tired. "I would give anything if I could undo the hurt I have caused my children."

There was so much pain in his voice I thought my heart would break. Though he said no more, his grief was obvious, and his words carried me back to another time and place. To the sorrowful words of another minister who also found himself face-to-face with his own sinful failure and the inevitable consequences.

A Case Study in Regret

Painfully that fallen minister related his experience:

Somehow I made it through the public confession, on adrenalin I think, but following the benediction an awful weariness settled

169

upon me. Like a sleep walker I made my way down the center aisle to the front doors. Years of weekly repetition gave my handshake firmness, my smile a warmth I didn't feel, and my words a person-ableness which belied the awful emptiness within. Eventually the last worshipper departed and I re-entered the now empty sanctuary and looked around in despair. The silence was overwhelming, almost erie. I made my way to the altar, then to the pulpit.

Standing there it all came back—my call to the ministry, the skimpy years when we both had to work so I could finish seminary, my first sermon, the night I was ordained, our first church. Then I began to weep, soundlessly at first, just huge tears running down my cheeks, then harder until my whole body shook. Great heaving sobs rent my soul. I wept for what might have been, what should have been. I cried for my wife, for the terrible pain I had caused her, for the anguish that now locked her in painful silence. I cried for my church. They deserved better than this. They had trusted me, loved me, and I betrayed them. And I cried for me, for the man I might have been.

I stood behind the pulpit, touched it, ran my fingers over the smooth wood and realized as never before what a sacred place it was. And with that realization came guilt so great that I couldn't breathe. The magnitude of my sin, my betrayal, drove me from the pulpit and I stumbled to the altar and sat down. An accusing voice inside of me whispered, "How are the mighty fallen."

There was no reason to stay, no reason to linger longer, but I couldn't tear myself away. My life was ending, unraveling thread by thread, and I was powerless to stop it. Over the years, I had told ministers, again and again, that they had identity as persons not just as preachers, but now I discovered it wasn't true for me. Without the pulpit, the church, the ministry, I had no self. I could feel myself becoming invisible, turning into a nonentity—breathing and taking up space but having absolutely no reason to exist.[1]

Though Bill hadn't said so in so many words, I was left with the impression that, like that grieving minister, he, too, was eaten up with regret. How different this Bill was from the outgoing and fun-loving man I once knew as a friend. How different he was from the arrogant man of a year ago, the one who was so sure he knew what was best for himself. No longer was he the selfish man who was determined to have his own way no matter whom it might hurt. Now he was a grieving man, unsure of himself and filled with a wordless regret.

Regret Can Be a Wake-Up Call

Sin does that to a person. In the mouth it tastes as sweet as honey, but in the belly it is as bitter as bile. There are moments of sinful pleasure to be sure, but the end is death. Sin always takes a person further than he ever wanted to go. It always costs him more than he ever intended to pay. It cost Bill his marriage, his ministry, and the respect of his children, not to mention his self-respect.

But all need not be lost. Regret doesn't have to be just a place of torment. It can be a wake-up call as well. It was for the prodigal son in Luke 15.

We are the object of His love, but not the cause of it.

In this, the most familiar of all of Jesus' parables, the youngest son of a wealthy landowner demanded his inheritance and set out to make his own way in the world. In short order he squandered all of his wealth in wild living and ended up destitute. In the words of Scripture, "he began to be in want. . . . and no one gave him anything" (15:14, 16).

Finally he came to his senses and realized what a tragic wreck he had made of his life. In that moment, regret turned his thoughts toward home. And he said, "How many of my father's hired servants have bread enough and to spare, and I perish with hunger! I will arise and go to my father, and will say to him, 'Father, I have sinned against heaven and before you, and I am no longer worthy to be called your son. Make me like one of your hired servants.' And he arose and came to his father" (15:17–20).

Notice how much he changed. Gone was the arrogant young man with all the answers; in his place was a penitent sinner. He left his father's house saying, "Give me" (15:12). He returned saying, "Make me" (15:19). Make me the kind of man I ought to be. Make me the son I should have been. Make something good and decent out of me.

Unfortunately not every person who falls on hard times comes to his senses. For some, regret simply turns to bitterness. Instead of taking responsibility for their sinful choices and the resulting consequences, they blame others, even God. Proverbs 19:3 describes such a man: "A man's own folly ruins his life, yet his heart rages against the LORD" (NIV).

Make no mistake. Taking responsibility for one's actions is never easy. It's a choice—a tough choice, but a wise one. The prodigal made that choice, and he was welcomed back into his father's house. He did not plead bad luck or a downturn in the economy or even extenuating circumstances. He simply said, "Father, I have sinned against heaven and before you, and I am no longer worthy to be called your son" (15:18–19). He returned home, seeking not pity but pardon, not understanding but mercy.

And because he took full responsibility for his actions and threw himself on his father's mercy, he was forgiven and restored. "But when he was still a great way off, his father saw him and had compassion, and ran and fell on his neck and kissed him. . . . 'Let us eat and be merry [he said]; for this my son was dead and is alive again; he was lost and is found'" (15:20, 23–24).

The Real Hero

Of course the hero of this story was not the wandering boy, but the waiting father and what he taught us about our Father in heaven. You see, like this waiting father, God loves us unconditionally. There is absolutely nothing we can do to make Him love us less—no sinful act, no degenerate deed no matter how foul, nothing. By the same token there is nothing we can do to make God love us more. He already loves us completely and unconditionally. We are the object of His love, but not the cause of it.

Having said that I must hasten to add that although God loves us unconditionally, He will not fellowship with us unless we walk in the light as He is in the light (1 John 1:7). Like the father in our Lord's parable, He yearns to fellowship with us and stands ready to forgive us, but we must repent and turn toward home before we can be restored to fellowship.

After a long and sinful life, the artist Camillo painted a picture of Christ as *The Man of Sorrows*. When he finished he discovered that the eyes of Jesus had such an appealing and searching look that he had to veil the picture. One day he described the painting to a minister and told him of the effect the eyes had had upon him. The minister told him to unveil the picture and let the eyes do their work.

Returning to his studio, Camillo did just that, and what a work those eyes did. They seemed to look right into Camillo's soul, searching out every hidden thing. They told him to make restitution to every person he had wronged. They told him to buy up and destroy every inch of canvas he had ever painted that might suggest evil thoughts. For weeks he did everything in his power to repair the damage he had caused. Yet, in his heart there was still no peace.

Finally in desperation he fell to his knees and told Jesus that he had sinned against Him as well as against his fellowmen. In that moment a miracle happened, a miracle of grace. Camillo became a new creation in Christ. Old things passed away, and all things became new.[2]

In the end Camillo discovered that he could not change the past. He could not undo the wrong he had done, *nor did he have to*. All that was required of him was that he take full responsibility for his sinful actions and call upon the name of the Lord in repentance and faith. Whether we are talking about the prodigal son, or Camillo, or Bill, or any one of us, the way home is the same. Now arise and come home. The Father is waiting.

If we say that we have no sin, we deceive ourselves, and the truth is not in us. If we confess our sins, He is faithful and just to forgive us our sins and to cleanse us from all unrighteousness.
(1 John 1:8–9)

Reflecting on Him

1. *How does bitter regret differ from the idea of "secret regrets" from Chapter 1?*

2. *When you recall the almighty "I" of Chapter 2, would you consider the absence of regret a symptom of serious problems with self-centeredness?*

3. *How can God turn bitter regret into redemption? Consider Samson.*

19

RESTORATION

Return with me for just a moment to the night Jesus was betrayed. It was now quite late and a strained silence filled the courtyard following Simon Peter's profane denial. In the distance a rooster crowed and at that very instant the Lord turned and looked straight at Peter. For a moment their eyes locked and Peter wondered briefly if Jesus had heard his denial. Surely not, for the distance was too great, and there was no judgment in the look Jesus gave him—just love, a faithful love. Still, it was all Peter could do to meet His gaze, for even if Jesus didn't know what he had done, Peter knew.

The crowing of the rooster seemed to fill the space between them, and then Peter remembered the words of Jesus: "Before the rooster crows, you will deny Me three times" (Luke 22:61). Shame flooded his soul, driving him into the darkness where he wept bitterly.

Hard Choices

Alone with his guilt, Peter was faced with some hard choices. He could succumb to self-pity, but if he did he would become a tragic figure wallowing in his own guilt, of no use to either God or man. Still, it was a tempting choice. When we fail, not just the Lord, but ourselves as well—we feel that we have a right, even an obligation, to suffer. The judgment we suffer, however, is our own, for whereas God is merciful, few of us are very good at extending mercy toward ourselves.

175

A second possibility was to pretend it never happened. Since none of the disciples witnessed his shameful denial, who would be the wiser? An attractive choice but a burdensome one. If Peter chose this route he would have to live a lie, pretending to be something he was not. Always he would live in fear of being found out.

His third choice was to confess his sin and seek forgiveness. Not an easy thing for anyone, especially a man like Peter who was proud and unaccustomed to failure. Still, it was the only way if he wanted to be fully restored.

While Peter may have initially succumbed to self-pity, or even flirted with the possibility of acting as though his shameful denial never happened, in the end he decided to come clean. How do I know this, since his confession is not recorded in the Bible?

It's simple enough. The man we see dominating the Scriptures immediately following the resurrection of Jesus and during the early years of the church literally glows with forgiveness. He was neither guilt-ridden nor playacting. His fervent faith and passionate message could only be the products of God's grace. As Jesus said, he who has been forgiven much loves much (Luke 7:36–48).

Then there is the biblical record of Peter's shameful denial. Matthew, Mark, and Luke all include it in their gospels. Since none of them were there, how did they find out about it? Did God just tell them? Perhaps. But I believe it is more likely that they learned it from Peter himself.

If Peter was anything at all, he was a straightforward kind of guy. With him, what you saw was what you got. If he had a thought, he blurted it out. If he had a feeling, it was written all over his face. It would be easier for him to "unsay" the shameful words he uttered in Caiaphas's courtyard than to pretend with the disciples. For him it was either confess all to them or cut and run. Since we know he didn't cut and run, I have to believe that he told them everything. And to their everlasting credit, they did not ridicule him or cast him out. Instead they forgave him and restored him to their fellowship. And well they should have, after all, with the exception of John, none of them did any better.

Material for Ministry

Undoubtedly Peter thought of his denial of Jesus in only the most negative terms—the worst moment of his life, his most shameful failure, or something along those lines. I dare say that in his wildest dreams he never imagined that anything good could come out of his appalling debacle. But in the centuries since that fateful night countless men and women have taken hope from Peter's experience. Instead of giving up on themselves they dared to believe that the God who forgave Peter and restored him would do the same for them. And if God could use Peter—in spite of his colossal blunder—then just maybe He could still find a way to use them as well.

I understand this principle best in light of an amusing, but profound, parable I heard years ago. According to the parable there was a boy who lived on a dairy farm. A part of his first job was picking up cow manure in the pasture and hauling it to a pile in the barnyard. Of course he hated it. It was dirty and smelly. Then one day the Word of the Lord came to him in a 4-H meeting. There he discovered that what he was picking up was not manure at all, but fertilizer!

When we first deny our Lord and fall far short of our high ideals, we can only think of our sins as manure. Desperately we try to hide them from public gaze. Sometimes we even try to hide them from ourselves. And of course we try to hide them from God, but when we do they become rancid.

But when we finally confess our sinful failures to the Lord He touches them with His grace, and they are changed from manure into fertilizer. The very thing the enemy intended for our soul's destruction now becomes material for ministry. And more often than not it is our disclosure of a personal failure, redeemed and overcome by God's grace, that becomes our most effective tool for ministry.

Brenda and I are privileged to witness this incredible principle being lived out nearly forty weekends a year as we conduct "Forever in Love" marriage seminars across the country. We are often told how helpful our ministry is. I suppose there are a number of factors that contribute to our effectiveness: a marriage spanning more than thirty years, strong biblical principles, and practical advice. Yet when we talk to the couples who seem to have benefited most from our seminars, those are not the things that stand out in their minds. More often than not they allude to our struggles, to the things we have overcome with God's help. They say things like: "If God could restore your marriage, then surely there is hope for ours."

In the early years of our marriage we struggled with the "little" things that plague all newlyweds—unrealistic expectations, conflicting marriage models, financial difficulties, and sexual differences. Those we were able to resolve without too much difficulty. The thing that nearly destroyed our marriage was my temper. Although I never physically abused Brenda, I did wound her with my words. After thirteen years, she could take no more, and on a hot Sunday afternoon in August she uttered the words that finally brought me to my senses.

"I hate you, Richard," she sobbed. "I hate you. Once I loved you as much as any woman could love a man, but not anymore. Your anger has killed my love."

Trembling with sorrowful rage, she stood before me gasping for breath. And then she spoke the words that seemed to seal our fate. "I can't live like this," she said. "I won't! When Leah graduates, I am going to divorce you."

Stumbling beneath the awful weight of her terrible pain, she fled the room, leaving an unbearable emptiness in her wake. I heard the bathroom door close, then lock. A heavy sadness enveloped me. *This is what I have done*, I remember thinking, *this is my doing.*

The very thing the enemy intended for our soul's destruction now becomes material for ministry.

We never spoke of that tragic Sunday afternoon again. What was there to say? Brenda could not take back what she had said, for she had meant every word. And I could not apologize for my angry outbursts, for to Brenda's thinking my words were empty and insincere, incapable of undoing the terrible damage my anger had wrought. For years, nine years and four months to be exact, that painful moment lay like a piece of misplaced furniture in the soul of our marriage. Neither of us ever talked about it, but anytime we tried to get close to each other, we bumped into it.

Only Jesus knows what private commitments Brenda made to our marriage in those years, for we did not speak of them. In my heart I determined to make up for the pain and sadness I had inflicted on her, albeit unintentionally. With God's help I would become a godly husband. I read everything I could find on marriage and enrolled in a number of marriage workshops. As far as anyone knew I was simply participating in a program of continuing education to enhance my pastoral skills. Only I knew the real reason: I was determined to become the best husband possible.

As the years passed, things continued to improve between us. Many a night I would lie on the bed watching her as she prepared to join me and think how blessed we were. Not infrequently I would ask her, "Do you think anyone is as happy as we are?" Giving me a quick smile and a hug before turning out the light, she would say, "I'm sure there are others just as happy."

Lying in the darkness I would think, *It's going to be all right. She's happier now, I can tell.* But oh, how I longed to hear her say, "Richard, all is forgiven. I don't hate you anymore. I love you. I could never divorce you." I couldn't ask, though, lest I awaken her old hurts. I could only wait. And hope.

The years passed, and we continued to grow closer, having learned how to avoid that piece of misplaced furniture in the soul of our relationship without ever speaking of it. In May 1988 Leah graduated, and shortly thereafter she left home to start a life of her own. Now it was just Brenda and me.

June turned into December, and before we knew it, it was Christmas Eve. I built a fire in the fireplace and lit the kerosene lamps on the mantel. Carols emanated from the stereo, and in the kitchen Brenda prepared eggnog. After a bit she came to join me in front of the fire, but instead of sitting beside me on the love seat, she knelt behind me and put both arms around my neck. "I have something for you," she said, handing me a red envelope.

A Christmas card, I thought. *How nice.* Then I saw a handwritten note beneath the printed verse. As I began to read it my eyes grew misty and my throat ached, so great was the lump that had formed there. This was what I had yearned for since that tragic Sunday afternoon in August nearly ten years before. This was what I was dying to receive, but could not ask for. This was what I so desperately needed, but did not deserve—Brenda's love and her forgiveness.

Through tear-blurred eyes I read:

I Brenda Starr take thee Richard Dean to be my lawfully wedded husband. To have and to hold from this day forward. For richer, for poorer, in sickness and in health, till death do us

*part. To love, honor, cherish and obey. Forsaking all others
and thereto I plight thee my troth. In the name of the Father,
the Son and the Holy Ghost.*

*It looks like you're stuck with me! I'm not going anywhere!
Always remember "I'll never leave thee nor forsake thee."*

*Your Devoted Wife & Lover,
Brenda Starr*

Think about it. Only God could turn the manure of hurt and anger into fertilizer for healing and redeeming countless other troubled marriages. But He was able to do it only when I confessed my sin and renounced it. And He can do the same for you.

Divine Provision

This in no way minimizes the seriousness of sin. Whether we are talking about Peter's denial, my temper, or some other sinful failure, we must never make light of them. The wages of sin is *always* death (Rom. 6:23). And if ever we are tempted to think that our sin is no big thing, all we have to do is take a look at the Cross. See Jesus bleeding and dying there, alone in the darkness, abandoned by God and man. *That is what God thinks of sin.* It must be punished!

On the cross the sinless Son of God suffered and died for our sins, each and every one. God Himself imputed to Jesus all the sins of Adam's lost race—past, present, and future. Then God discharged upon Jesus the full weight of His holy wrath. And through His death Jesus fully satisfied the just demands of a righteous God, thereby making it possible for God to forgive our sins.

Peter's sin could be forgiven, his shameful act redeemed, because it had already been punished. From firsthand experience he wrote, "[Jesus] Himself bore our sins in His own body on the tree, that we, having died to sins, might live for righteousness" (1 Peter 2:24).

My sinful failures can be redeemed, as can yours, and those of every man and woman who calls on the name of Jesus. Because He paid the penalty for our sins, we can be forgiven and restored. And even as His sacrificial death transformed the Cross into an emblem of mercy, so does He redeem our most shameful deeds. The very things we were sure would forever disqualify us from kingdom service have now become material for ministry. This is the Lord's doing, and it is *marvelous* in our eyes.

Like many of you, I'm impressed by Peter's triumphs, by those moments when his faith shone with otherworldly brilliance, but if that was all I knew about him he would be an intimidating figure indeed. By the same token, if all I knew of him were his failures, he would be forgettable at best—perhaps even tragic. But when I see Peter's spiritual accomplishments against the backdrop of his failures I am truly inspired. I find myself saying, "If God could use a man like Peter, with his obvious feet of clay, then maybe, just maybe, He can use a man like me."

Reflecting on Him

1. *What was Peter's final legacy to the church?*

2. *What do you want your legacy to be for your children and younger Christians? In other words, how do you want to be remembered at your church?*

3. *As you look at Peter's final life of commitment to Christ, make a list of adjectives that describe his redeemed character. List as many as you can, then complete the following sentences with the adjectives.*

   Peter became _____, and I, too, can become _____.

   E.g., Peter became <u>courageous</u>, and I, too, can become <u>courageous</u>.

   E.g., Peter became <u>faithful</u>, and I, too, can become <u>faithful</u>.

   E.g., Peter became <u>consistent in his faith</u>, and I, too, can become <u>consistent in my faith</u>.

SEXUAL TEMPTATION

If you are battling with a secret sexual sin, you know how easy it is to become discouraged. After all, you have prayed and fought this battle for years with only the most limited success. In the depths of despair, following yet another sinful failure, it would be easy to conclude that while God can deliver you from the eternal penalty of sin, He cannot deliver you from its present power. Although your disappointments may far outnumber your victories, you must not allow personal failures to define your theology. They in no way nullify the truth of the gospel's redemptive power. According to the Scriptures the Cross not only provides justification, but redemption and deliverance as well!

In reality, lust can only be defeated by a combination of divine deliverance and daily discipline. Without the direct intervention of the Holy Spirit making the finished work of Christ a present reality in our lives, all attempts at spiritual discipline will be to no avail. On the other hand, deliverance is fleeting at best unless it is lived out day by day. Galatians 5:16 says, "Walk in the Spirit, and you shall not fulfill the lust of the flesh."

20

LUST:
THE ENEMY WITHIN

As he stepped into my office I could not help noticing the stylish cut of his suit, his monogrammed shirt, and his expensive shoes. He was a man familiar with success, well respected by both his family and his colleagues. Unfortunately, neither his designer clothes nor his pseudoconfidence could totally mask the misery that was eating at his soul.

He was a respected leader in his church, a husband, and a father. Yet this was only part of the story, for he had another side, a dark side where lust reigned. Like so many others, he was a man with a secret life.

His foray into sin's clandestine world started innocently enough with coffee at a neighborhood convenience store. Then one morning he began browsing through the pornographic magazines on the counter while drinking his coffee. Then he purchased one, then another.

From magazines he progressed to X-rated videos and adult theaters; finally, he secured the services of a prostitute. Of course, this degeneration didn't happen overnight. It took place over several months, and with each step he told himself he would go no further, but he seemed powerless to stop.

Soon he was living in a self-made hell. There were moments of lustful pleasure to be sure, but they were followed by hours of shame, days and weeks of unspeakable regret. Yet even in his shame he was irresistibly drawn toward the very thing he hated.

"I can't concentrate on anything," he confided, "without making plans for my next 'fix.' A fifteen-minute trip to the neighborhood drugstore turns into a two-hour trip across town to the adult theater."

Guilt and fear tormented him. What if someone saw him? What if his wife found out or someone from the church? Even if his double life was never exposed, he knew what he had become and that knowledge was nearly more than he could bear. "It is a terrible thing," he told me, "to know that you are not the godly man your family and friends think you are."

He wanted out, but something seemed to drive him. Too late he had discovered that more is never enough! Even his desperate prayers now seemed powerless against the demons within.

The Secret Fraternity

Unfortunately he is not alone. He is far from an isolated case. My experience as a pastor and a speaker for numerous men's conferences and retreats has convinced me that the problem is church-wide, affecting ministers and laity alike. I believe I can safely say that more men sin sexually through the use of pornography than in any other way. In fact, studies suggest that more than half of American midlife males (both Christian and non-Christian) live with at least one secret somewhere in their past. For many the secret is ongoing. Like the aforementioned man, they are trapped in some form of sexual sin: pornography, adultery, or homosexuality. They are convinced of the catastrophic consequences should their secret be discovered.

One man—a minister—desperate to be free, took a chance and bared his soul to a trusted colleague. Of that experience he writes:

> I had never shared intimate details of my lust life with anyone before, but the schizophrenia was building to such a point I felt I must. He listened quietly, with compassion and great sensitivity as I recounted a few incidents, skipping over those that showed me in the worst light, and described some of my fears to him.
>
> He sat for a long time with sad eyes after I had finished speaking. We both watched our freshly refilled cups of coffee steam, then stop steaming, then grow cold. I waited for his words of advice or comfort or healing or something. I needed a priest at that moment, someone to say, "Your sins are forgiven."

But my friend was no priest. He did something I never expected. His lip quivered at first, the skin on his face began twitching, and finally he started sobbing—great, huge, wretched sobs such as I had seen only at funerals.

In a few moments, when he had recovered some semblance of self-control, I learned the truth. My friend was not sobbing for me; he was sobbing for himself. He began to tell me of his own expedition into lust. He had been where I was—five years before. Since that time, he had taken lust to its logical consequences. I will not dwell on sordid details, but my friend had tried it all: bondage, prostitution, bi-sexualism, orgies. He reached inside his vest pocket and pulled out a pad of paper showing the prescriptions he took to fight the venereal disease and anal infections he had picked up along the way. He carries the pad with him on trips, he explained, to buy the drugs in cities where he is anonymous.

I saw my friend dozens of times after that and learned every horrific detail of his hellish life. I worried about cognitive dissonance; he brooded on suicide. I read about deviance; he performed it. I winced at subtle fissures in my marriage; he was in divorce litigation.[1]

How, you may be wondering, could a Christian become entangled in such a sordid mess? You can be sure it did not happen overnight, nor is it likely that he consciously chose to become a slave to his lust. Most likely it was a chance encounter, a seemingly innocent temptation that he indulged out of curiosity, only to discover that he had given birth to a monster with an insatiable appetite.

In reality, lust can only be defeated by a combination of divine deliverance and daily discipline.

Another man traced his obsession to something that happened when he was fourteen years old. He said, "I was riding my bicycle across an open field on my way home from school when I found a pornographic magazine. That discovery introduced me to masturbation and eventually fornication. The addiction has never left me, not even after I married."

"Shortly after going on the Internet," another confided, "I discovered that porno garbage was everywhere! Out of curiosity I took a peek. What a mistake that was. Within a short time I was addicted, and I couldn't tear myself away. I felt horrible because I could not believe a Christian could have this kind of problem."

Another man, also a Christian, confessed, "Although I struggled with pornography before I gave my life to Jesus Christ, I was not really tempted by it for about two years after my conversion. Then I discovered the Net, and somehow I got drawn into it again. I was tempted by how easy it was to view and read pornography without anyone ever knowing. Over the past year I have almost become addicted to it."

He went on to say, "I realize it is wrong and feel like the biggest hypocrite, because everyone who knows me considers me a strong Christian."

The power of this kind of sexual temptation is rooted in its secrecy. It flourishes in the dark, behind closed doors, denied and unacknowledged, except for those terrifying times when it exacts its terrible toll. Then it leaves its victim shamed and guilt-ridden, determined that it will never happen again, but still locked in his debilitating silence.

Dietrich Bonhoeffer wrote,

> He who is alone with his sin is utterly alone. . . . The pious fellowship permits no one to be a sinner. So everyone must conceal his sin from himself and from the fellowship. We dare not be sinners. . . . So we remain alone with our sin, living in lies and hypocrisy. The fact is that we are sinners![2]

Sinners we may very well be, but we dare not confess either our sins or our temptations, especially if they are of a sexual nature. And the more respected a person is, the harder it is for him to risk a confession. He has too much to lose; too many people will be hurt. He has a reputation to maintain, an image to protect; only that is all it is—an image. In truth he is a tormented man, fighting a lonely and losing battle against the sinful habits of a lifetime. He is not a bad man, not a hypocrite. He hates himself for what he has become—a man of God with a secret life.

If the truth were known, he has probably spent many a night in desperate prayer only to succumb again. He really does love the Lord and his wife and children, but he does not know how to find the deliverance he so desperately needs. And if his secret addiction is not overcome it will destroy him, not immediately perhaps, but eventually. In the end, sin will exact its just due.

A Theology of Deliverance

If you are battling with a secret sexual sin, you know how easy it is to become discouraged. After all, you have prayed and fought this battle for years with only the most limited success. In the depths of despair, following yet another sinful failure, it would be easy to conclude that while God can deliver you from the *eternal penalty* of sin, He cannot deliver you from its *present power*. Although your disappointments may far outnumber your victories, you must not allow personal failures to define your theology. They in no way nullify the truth of the gospel's redemptive power. According to the Scriptures the Cross not only provides justification, but redemption and deliverance as well!

The fact of our victory over sin was accomplished when Jesus died on the cross. It becomes a present reality in our lives as we "count [ourselves] dead to sin but alive to God in Christ Jesus," (Rom. 6:11 NIV). This is not simply wishful thinking but truth, carefully considered and documented by the Scriptures. *When Jesus died, He not only died for our sins, but also as sin.* Paul says, "For He made Him who knew no sin to be sin for us" (2 Cor. 5:21). Therefore when He died, sin died—that is, its stranglehold on the human will was broken; it was rendered powerless. Now the only power sin has in the believer's life is what he gives it.

What does all of this theology have to do with the enemy within? Everything! Lust is not the result of an overactive sex drive; it is not a biological phenomenon, nor the by-product of our glands. If it were, then it could be satisfied with a sexual experience, like a glass of water quenches our thirst, or a good meal satisfies our appetite; but alas, the more we attempt to appease our lust, the more demanding it becomes. There is simply not enough erotica in the world to satisfy its insatiable appetite.

When we "count [ourselves] dead to sin" (Rom. 6:11 NIV), when we crucify "the flesh with its passions and desires" (Gal. 5:24) by denying our lustful obsessions, we are not repressing a legitimate drive; rather, we are putting to death an aberration. Lust is to the gift of sex what cancer is to a normal cell. Therefore we deny it, not in order to become sexless saints, but in order to be fully alive to God, which includes the full and uninhibited expression of our sexual being within the God-given context of marriage.

Romans 8:13 declares, "If you live according to the flesh you will die; but if by the Spirit you put to death the deeds of the body, you will live."

In reality, lust can only be defeated by a combination of *divine deliverance* and *daily discipline*. Without the direct intervention of the Holy Spirit making the finished work of Christ a present reality in our lives, all attempts at spiritual discipline will be to no avail. On the other hand, deliverance is fleeting at best unless it is lived out day by day. Galatians 5:16 says, "Walk in the Spirit, and you shall not fulfill the lust of the flesh."

Daily Discipline

Let's return for a moment to the man who came to my office to confess his bondage to pornography and prostitution. In order to remain free there were certain things he could not continue to do, certain places he could not go—not because they were sinful in themselves—but because of his propensity for sin. For instance, he could not go to a convenience store; the risk was simply too great. Nor could he go to a place that rented videos. Extreme? Perhaps, but we were dealing with matters of life and death. Jesus said: "If your right eye causes you to sin, pluck it out and cast it from you; for it is more profitable for you that one of your members perish, than for your whole body to be cast into hell" (Matt. 5:29).

An important key in overcoming temptation of any kind, but especially lust, is to deal with it in its *earliest* stages. Far too often we are oblivious to the daily patterns that lead us into temptation; consequently, we seldom confront our sinful desires until they are full-blown, making failure nearly a foregone conclusion. If we are serious about overcoming sexual temptation, let us examine our lives and identify the places, the people, and the circumstances when we are most vulnerable to temptation. Once we have identified them let us make whatever changes are necessary to eliminate them from our lives.

One man, whose business made it necessary for him to travel extensively, told me that he discovered he was most vulnerable to lust when he was alone in a hotel room late at night. With the pornographic offerings of the X-rated channel just the flip of a switch away, he found himself repeatedly succumbing to temptation. No matter how much he prayed and studied the Word, he seemed powerless to resist the sinful offerings of the in-room adult channel. After numerous failures he began to call ahead and ask the hotel to remove the television from his room prior to his arrival. They always refused.

Being desperate, he decided to take matters into his own hands. Since the hotel refused to remove the television from his room, he began disabling it as soon as he entered his room. He accomplished this by cutting the signal cable with a pair of wire cutters. Although no hotel ever confronted him about the vandalism, he never felt right about the destruction of their property.

Eventually he designed a plug lock that was made from a piece of PVC tubing, two end caps, and a bicycle lock. He cut a slot into the tube beginning at one end and running along the tube for several inches but not completely to the other end. After gluing one of the caps to the end without the slot, he then put the other cap on the other end of the tube and drilled a hole through the cap and the tube. Now when he goes to a hotel he slides the television plug into the tube being careful to pull the cord into the slot. Next he puts the other cap on the tube and threads his bicycle lock through the hole and locks it. Finally he takes the key to the front desk and asks them to keep it in the safe for him.

Now the television cannot be plugged in because the plug is locked in the tube and the key is in the safe at the front desk. This puts enough distance between him and temptation that he is able to handle it as long as he continues to pray and rely on the Lord.

To some this may seem extreme, but in reality he is simply recognizing his limitations and dealing with temptation from a position of strength rather than weakness. By being proactive, he is winning the war against lust!

Another important step is to confess your temptations and your sin to someone you can trust. Over the years it has been my experience that temptation, which flourishes in secret, somehow loses much of its mesmerizing power when it is confessed and exposed to the light of Christian love. If the body of Christ is serious about helping one another overcome sexual temptation of all kinds, but especially the secret sin of lust, then we must be about the business of establishing a spiritual support system, in which we can encourage and strengthen one another. It is not likely a person will trust someone enough to share a problem of this magnitude unless he has had opportunity to test the waters by sharing confidences of a less threatening nature.

Recently at a minister's conference a well-known minister was invited to share his testimony. He told those present that after having achieved enormous success in the ministry he fell prey to sexual temptation. Somehow he managed to lead a double life for a number of years. Eventually, however, his secret life was exposed, and he was defrocked by his denomination. Following his dismissal he entered his denomination's rehabilitation program and was later restored to the ministry.

The thing I remember most about his testimony was not the painful details of his failure and the subsequent loss of nearly everything dear to him, but a remark he made in closing. He said soberly,

If you are already involved in sexual sin this message will probably be of little or no help to you. While trapped in my secret life I heard many messages like this. I would return to my hotel room under great conviction, get down on my knees, and confess my sin to God. Begging Him for forgiveness, I would promise never to yield to sexual temptation again. Though I was sincere, it was all to no avail. Within days, sometimes within hours, I was involved in the same sordid mess. I can only conclude that once a man becomes ensnared in sexual sin, he will never be free until his sin is exposed.

I do not believe a person's sin has to be exposed publicly before he can be delivered. I do, however, believe he has to acknowledge his sin to a mature brother in the Lord. In addition he must make himself accountable to that person. As his sin and temptation are exposed to the holy light of Christian fellowship they will lose much of their seductive power. Sin is a creature of darkness, and it cannot long survive in that kind of light.

As Christians we are charged with the responsibility for modeling this kind of transparency in order to create a climate where sin can be confessed and forgiven. We are charged to acknowledge our own struggles and temptations so others will feel free to confess their needs without fear of rejection or misunderstanding. As Richard Foster writes,

If we know that the people of God are first a fellowship of sinners we are freed to hear the unconditional call of God's love and to confess our need openly before our brothers and sisters. We know we are not alone in our sin. The fear and pride which cling to us like barnacles cling to others also. We are sinners together. In acts of mutual confession we release the power that heals. Our humanity is no longer denied but transformed.[3]

Reflecting on Him

1. *What are the places, people, and circumstances which produce the most dangerous mixture of sexual temptation for you?*

2. *How can you change your life so that you can successfully avoid this situation?*

21

THE TENDER TRAP

Craig and Lisa are in their early thirties. Last month they celebrated their eleventh wedding anniversary. They have two children—a boy and a girl—who are bright and well behaved. If you saw them in church, you would think they were the ideal Christian family. In many ways they are, or perhaps I should say were, for their marriage is now fractured by infidelity.

Much to her dismay Lisa discovered Craig was having an affair with her best friend, Donna. She was crushed. You can imagine how betrayed she feels. Craig is confused. As a Christian, he wants to save his marriage, but another part of him is convinced he has found something with Donna that he desperately needs—something he has never had with Lisa.

"I just don't understand it," Lisa sobs. "We are all supposed to be born-again Christians. In fact, if we had not all been going to the same church we probably never would have met. And to think Donna and her husband were our best friends. How could they do that to us?"

Craig breaks his dazed silence to lament, "This doesn't say much for our Christianity, does it?"

An Emotional Maelstrom

Perhaps you know exactly how Lisa and Craig are feeling. You know because you've been there, in fact you may be walking in their shoes right now.

If you are the betrayed spouse you are probably feeling crushed. The person you trusted most in the whole world has betrayed you. If your situation is like Craig and Lisa's you feel doubly betrayed. First by your spouse and then by your best friend.

Hurt has become a permanent pain deep in your chest. Sometimes it recedes for a little while, but it never goes away. A host of questions haunt your tormented mind: *When did it start? Why? How could they do this?*

You have painful flashbacks in which you see them together in your mind's eye. The very thought is nauseating, yet you seem to have a morbid fascination for the details.

Sometimes you awake in the morning and for a moment everything seems right with the world. Sunlight is streaming through the bedroom window, and you can hear the chirping of birds in the backyard. Then you remember, and it is like a dark cloud blocking out the sun. The painful humiliation comes rushing back as fresh and as devastating as it was the moment you first learned of the affair. Your mood changes. That sick feeling returns to the pit of your stomach.

It is important to establish appropriate guidelines for our relationships before we are tempted to stray.

If you are the guilty spouse, the adulterer or adulteress, you have troubling emotions of your own. Now you feel trapped, torn. Maybe your marriage was not all it could have been, but now that it might end you are beginning to realize how much it means to you—the children, the house, the shared memories. Yet your affair has given you an excitement you have not known in years. You feel attractive to the opposite sex. You feel alive, really alive, when you are with your lover. Still, you know it cannot go on like this. Something has to give.

Guilt has become your constant companion. It clings to you like a shadow. You hate yourself every time you see the hurt in your spouse's eyes. His constant sadness cuts you like a knife. And the kids. Oh God, what have you done to the kids? Every time you look in the mirror you experience a wave of self-disgust. You have not only betrayed your husband and family, but yourself as well.

You are not the person you thought you were, not the godly wife and mother everyone thinks you are.

You have probably prayed, or tried to pray, only to discover that prayer has lost its meaning. You are sick at heart, homesick of soul, yet you cannot bring yourself to repent and break off the affair. Even as you promise God you will end it, another part of your mind is planning the next clandestine meeting. *How*, you ask yourself in disbelief, *did I become an adulteress?*

How an Affair Begins

Contrary to popular belief most affairs begin for nonsexual reasons. The lack of need fulfillment and intimacy creates an intense vacuum, making the desire for emotional intimacy the primary reason why people have an extramarital affair. Many a shocked husband has said, after discovering that his wife is having an affair, "What does she see in him?" His wife's response? "He listens, cares, and he doesn't criticize me!"

Don't misunderstand me. I am not excusing infidelity. There are no extenuating circumstances, no situation where adultery can be justified. I mention emotional deprivation as a warning signal only. When the need for closeness, goodness, kindness, and togetherness—what I call our "ness" needs—is not being met on a regular basis in a marriage, the temptation may be to find a person who will be good to us, touch us, hold us, give us a feeling of closeness. Sexual fulfillment may, indeed, become an important part of an extramarital relationship, but for most men and women, the "ness" needs are initially more important.

Dr. Carlfred Broderick, marriage counselor and author, has talked to dozens of couples who have been fully committed to fidelity, yet found themselves involved in affairs. He writes: "I am convinced that more people get themselves into the pain of infidelity through empathy, concern and compassion than through any base motive. The world is full of lonely and vulnerable people, hungry for a sympathetic ear and a shoulder to cry on."[1]

What am I trying to say? Simply this: An innocent get-together like working together on a project, helping a neighbor, or even meeting for coffee, can begin a pattern of meetings that become increasingly mutually fulfilling. Soon the parties are sharing deeply, which gives birth to emotional intimacy, which inexorably leads to adultery. Or as one man put it, "In two weeks we were in bed together. I just can't believe it's happening to me!"

It is crucial that the relationship be terminated before that emotional bond forms. Should you fail to do so, the power of passion takes over, distorting reality and rendering you incapable of making spiritually sound decisions.

Hedges

It is important to establish appropriate guidelines for our relationships before we are tempted to stray. For instance, experience has taught me that I should not form a close friendship with a member of the opposite sex. It is simply too dangerous. Rigid? Perhaps, but hardly when one considers the tragedies befalling so many couples.

R. Kent Hughes, author of *Disciplines of a Godly Man,* wrote:

> Men, put disciplined hedges around your life—especially if you work with women. Refrain from verbal intimacy with women other than your spouse. Do not bare your heart to another woman, or pour forth your troubles to her. Intimacy is a great need in most people's lives—and talking about personal matters, especially one's problems, can fill another's need of intimacy, awakening a desire for more. Many affairs begin in just this way.
>
> On the practical level, do not touch. Do not treat women with the casual affection you extend to females in your family. How many tragedies have begun with brotherly or fatherly touches and then sympathetic shoulders. You may have to run the risk of being wrongly considered "distant" or "cold" by some women.
>
> Never flirt—even in jest. Flirtation is intrinsically flattering. You may think you are being cute, but it often arouses unrequited desires in another.[2]

For some the journey into the spiritual and emotional pitfalls of adultery begins right here—with some "innocent flirting" that is carefully couched in double meanings. If the one being flirted with fails to respond or becomes offended, the person doing the flirting can protest his innocence, claiming he was misunderstood. On the other hand, if the "flirtee" responds in kind, the chase is on, and excitement is high. Neither person has yet made a conscious decision to commit adultery, but subconsciously they are committed to it.

I use the term "innocent flirting" with tongue in cheek because it is this kind of coded conversation that fans the flames of imagination. Flirting of this type is usually done in public, even in the presence of each other's spouse. For instance a man might say to his friend, "You're a lucky man to have such a beautiful wife." Or a woman might say something like, "I hope you appreciate what a sensitive man your husband is." Of course he or she makes those remarks where his or her friend's spouse cannot help but hear. If the spouse is secure and fulfilled in his or her marriage, he or she may disregard such comments without a second thought. But if he or she is restless it can spark the kind of interest that leads to other things.

Even as a couple building a relationship with another couple, you must make a conscious effort to maintain appropriate boundaries, especially in the areas of personal conversation and physical contact. Dr. Richard Dobbins, founder and director of EMERGE Ministries, a Christian counseling center, wrote,

> As friendships among couples grow more intimate, there is a tendency to become too personal and permissive in discussing the sexual side of life. . . . When personal boundaries are ignored over a long period of time, the frequency and intimacy of contacts allowed between close friends can threaten to lead the best intentioned of person to an emotional "point of no return" which can be disastrous.[3]

The "Moment of Maybe"

When a Christian succumbs to sexual sin it is seldom a sudden thing, rather it is the culmination of a series of small temptations. Therefore it is critical that we develop the ability to recognize temptation the moment it first whispers its beguiling suggestions. Walter Wangerin Jr. calls this first subtle temptation a "moment of maybe."

> Early on in an extramarital friendship there often comes a moment of "maybe." Even when that friendship is altogether innocent, your friend may send the signal, or you may sense the feeling, of further possibility. It occurs in a glance more meaningful

than mere friends exchange. It arises from a touch, a hug, a brushing of flesh that tingled rather more than you expected—and you remembered the sensation. . . . In that moment nothing more is communicated than this: our friendship could turn into something else. Neither of you need say, or even think, what that "something else" might be. . . . It is precisely here that the drama toward adultery begins. Whether it also ends here, or whether it continues hereafter, is a terribly critical question. For a door has opened up.

If, in this moment, you do nothing at all, then you enter the door. If you make no decision (privately but consciously) to close the door and carefully to restrict this relationship, the drama continues. For though a promise has not been made in the moment of "maybe," it hasn't been denied either. And though you may not yet love each other, neither have you said no to love. You permit, by making no decision at all, the "maybe." And "maybe" takes on a life of its own.

When a desire is born in us, we have a choice. When it exists still in its infancy, we have a choice. We can carefully refuse its existence altogether, since it needs our complicity to exist . . . Or else we can attend to it, think about it, fantasize it into greater existence—feed it! . . . But if we do the latter, if we give it attention in our souls, soon we will be giving it our souls. We've lost free will and the opportunity to choose. The desire itself overpowers us, commanding action, demanding satisfaction.[4]

When a Christian succumbs to sexual sin it is seldom a sudden thing, rather it is the culmination of a series of small temptations.

Since temptation is so subtle, you may protest, it is not always easy to recognize a "moment of maybe." True enough, especially if you are inclined toward rationalization. In your defense, you reason that being a Christian friend requires you to be sensitive, supportive, and caring. And it does, but there is a point at which your concern becomes more than friendship, a point at which you find yourself meeting emotional needs for him, and he for you, that can be met legitimately only by one's spouse. Although you haven't yet done anything sexually inappropriate you are, nonetheless, guilty of emotional adultery. And if you do not take immediate steps to rectify the situation it is only a matter of time until you will find yourself entangled in a full-blown affair.

Early Warning Signals

Determine early on, before you become emotionally entangled, that you will recognize and respond to the earliest warning signals. These include, but are not limited to:

1. *A growing fascination with this other person.* Beware when he or she regularly intrudes upon your thoughts, even when you are with your spouse and family.

2. *A heightened sense of anticipation when you have an opportunity to be with him or her.* Beware when you find yourself looking forward to those "ministry" opportunities when you can legitimately be alone with him or her, or when you volunteer for church projects so the two of you can be together.

3. *A growing desire to confide in him or her.* Beware when you are tempted to share with him or her the frustrations and disappointments in your own marriage.

4. *An increased sense of responsibility for his or her happiness and well-being.* Beware when you think more about his or her needs than the needs of your own spouse and family.

5. *Emotional distancing from your spouse.* Beware when you have an increasing need to keep your thoughts and feelings for him or her secret from your spouse.[5]

Ignore these early warning signs, and disaster is virtually unavoidable. If by some freak chance you stop short of physical adultery—a most unlikely possibility—you have still done a grave disservice to your marriage. By forming that kind of emotional bond with someone other than your spouse you have committed "emotional adultery." If you doubt the validity of my conclusions, just ask yourself how you would feel if your spouse were getting his or her emotional needs met by another person.

The power of sexual temptation is so great that unless a stake is driven into its heart immediately, it may well overwhelm us. Kings have renounced their thrones, saints their God, and spouses their lifetime partners. People have been known to sell their souls, jobs, reputations, children, marriage—they have literally chucked everything for a brief moment of sexual pleasure.

With Christ everything is possible. We can resist sexual temptation, but we must act with ruthless urgency!

But you, O man of God, flee these things and pursue righteousness, godliness, faith, love, patience, gentleness. Fight the good fight of faith, lay hold on eternal life, to which you were also called and have confessed the good confession in the presence of many witnesses. . . . Guard what was committed to your trust. *(1 Tim. 6:11–12, 20)*

The Deadly Descent

If we fail to heed the early warning signals, the descent toward infidelity will continue. Once that deadly descent begins, it rapidly advances from one stage to the next. Initially the potential adulterers will probably spend significant amounts of time fantasizing about each other. As the "affair" progresses these fantasies become more explicit. For the man they will often be sexual in nature, though not always, while for the woman they usually will be romantic. In either case they are deadly, for Jesus said, "Whoever looks at a woman to lust for her has already committed adultery with her in his heart" (Matt. 5:28).

The next stage is talking, sharing deeply with one another. Again it starts innocently enough, usually under the pretext of passing along an announcement or an invitation. Then the conversation shifts to more personal things, a favorite book or movie, plans for the future, a childhood experience, or even some personal problem.

During this stage both parties are careful to assure themselves that they are just friends. They may even acknowledge a growing attraction for each other, but they are determined to build a relationship rather than have an affair. Unfortunately they are already involved in an affair—an affair of the heart. Someone other than their spouse is satisfying their need for closeness, tenderness, and togetherness.

By now they are undoubtedly doing a considerable amount of rationalization in an attempt to appease their consciences. The Holy Spirit knows what is going on and He convicts them, but to no avail. Their relationship is too meaningful to give up. He makes her feel cherished and attractive. She believes he loves her for who she is and not just for her body, after all they will never have sex. She makes him feel special, hangs on every word he says. She understands him in ways no one else ever has.

Now they begin to justify their relationship—carefully cataloging every failure in their respective marriages. They recite their spouse's shortcomings in deadly detail. They remember and magnify every problem. Their spouse is insensitive and unresponsive. Surely God doesn't expect them to live their entire lives in such an unhappy state. With a little help from such rationalization their compatibility leads smoothly into tenderness, the tenderness to a need for privacy, the privacy to physical consolation, and the consolation straight to bed.

Once they physically commit adultery, the adulterers find themselves in a maelstrom of emotions. Guilt and fear haunt them. Their self-esteem falters. They live with the constant fear of being found out. Prayer seems impossible. How can they face God? Yet even as they writhe in remorse, they are driven with excitement and desire. They hate what they are doing, but they feel powerless to stop. They vow to break it off, to go back to just being friends, but to no avail. Their good intentions are just that—good intentions—nothing more. Like moths drawn irresistibly to a flame they seem destined to self-destruct.

As the affair progresses, their excitement wears off while their guilt and fear increase. Now they feel trapped. There is no way out of the relationship without hurting the other person, yet they can't continue like this indefinitely either. No matter what they do now someone is going to get hurt and hurt bad!

Now they must face the spouse they have betrayed, the children they have abandoned, and the God they have disobeyed. The consequences of their sin will reverberate through eternity, hurting the innocent as certainly as the guilty. The consequences are inevitable:

> Can a man scoop fire into his lap
> without his clothes being burned?
> Can a man walk on hot coals
> without his feet being scorched?
> So is he who sleeps with another
> man's wife;
> no one who touches her will go
> unpunished. . . .
> But a man who commits adultery
> lacks judgment;
> Whoever does so destroys himself.
> (Prov. 6:27–29, 32 NIV)

Taking Action

If you have caught a glimpse of yourself or your marriage, now is the time to take corrective action. If there is anything dangerous or inappropriate about any relationship in your life, confess it to God and renounce it. Terminate the friendship immediately, and make yourself accountable to a trusted Christian friend or to your pastor.

Although adultery is an unspeakable tragedy it is not the unpardonable sin. God's grace is greater still: "God does not take away a life; but He devises means, so that His banished ones are not expelled from Him" (2 Sam. 14:14). Through the sacrificial death of Jesus Christ, God has made a way to forgive the adulterer and to reconcile him to Himself.

"'Come now, and let us reason together,' / Says the Lord, / 'Though your sins are like scarlet, / They shall be as white as snow; / Though they are red like crimson, / They shall be as wool'" (Isa. 1:18).

While temptation is inevitable, *defeat is not.* Temptation *can* be resisted and overcome. "God is faithful, who will not allow you to be tempted beyond what you are able, but with the temptation will also make the way of escape, that you may be able to bear it" (1 Cor. 10:13).

If we are serious about overcoming the kinds of sexual temptations that lead to adultery, not only will we establish appropriate guidelines for our relationships and respond to the earliest warning signals, but we will also give our marriage first priority. We will invest quality time and energy in the relationship, pledging ourselves not only to physical faithfulness but to emotional fidelity as well. "So guard yourself in your spirit, and do not break faith with the wife of your youth" (Mal. 2:15 NIV).

Maintaining a healthy marriage does not eliminate temptation, but it does minimize its impact. When our deepest spiritual and emotional needs are met in relationship with God and our spouse, we will not need to use other relationships in a misguided attempt to establish our value as persons. We may still be tempted, but now we can respond out of wholeness rather than need.

Reflecting on Him

1. *How are you attending to the "ness" needs (closeness, goodness, kindness, and togetherness) of your spouse on a regular basis?*

2. *Are you, even at this instant, aware of a "moment of maybe" within your life? If so, honestly confess it to God and take immediate steps to build a spiritual hedge around your marriage by investing extra in the "ness" needs of your spouse.*

3. *If you answered yes to question two, you have not sinned. But, it is critical that you be honest before God with your present state. To do so, review the five warning signals and take immediate action to protect yourself and your spouse. Take out two index cards. On one card write out the complete Scripture verse from Malachi 2:15—give this card to a trusted Christian friend or your pastor and ask him to pray for you daily and to hold you accountable for this scripture. On the other card write out 1 Corinthians 10:13—keep this card in a prominent place where you can see it daily. Make it a habit to read it over and over each day, for this is God's promise of deliverance for you.*

22

MIDLIFE AFFAIRS

Oscar Wilde once wrote, "In this world, there are only two tragedies. One is not getting what one wants, and the other is getting it."[1] Nowhere is the truth of this axiom more apparent than in midlife. By midlife many people have achieved more success than they ever imagined possible only to discover that they are desperately unfulfilled. This phenomenon often results in a midlife affair or at least strong temptation in that direction.

Gordon MacDonald, author of *Ordering Your Private World*, and past president of InterVarsity Christian Fellowship, is a tragic example of a man who fell prey to this kind of affair. I refer to him by name, not to cause him or his family further pain, but only that we might learn from the failure that he has been so courageous to overcome and share. In an interview with *Christianity Today* he urged us to "take a hard look at what happened to me and resolve that it won't happen to . . . [you]."[2]

In that same interview he identified some of the circumstances that contributed to his adultery. He was in midlife, at the height of his career, and for years he had driven himself. He said,

> From about 1982 on I was desperately weary in spirit and in body. I was working harder and enjoying it less. . . . In addition, I now realize I was lacking in mutual accountability through personal relationships. We need friendships where one man regularly looks another man in the eye and asks hard questions about our moral life, our lust, our ambitions, our ego.[3]

Of course, for that kind of relationship to work you have to tell the absolute truth when asked.

Daniel Levinson, author of *The Seasons of a Man's Life*, is careful to differentiate between this type of extramarital relationship and what he calls "the kind of casual affairs" men have just for "kicks" when they are younger. He says, "People [who are in the midst of a midlife crisis] enter an affair because they feel that something important is missing in their marriage and they are looking to find it elsewhere."[4] In many cases it is not just the marriage that is found lacking, but a person's entire life.

While this crisis occurs during midlife, *it is really the result of choices they have been making their entire lives*. It has been pointed out that our lives are generally made up of three components. First there is the *vocational*—a person's career. Second, there is the *relational*—one's interaction with significant others such as spouse, children, parents, and peers. Third, there's the realm of the *personal*—the part of one's self that is genuinely unique and is expressed simply for one's own private delight. I would like to add a fourth: the *spiritual*—one's relationship with God. It has been suggested that all of us tend to overinvest in one or the other of these components in our earlier years and that during the midlife crisis, the effects of this imbalance begin to surface. Consider, for example, King David's tragic affair with Bathsheba.

King David's Midlife Affair

While the term *midlife crisis* is relatively new, the experience itself is probably as old as mankind. There are several cases in the Scriptures, but none is as obvious as the case involving King David.[5] The roots of his crisis probably go clear back to his childhood. As the youngest child he was neglected and overlooked in his family, especially by his father, and by his older brothers as well (1 Sam. 16:1–13 and 17:28). As a result he became a big-time overachiever in a futile attempt to make up for the approval his father never gave him. In modern terms he would probably be called a workaholic. In five short decades he rose from the obscurity of tending sheep to become the uncontested ruler of a huge area stretching from the Nile to the Euphrates. Many factors contributed to his success, including the anointing of God; but we dare not overlook his remarkable ability to give himself completely to the task at hand. He did not do it for selfish reasons either; but the cost at midlife was extravagant just the same.

David showed us how to make a difference in the world by investing ourselves totally in our careers. Unfortunately he also showed us what happens when there is not concomitant growth on the other frontiers of our lives. When we examine his biography it becomes evident that his overinvestment in the vocational area led to tragic neglect in the other facets of his existence, particularly the relational area.

After Jonathan's death there is no indication that David ever established a relationship of authentic intimacy with any other person. He had many wives but no deep relationship, and as a result he grew lonelier and lonelier as the years went by. His failure in the area of intimacy extended to his children as well. He had a number of them: The Bible lists at least nineteen sons, and there is no telling how many daughters there were. From the way they later fought and connived and betrayed each other, it seems clear that they had little contact with, or guidance from, their famous father.

Initially it is much easier, as David undoubtedly found out, to substitute the creation of several superficial relationships for the task of building one primary relationship in life, but the outcome is not the same. Apparently every time he had difficulty with one of his wives, instead of using the occasion to deepen and strengthen their bond, David slid off sideways and began a new marriage. Ultimately this behavioral pattern resulted in moral failure of the gravest kind.

One spring David decided to remain in Jerusalem rather than go to battle with his armies. He was now firmly established as king and had no further need to prove himself. Therefore he delegated to Joab the leadership of the army in the field. Of course he would arrive in time to participate in the final battle and thus take credit for the victory, but emotionally it was not the same as being in the thick of things.

While Joab and the armies of Israel were laying siege to Rabbah, David was idling away his time in the palace. He now had leisure he was not equipped to enjoy. As Kenneth Chafin points out, "He was a man of action with a bit of time on his hands, a warrior who now took naps in the afternoon, and he may have felt the need for some excitement, for a new interest, or for an escape."[6]

Whatever the case he arose late one afternoon and went to the roof of the palace to enjoy the cool evening breeze. As he paced back and forth it was apparent that he was more restless than relaxed. Having achieved more than he ever imagined possible, he may have been chagrined at discovering that for all his success he did not feel the way he thought he would feel, which is a typical midlife experience. Perhaps he was painfully evaluating his life in terms of meaningfulness and fulfillment. Maybe this once he stayed at home because he wanted to begin to develop the relational area of his life. That being the case, he was surely disappointed. His wives and his children had all learned long ago to fare for themselves. He was a stranger to them, and they had little feeling for him.

The first step in avoiding a midlife affair is to invest ourselves proportionately in the four main areas of our lives: vocational, relational, personal, and spiritual.

All of which simply suggests that the forces that drove David to have an affair with Bathsheba did not begin the evening he caught sight of her bathing. They began years earlier, when he gave himself exclusively to his career, ignoring his need for deep interpersonal relationships, as well as his need to develop his personal uniqueness. This was more than just a lifestyle. It was a reflection of the kind of person David was. Not infrequently the person who lives his life this way is doing so in a desperate attempt to cope with long-standing personal pain. In addition to the unfulfilling relationship David had with his father and older brothers there was the pain of his failed relationship with King Saul, not to mention Jonathan's death. No matter what David achieved it never seemed enough to still the pain within.

It should also be noted that although David maintained his relationship with the Lord throughout all the seasons of his life, it did not make him immune to the consequences of his negligence in these other areas. How else can we explain his tragic moral failures?

What can we learn from all of this? Much I hope, for the integrity of our lives and our marriages, may well depend on it.

Goal-Gap Midlife Crises

H. Norman Wright, in his book *Seasons of a Marriage,* has identified two primary causes of the male midlife crisis. The first is what he calls a *goal-gap midlife crisis.* "This refers to the distance a man perceives between the goals he has set for himself and the achievements he has actually attained."[7] In other words, at midlife, he is often brought face-to-face with reality. Not only have the goals he set for himself not been attained, but in all likelihood he never will attain them. This can be a most distressing realization, especially if his career has been the foundation of his personal identity.

One of the best examples I know of this "goal-gap midlife crisis" involved a forty-year-old salesman. His situation and his symptoms were classic. His fortieth birthday was traumatic, and shortly thereafter he dyed his hair, lost more than thirty pounds, bought a new "mod" wardrobe, and returned to college.

Those of us who knew him were more amused than concerned, after all his "crisis" was not serious. I mean, he could have quit his job, divorced his wife, bought a motorcycle, and headed for the West Coast. I now realize that we should have taken him more seriously. His new clothes and return to college were just the tip of the iceberg. The months that followed produced one disconcerting disclosure after another.

First was an incident involving a young woman, a coworker, who accused him of trying to kiss her. Of course he denied it, and we all laughed it off as being totally out of character for him. There were other symptoms, too, which are obvious in retrospect: a growing disillusionment with his job, talk about a new career in another field, a sudden interest in rock music. Ultimately he left his job and his wife after becoming involved with a woman fifteen years younger than himself.

It's not unusual for a man to feel frustrated and unfulfilled when he comes face-to-face with the harsh realization that he is never going to achieve the career goals he set for himself. Most men, however, respond in a positive way once they have gotten over the initial shock. Many cope by establishing more realistic goals and by reordering the priorities in their lives. For many, spiritual character becomes more important than success, relationships of more value than status symbols such as job titles, office size, or salary. As a result, the midlife years are often the most fulfilling years of their lives.

King of the Mountain

The second cause that Wright identifies is on the opposite end of the spectrum. He wrote, "Some men experience a career crisis because . . . they have attained their goals."[8] There are no more worlds to conquer. Suddenly the middle-aged man finds himself king of the mountain—only the top of the mountain is an awfully lonely place. In his single-minded quest for success he has ignored his family and alienated his friends. Now he has everything he ever wanted, only he does not feel the way he is supposed to feel. Where is the inner contentment? Where is the sense of achievement? Belatedly he realizes that success without someone to share it with is not success at all. Achievement without relationships is empty indeed!

What happens next depends not only on the way that he responds to this crisis but on his wife's response as well. While he has been busy with his business, she has been coping with her own responsibilities—and some of his too: rearing the children, running the home, and maybe even building her own career. Now she is experiencing a midlife crisis of her own, or if not a crisis, at least some significant midlife changes.

Wright said that in midlife, "women tend to become more autonomous, aggressive and cognitive. They now seek more instrumental roles such as a career, money, influence."[9] Their husbands, on the other hand, have finally seen the futility of a life lived only for their career, and they are now ready to reestablish contact with their mates. Rather than being affirmed and excited by their husband's sudden interest, many wives see it as just another way of keeping them in "their place."

It's a sad picture indeed, and an all too familiar one. A lot of marital tragedy takes place right here. Just as the husband is turning toward his wife in search of intimacy and closeness, she turns away from him toward a new career and new interests in life.

A few days ago I received a telephone call from a distraught husband who found himself in just such a situation. Following their youngest child's departure for college, his wife informed him that she didn't love him anymore. After more than twenty years of marriage, she was fed up with his controlling ways. From now on she was going to be her own person. She would come and go as she pleased, and if he didn't like it—tough! Now that the children were out of the house, she intended to pursue her own interests, and at the present those interests did not include her husband. She also demanded that he move his things into the guest room, as they would no longer be sharing the same bed.

It is not hard to imagine what will likely happen next. In the course of her professional duties this unhappy wife will probably find herself working with a number of interesting men—men whom she perceives see her as a person in her own right and not just an appendage of their ego, as her husband sees her. Working together on important projects she will likely find herself spending a lot of time with one or more of them.

Some night after working late one of the men will probably suggest they get something to eat before going home. She will readily agree, although she knows that given her state of mind, it is not a wise thing to do. During dinner they will discover they have a number of things in common, including less than ideal marriages. Without consciously deciding to, they will find themselves disclosing the shortcomings of their individual spouses. His inner emptiness mirrors her own, and almost without realizing what is happening they will forge an emotional bond. Here is a man who appreciates her as a person. He listens to her and really cares about the things she feels. For the first time, in longer than she can remember, she feels alive. In a matter of weeks, sometimes just days, they will find themselves involved in a torrid affair.

This midlife affair actually started years ago and initially had almost nothing to do with sex. Her husband overinvested in his work and his career, at the expense of his relationship with his family and her. For her part, she internalized her resentment until it turned into the acid of hatred. She blames her husband for everything she thought she had missed in life, and now she is determined to make up for lost time. Although she knows it is wrong, she doesn't care. At least she doesn't care enough to do anything about it.

Overcoming Midlife Temptations

The first step in avoiding a midlife affair is to invest ourselves proportionately in the four main areas of our lives: vocational, relational, personal, and spiritual. As already noted, during our early years most of us tend to overinvest in at least one of these areas at the expense of the others, suffering the consequences at midlife. Most men tend to pour themselves into their work. It's easy to justify the long hours, the travel, and the weekends away from the family. He is doing it for them. He has to become established. It is only for a time. And herein lies the trap—by the time he has established himself, he has developed workaholic tendencies that are almost impossible to break.

When a man overinvests in his work for an extended period of time, at least two things happen. First, he distances himself from his wife and family. The relationship that should be at the center of his being gets shoved to the ragged edge. His marriage gets the leftovers, the scraps at the end of a demanding day—hardly the stuff of which meaningful marriages are made. And it goes without saying that when his marriage is not in good repair, he is susceptible to sexual temptation, as is his wife. By midlife this lack of emotional closeness usually produces a crisis for both the husband and the wife.

For her part she is resentful, tired of playing second fiddle to his career, and tired of being controlled. Now that the children are out of the house she is ready to try her wings. She feels she can now accept that promotion that requires her to travel two or three days each week. To her way of thinking it is time she thought about her own needs—a mind-set that leaves her vulnerable to all kinds of temptation. If these differences cannot be resolved, a midlife affair is likely.

The first step in rebuilding the marital relationship is for each spouse to honestly own their mistakes without attempting to justify or rationalize their behavior. The husband who says, "I was doing it for you and the children" only succeeds in further alienating his wife. She knows he was chasing the brass ring for himself, his protests to the contrary notwithstanding. The only question she has is whether or not he is willing to take responsibility for his actions. If he cannot, then it will probably be impossible for her to believe he is serious about giving their marriage first priority, regardless of what else he might say to the contrary.

She, too, must be willing to take responsibility for her own feelings. Although her husband's behavior may have created a climate in which it was easy for her to become resentful and even bitter, it was still her choice. By owning her mistakes she can take the first step in moving from resentment to reconciliation.

As the spouses make new commitments to the marriage, there may be a temptation to expect the emotional climate of the relationship to improve overnight. While that might happen, it is not likely. Each of you has been hurt, trust has been eroded, and it will take time to rebuild it. Now comes the hard part: living out your new commitments day by day even when there is no corresponding emotional resonance. Your faithfulness during this difficult time will go a long way in determining the future of your relationship.

The second consequence of overinvesting in the vocational area of life is burnout! By midlife the workaholic is physically and emotionally worn out. Consequently, when he struggles with temptation he has neither the inner strength nor the spiritual resources to resist. He succumbs, I think, oftentimes more out of an inner emptiness than any evil desire.

Another misconception that sets a person up for a midlife affair is the confusion about his or her identity and self-worth. Many people labor a lifetime believing that if they can just reach their goals they will finally feel accepted and worthy. Not true! There is not enough success in the world to quiet the discordant voices within. Self-esteem is not the by-product of achievement, but the natural consequence of a healthy relationship with one's parents, spouse, and God. It is a matter of who we are in Christ, not what we have done. Tragically, the person who labors a lifetime only to discover that he or she chased the wrong dream often becomes a prime candidate for a midlife affair.

I Don't Believe This is an Accurate statement

Mutual Accountability

The man who is serious about overcoming the temptations of midlife will make building friendships with godly men a high priority. He will search for men who are deeply committed to the things of God, who share his love for the Scriptures and the work of the kingdom. In relationships of mutual accountability he will find strength, correction, and love. Only God knows how many men have escaped the tempter's snare through the counsel and prayers of a spiritual friend. Solomon said,

> Two are better than one,
> because they have a good return
> for their work:

> If one falls down,
>   his friend can help him up.
> But pity the man who falls
>   and has no one to help him up!
> Also, if two lie down together, they
>   will keep warm.
> But how can one keep warm alone?
> Though one may be overpowered,
>   two can defend themselves.
> A cord of three strands is not
>   quickly broken. *(Eccl. 4:9–12 NIV)*

Ideally a man's wife should be his *best* friend, but he dare not make her his *only* friend. If he does he will likely overwhelm her with his neediness. When she cannot meet all of his belonging needs, he will experience disappointment and frustration, while she is made to feel inadequate—a situation that will put no little strain on the relationship.

Interestingly enough, if he will develop a small circle of friends who are godly men, he will discover that rather than distracting from his relationship with his wife, it actually will enhance it. Freed from the burden of being her husband's *only* friend, she can enjoy being his *best* friend!

The key element in developing these kinds of relationships is *time*. Whether we are talking about marriage or friendship, the key is the same—*time*! Relationships are demanding, I'll grant you that, but the benefits more than justify the investment.

One of the best friends I've ever had is a Methodist minister who reached out to Brenda and me when we were just kids serving our first church in a little place called Holly, Colorado. His friendship made two of the most difficult years of our lives not only bearable but blessed. My life bears the imprint of his influence still, almost thirty years later. Many times since I've wished I could find another friend like him. I've even prayed to that end. Gently the Lord rebukes me, "Don't pray 'Let me find a friend like that.' Instead pray, 'Let me be a friend like that.'"

Conclusion

The time to prepare for midlife is right now! In order to avoid a midlife crisis and the possibility of a midlife affair, develop a network of spiritual friends, a support system, with your spouse at the very center. Set realistic goals that you can attain but not out-grow. Personal identity must be firmly rooted in who we are in Christ rather than what we have done. And finally, maintain a per-sonal relationship with the living God. Do this faithfully, and you will have nothing to fear when midlife's inevitable temptations come.

Reflecting on Him

1. *Midlife is a time when you experience multiple changes that produce significant stress on most individuals. What are you doing during this time of great change to assure that you grow closer to God and your spouse?*

2. *What proportion of your emotional, physical, and spiritual energy do you devote to your career/vocation, your relation-ships with others, your personal satisfaction, and your spiri-tual walk with Christ? Do you believe that you are maintaining an appropriate balance in these areas?*

3. *Are you doing things "for" or "with" God, your family, your friends, your coworkers, etc.? In your own words, why is it more important to do "with" rather than "for"?*

OVERCOMING TEMPTATION

Only when a person embraces his propensity for sin will he take the steps necessary to escape it. As long as he pretends that sin is not a problem for him, he will continue to place himself in situations that make it nearly impossible for him to resist temptation. And given the right circumstances, the best among us are capable of the most horrific sins. The sooner we come to grips with this painful truth, the sooner we can be about the business of overcoming temptation.

23

KNOW
YOUR LIMITATIONS

As I write this I am sitting in a small cabin in the Ozark Mountains in northwest Arkansas. It is an almost perfect place to write. Being located twenty-five miles from town and nearly ten miles from the nearest paved road, there are few distractions. To my knowledge no one has ever just dropped in on us. There is one drawback, however—the cabin sits on the side of a mountain just about one hundred feet above Beaver Lake. Since I am an avid fisherman this has proved to be an almost irresistible temptation.

When we arrived a few days ago, I knew there would be no time for fishing. I was behind schedule on this book and working on a strict deadline. Every waking hour would have to be spent at the computer—no easy task for me. In the past I have had a history of spending some time on the lake every day, no matter how pressing the project. This time I didn't dare, or I would never meet my publisher's schedule.

Given my history, I knew the situation called for drastic action, so I decided to leave my boat on the trailer. Usually the first thing I do upon arriving at the cabin is to put the boat in the water where it remains for the duration of our stay. This makes it easy for me to go fishing. All I have to do is run down to the dock and get in the boat—a temptation I've seldom been able to resist.

By recognizing my weakness and taking steps to deal with it before I am tempted, I am succeeding. Thus far I have not gone fishing a single time, nor do I intend to do so until this manuscript is finished and in the hands of my publisher. Why am I succeeding this time, when I have failed so often in the past? Because I have made temptation terribly inconvenient; therefore, it is easier to resist. It is just too much trouble to haul the boat to the lake and launch it every time I want to go fishing.

The point I am trying to make should be readily obvious: Only when a person embraces his propensity for sin will he take the steps necessary to escape it. As long as he pretends that sin is not a problem for him, he will continue to place himself in situations that make it nearly impossible for him to resist temptation. And given the right circumstances, the best among us are capable of the most horrific sins. The sooner we come to grips with this painful truth, the sooner we can be about the business of overcoming temptation.

The Risk Taker

When battling temptation nothing is more deadly than overconfidence. It causes a person to rush in where angels fear to tread. Therefore the apostle Paul warned, "Let him who thinks he stands take heed lest he fall" (1 Cor. 10:12). Although overconfidence manifests itself in a variety of ways, the two most common are spiritual naïveté and risk taking.

The spiritually naive person is simply out of touch with his own humanity. To him the possibility of committing a serious sin is inconceivable. Consequently, he may place himself in compromising situations without ever realizing the risks he is taking. When the inevitable temptation comes, it blindsides him, and he succumbs in short order. Afterward he is devastated. He never imagined himself capable of such a thing.

The risk taker, on the other hand, is an adventurer. He is addicted to danger and excitement. He recognizes the possibility of a sinful failure—in fact, it is that very possibility that excites him. Not that he would ever actually do it but . . . tragically the risk taker almost always overestimates his moral resolve. He is simply no match for the tempter.

Samson, of Old Testament fame, was a classic risk taker. His biography fascinates Bible scholars and moviemakers alike. He was the only child of godly parents, who dedicated him to the Lord from the day of his birth. By God's instruction, no razor was ever to touch the hair of his head, nor was he ever to drink wine or strong drink of any kind. He was a Nazirite to God (Judg. 13:3–5).

The Spirit of the Lord came upon him from time to time (Judg. 13:25; 14:6, 19; 15:14), and he did great exploits. While he was a man used by God, he was hardly a man of God. He did mighty feats when the Spirit was upon him, but he was not a man who walked in the Spirit.

His was the original "fatal attraction"—he had a weakness for forbidden women. Repeatedly he fell in love with the daughters of his enemies. First it was a woman in Timnah. "So he went up and told his father and mother, saying, 'I have seen a woman in Timnah of the daughters of the Philistines; now therefore, get her for me as a wife'" (14:2–3).

Against their better judgement his parents made the arrangements, and during the seven-day wedding feast Samson posed a riddle to her Philistine friends. Of course they could not solve it so they turned to his bride for help. "Then Samson's wife wept on him, and said, 'You only hate me! You do not love me! You have posed a riddle to the sons of my people, but you have not explained it to me'" (Judg. 14:16). By the seventh day Samson could bear no more of her whining, so he explained the riddle to her, whereupon she conveyed that information to the sons of her people.

Just before sunset on the seventh day the Philistines came to Samson with the solution to the riddle. Instantly he realized his wife had betrayed him. Bitterly he said, "If you had not plowed with my heifer, / You would not have solved my riddle!" (Judg. 14:18).

Samson should have learned his lesson, but apparently he did not. Some years later he fell in love with another Philistine woman named Delilah. Quickly the lords of the Philistines moved to take advantage of the situation. They offered Delilah a considerable sum of money to find the source of Samson's great strength. Thus began one of the most unusual accounts in all of Scripture.

Three times Delilah pressed Samson to tell her the secret of his strength and how he might be bound. Each time he told her something different. First he said, "If they bind me with seven fresh bowstrings, not yet dried, then I shall become weak, and be like any other man" (16:7). When that proved not to be the case, she tried again. This time he told her that if he was bound with new ropes that had never been used that would do the trick (16:11). Of course that did not work, either, and she continued to press him: "Until now you have mocked me and told me lies. Tell me what you may be bound with" (16:13). Finally he said, "If you weave the seven locks of my head into the web of the loom" (16:13). Of course this proved to be no more effective than virgin bowstrings or new ropes, leaving her looking like a fool in the eyes of the Philistine lords.

> Then she said to him, "How can you say, 'I love you,' when your heart is not with me? You have mocked me these three times, and have not told me where your great strength lies." And it came to pass, when she pestered him daily with her words and pressed him, so that his soul was vexed to death, that he told her all his heart, and said to her, "No razor has ever come upon my head, for I have been a Nazirite to God from my mother's womb. If I am shaven, then my strength will leave me, and I shall become weak, and be like any other man. . . ." Then she lulled him to sleep on her knees, and called for a man and had him shave off the seven locks of his head. Then she began to torment him, and his strength left him. And she said, "The Philistines are upon you, Samson!" So he awoke from his sleep, and said, "I will go out as before, at other times, and shake myself free!" But he did not know that the LORD had departed from him. Then the Philistines took him and put out his eyes, and brought him down to Gaza. They bound him with bronze fetters, and he became a grinder in the prison. *(Judg. 16:15–17; 19–21)*

For years I thought Samson had to be the dumbest man who ever walked the face of the earth. How else could his relationship with Delilah be explained? Each time he gave her false information regarding the source of his strength she *immediately* used it against him. Even the most dimwitted clod would have had to realize that she was in cahoots with the Philistine lords. Still Samson bared his heart to her and suffered the consequences.

Now that I am older, and hopefully somewhat wiser, I no longer think Samson was lacking in intelligence. He was no backward country bumpkin taken in by Delilah's feminine charms. He knew exactly what she was doing. Why then did he share his whole heart with her? Because he enjoyed the risk. He was using her even as she was trying to use him. Flirting with danger gave him a rush. Besides he was convinced that even if she shaved his head he would still be more than a match for the fumbling Philistines.

Overconfidence, not Delilah, was Samson's undoing!

Living Within Your Limits

The person who is serious about overcoming temptation will never deliberately put himself in tempting situations as Samson did. He will not flirt with danger! If he wants a rush he will go bungee jumping. He will not overestimate his own spiritual resources, nor will he underestimate his capacity for sin. By realistically appraising both his strengths and his weaknesses, he will be able to live within his limits, thus minimizing the risks of yielding to temptation.

Joseph is a case in point. As a seventeen-year-old boy he was sold by his jealous brothers to a caravan of Ishmaelite merchants who trafficked in slaves. They took him to Egypt where he was purchased by Potiphar, the captain of Pharaoh's guard. The Lord was with Joseph, and he found favor in his master's eyes. Soon Potiphar made him the steward of his entire estate and "the LORD blessed the Egyptian's house for Joseph's sake; and the blessing of the LORD was on all that he had in the house and in the field" (Gen. 39:5).

As the captain of Pharaoh's guard, Potiphar was gone from home a great deal. During one of his absences, his wife approached Joseph. The Bible describes it this way: "Now it came to pass after these things that his master's wife cast longing eyes on Joseph, and she said, 'Lie with me'" (Gen. 39:7).

"But he refused and said to his master's wife, 'Look, my master . . . has committed all that he has to my hand. There is no one greater in this house than I, nor has he kept back anything from me but you, because you are his wife. How then can I do this great wickedness, and sin against God?'" (Gen. 39:8–9).

Potiphar's wife did not give up. She simply changed her tactics. Day after day she spoke to Joseph. Possibly her conversation went something like this: "Joseph, can you ever forgive me for making such a fool of myself? I really don't want to lie with you. I just need someone to talk to, someone to be with. With Potiphar gone so much of the time I am terribly lonely, and there is no one else for me to talk to. You are the only man I can trust. You are not like other men. You are different, more sensitive, more understanding. Surely there cannot be any harm in talking with me?"

Thankfully Joseph was not taken in. "And though she spoke to Joseph day after day, he refused to go to bed with her or even be with her" (39:10 NIV).

Apparently Joseph realized his limitations and governed himself accordingly. Undoubtedly he knew that if he spent time with his master's wife it would only be a matter of time until they were in bed together. Because he did not want to compromise his integrity nor betray his master's trust, he did the only sensible thing—he refused even to be near her. He who does not want to be robbed does not invite a thief into his house!

Along this same line a young man approached his pastor and embarrassingly acknowledged that he was losing the battle with his sexual desires. His hormones were working overtime, and no matter how passionately he prayed or how determinedly he vowed to resist temptation, nothing seemed to work. As soon as he was alone with his girlfriend, his good resolve flew out the window.

After hearing him out, his pastor told him that if he was serious about fleeing youthful lusts, he would have to avoid tempting situations. Instead of stopping on the bluff overlooking the lake, he would have to drive his girlfriend directly home. When the young man replied that he thought that was a little extreme, his pastor pointed out that if he was going to win the war against lust, he was going to have to change the battlefield. Instead of doing battle in the backseat of a car, where his convictions had already proved to be no match for his hormones, he should determine to confront his temptations in the company of others, where he was much less likely to fail. "He who chooses the battlefield," counseled his pastor, "usually wins the war."

Earlier I shared an embarrassing incident that took place at a car rental counter in the airport (Chapter 17). Having failed to refuel the rental car I decided to try to bluff my way through the check-in procedures. Approaching the counter I felt apprehensive in my spirit, but I chose to ignore it. Instead I rationalized that it was no big deal—I had only driven the car a few miles, and the fuel gauge was still registering full. Of course, I ended up lying to the attendant who checked the car in.

At the time I was not willing to admit that I was lying, after all I was careful to tell the "exact" truth, if not the whole truth. By telling the attendant that the fuel gauge was reading full, I was using the truth to deceive, and that is dishonesty of the most serious kind. Of course the Lord chastened me in a most painful manner, causing me to see some things in my character that I had heretofore chosen to ignore.

Following that shameful incident I took immediate steps to see that it never happened again. Now when I rent a car I always take the fuel option, which allows me to purchase a full tank of gas in advance. It probably costs me a few dollars in unused fuel, but that seems a small price to pay in order to avoid temptation. Some may feel I have taken a cowardly way out. Perhaps they are right, but I do not really think so. Instead I view it as dealing with temptation from a position of strength rather than weakness.

All of us have areas where we are particularly susceptible to sin. Once you acknowledge your areas of weakness you can then address them with a strategy that enables you to overcome. Your tactics may be extreme—and others who do not struggle in that particular area may not need to go to the same lengths to gain the victory—but you will be dealing from a position of strength rather than weakness, thus increasing your chances of success.

Living Circumspectly

There are several factors that determine your vulnerability to temptation. The most obvious, of course, is circumstance. By allowing yourself to be in the *wrong place*, associating with the *wrong people* at the *wrong time,* you make overcoming temptation nearly impossible. You have stacked the deck against yourself!

A second factor is your personality, your temperament. By nature there are certain temptations that appeal to you more than others. For instance you may be the kind of person who will do almost anything to be accepted—making you especially susceptible to peer pressure. That being the case, choosing the right friends is doubly important if you hope to live an overcoming life.

A third factor is your personal history—those experiences that have shaped who you are. Studies indicate that children who come from abusive homes are more likely to grow up to be abusers than those who come from nonabusive families. Similar studies show that women who were victims of incest are more likely to be promiscuous than those who were not. That is not to say that you cannot overcome your past or the temptations it births, but only that it is a factor that must be worked into the equation. By recognizing the part your past plays in making you vulnerable to certain temptations, you can take whatever steps are necessary to neutralize its power.

If we are serious about overcoming temptation we will prayerfully examine ourselves, taking into account both our successes and our failures. We will ask the Lord to help us understand why we seem especially susceptible to one temptation and not another, why we are able to resist the offerings of the enemy one time and not the next. This is not morbid introspection but rather the sanctifying work of the Holy Spirit. As the Lord does His deep work—bringing to light our hidden anxieties and the sinful desires we have not even admitted to ourselves—He is in the process of transforming us. Little by little He is conforming us to His very own image.

This is searching prayer, lingering prayer (Ps. 139:23–24), and it brings to light the hidden things. In His holy presence we acknowledge our secret sins and receive forgiveness. He lays His healing hands on our wounded spirits, imparting wholeness. Now we are able not only to concede our selfish ambitions but to relinquish them. Not our will, but His will be done.

R. Kent Hughes, author of *Disciplines of a Godly Man* writes,

> Prayer is like a time exposure to God. Our souls function like photographic plates, and Christ's shining image is the light. The more we expose our lives to the white-hot sun of His righteous life (for say, five, ten, fifteen, thirty minutes, or an hour a day), the more His image will be burned into our character—His love, His compassion, His truth, His integrity, His humility.[1]

And as we are more and more fully conformed to His image we find ourselves ever more resistant to temptation.

Much of what happens in prayer is beneath the surface of our consciousness, but the part that deals with who we are and why we do the things we do is not. With tender mercy the Spirit brings to light our hidden motivations. Little by little we are able to understand how both our personality and our past make us vulnerable to certain temptations. As we prayerfully examine our "wilderness" experiences, we come to see that what we at first assumed to be the enemy's initial thrust was not that at all. Rather it was the culmination of a series of small compromises that led finally to the temptation that did us in. And when we were victorious we now realize it was because we resisted temptation immediately, rather than giving it a foothold in our lives.

> As painful as it may be, recall a sinful failure. See if you can identify the earliest moment of temptation. It was probably some small

thing, seemingly insignificant, hardly noticed. Now identify the successive steps leading up to the sinful act itself. Repeat the process with two or three other failures and see if you can identify a pattern. If you are repeatedly tempted in the same areas (i.e., lust, anger, greed, or some addictive behavior), examine your daily life and habits to see what behaviors make you susceptible to these temptations.[2]

Now ask the Lord to help you make whatever adjustments are necessary in your lifestyle in order to walk in victory.

I believe this is what the apostle Paul had in mind when he counseled the Ephesian believers to "walk circumspectly, not as fools but as wise" (Eph. 5:15). To walk circumspectly means to carefully consider all related circumstances before making a decision or pursuing a particular course of action. Do this faithfully, and you will become increasingly effective in resisting temptation.

Reflecting on Him

1. *What role does the almighty "I" play in your ability to recognize your limitations?*

2. *Does it mean that you are a "weak" person if you have to rely on strategies like those described at the beginning of this chapter to overcome temptation?*

3. *Identify at least two areas in your life where you continue to struggle with overcoming temptation that is clearly situational. What steps can you take to avoid these situations, and thus keep yourself safe? Jot down at least four or five strategies.*

24

DEVELOP AN EARLY WARNING SYSTEM

The sky over the small, central Texas town of Jarrell is black and boiling. Huge thunderheads tower tens of thousands of feet into the air. The sultry air is heavy, foreboding. For some longtime residents it is reminiscent of another spring day in 1989 when a tornado snaked down from the sky, bringing death and destruction with it. On that day one person died, twenty-eight more were injured, and nearly fifty homes were damaged or destroyed. Before this dreadful day is over, however, that tornado will prove to be nearly insignificant. At this very moment, about sixty miles to the north, a monster tornado is in the process of forming in the thunderheads swirling over Bell and McLennan counties.

The storm roars into Williamson County at about 3:45 P.M. on Wednesday, May 28, 1997. It comes with a rush of wind, hurling blinding sheets of rain as hard as pellets. Then it seems to ease just a little; the rain slackens, and the wind dies. For a minute or two the uneasy residents of Jarrell breathe easier. Maybe the worst of the storm is over. Maybe they will be spared this time.

A few brave souls venture out to study the sky in the eerie half-light while the tornado siren continued to wail, portending things to come. In the distance they hear an ominous rumble like the sound of an approaching freight train—only this is no train! The wind is still unnaturally calm, but no one in this ill-fated town is fooled. The storm is not over—not by a long shot!

Just before the blinding sheets of rain return, obliterating all visibility, a finger of darkness snake out of the bruise-colored cloud shelf approaching from the north. From a distance it is almost beautiful—especially to the undiscerning. Gracefully it seems to trail across the uneven terrain, touching down first one place, then another. But it is the finger of death, and in its wake there is no beauty, only devastation. The swath it cuts is nearly a mile long and two hundred yards wide. It totally wipes out the Double Creek Estates subdivision—entire houses are gone. Nothing remains but naked concrete slabs looking like giant headstones in an ill-kept cemetery.

When at last it is over, the survivors emerge into the rain-washed sunlight to discover a scene of horror: Bits of clothing hang from barbed-wire fences, telephone poles have been snapped in half, and a tractor-trailer lies on its back in the middle of a field. Stunned and covered in mud, they wander around in the wreckage, crying and consoling each other. A temporary morgue is set up at the volunteer fire department, and rescue workers search through the night for the dead and missing. Hearses trickled in as they begin retrieving bodies. By morning, the death toll totals thirty. No one in this tiny town, population one thousand, is untouched.

Surviving a Tornado

Having lived in "tornado alley" for the past seventeen years I have learned some things about surviving a tornado. Two things are absolutely mandatory: *advance warning* and *suitable shelter*. Since tornadoes usually form quickly, it is critically important to know when the atmospheric conditions are favorable to their formation. When those conditions are present the National Weather Service issues a *tornado watch*. Once an actual tornado is sighted, the alert is upgraded to a *tornado warning,* at which time residents are urged to take immediate shelter. The safest place is an underground storm cellar or a basement. Lacking that, a person should go to an inside room on the ground floor of his home.

Meteorologists tell us that the formation of a tornado is most likely when the temperature at ground level is between 65 degrees and 84 degrees with a dew point above 50 degrees. They are formed when a cold front or a line of hot, dry air collides with warm, humid air and crosscurrent winds create a horizontal spinning effect. Strong updrafts then pull the warm, moist air upward and create a giant vertical chimney of rotating air.

The most favorable place for tornado formation is the central plains—the flat region east of the Rocky Mountains. Oklahoma, for instance, has more tornadoes per square mile than any other state. It is here where moist air from the Gulf of Mexico collides with dry air flowing down the slopes of the Rockies. Inject a cold front from Canada, and the conditions are prime for tornado formation.

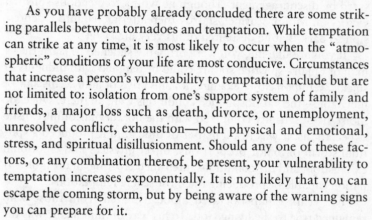

Like a killer tornado, temptation is most destructive when it takes us by surprise.

As you have probably already concluded there are some striking parallels between tornadoes and temptation. While temptation can strike at any time, it is most likely to occur when the "atmospheric" conditions of your life are most conducive. Circumstances that increase a person's vulnerability to temptation include but are not limited to: isolation from one's support system of family and friends, a major loss such as death, divorce, or unemployment, unresolved conflict, exhaustion—both physical and emotional, stress, and spiritual disillusionment. Should any one of these factors, or any combination thereof, be present, your vulnerability to temptation increases exponentially. It is not likely that you can escape the coming storm, but by being aware of the warning signs you can prepare for it.

Even a brief overview of the major Bible characters and their temptations will bear out the role these "atmospheric" conditions played in their vulnerability to the enemy. Take Peter for instance. On the night that he denied Jesus he was battered by internal storms, which left him stunned and ill-prepared to resist temptation. With the arrest of Jesus, the disciples fled, leaving Peter without a support system. For him, Jesus' arrest was a major loss, one that left him spiritually disillusioned. On top of everything else he was physically and emotionally exhausted. Had he been more aware of the spiritual and emotional dynamics that were at work in his life, he might have realized that he was in no condition to invade the enemy's territory, sparing him his most devastating failure.

Unfortunately, like Peter, few of us know how to read the warning signs. Unless we see a twister bearing down upon us we are largely unaware of the spiritual and emotional dynamics transpiring within. As John Gardener, author of *Self-Renewal* points out, "Self-knowledge is ruled out for most people by the increasingly effective self-deception they practice as they grow older. By middle age, most of us are accomplished fugitives from ourselves."[1] As a result temptation often catches us unaware, and if not unaware, at least unprepared. The consequences are often nothing less than tragic. Like a killer tornado, temptation is most destructive when it takes us by surprise.

Consider the case of Elijah the prophet. Following his showdown with the prophets of Baal (1 Kings 18, 19), he was blindsided by discouragement. Though he won a tremendous spiritual victory on Mount Carmel, shortly thereafter he fell into a depression so dark that he despaired of his very life (19:4).

If you are like me, you were probably shocked to learn that a man of Elijah's spiritual stature could be tempted with thoughts of suicide, yet upon closer examination, his crisis of faith seems almost inevitable—the "atmospheric" conditions were all there. Once the moist air of self-pity combined with the hot, dry air of unrealistic expectations, it was just a matter of time until it produced a spiritual storm of major proportions. Inject physical and emotional exhaustion, and the conditions intensified creating an unstable situation capable of producing the most severe temptations.

For years Elijah operated alone, isolated from those who remained true to the living God. To his way of thinking he was the only faithful man in all of Israel—a dangerous mind-set indeed. He had no prayer partner to encourage him when he became discouraged. No brother in the Lord to strengthen him when he grew weary in well-doing. No one to challenge his thinking when his thoughts tempted him to indulge in self-pity.

He cried, "I have been very zealous for the LORD God of hosts; for the children of Israel have forsaken Your covenant, torn down Your altars, and killed Your prophets with the sword. I alone am left; and they seek to take my life" (19:10).

A second factor was his physical and emotional exhaustion. A power encounter of the kind that Elijah had with the 450 false prophets on Mount Carmel was exhausting beyond words. Physically he was worn out from rebuilding the altar of the Lord and digging a deep trench around it, not to mention the fact that he had to kill and butcher a bull for the sacrifice. Then there was the physical and emotional letdown following the adrenaline high of facing down a wicked king and hundreds of false prophets. Finally there was the exhausting work of intercessory prayer and last, but not least, his thirteen-mile run ahead of King Ahab's chariot from Mount Carmel to the entrance of Jezreel. All of this was simply more than his body could bear, leaving him without the strength to battle his tormenting thoughts.

A final factor was disillusionment. Having expected a national revival following his victory on Mount Carmel, Elijah was devastated when Jezebel put a price on his head. Having entertained unrealistic expectations, he was now ready to throw in the towel. He had lost all hope; if the power demonstration that the Lord God displayed on Mount Carmel wasn't enough to bring Israel to her senses then nothing would. As far as he was concerned, his life had been a waste. There was no reason to go on living. Given these "atmospheric" conditions it is no wonder Elijah succumbed to temptation and prayed to die (19:4).

Tornado Warning

No one needs to be caught unaware when temptation strikes, for God is faithful to warn us. The first alert generally comes in the form of conviction—what I sometimes call a "check" in my spirit. By that I simply mean that I have an uneasy feeling, an inner sense that something is not quite right. It is kind of like the calm before the storm. The wind is still, but there is no peace—instead there is a sense of impending doom.

The human tendency at this point is to rationalize, to try to reason that uneasy feeling away. Don't! Instead, trust the Holy Spirit. He knows what the future holds. He knows where that relationship is going, where that business deal will take you. Your well-being is His only concern, and He is trying to protect you from the consequences of a bad decision.

In regard to the Holy Spirit's "tornado warnings" I want to be like the little boy who asked his mother what his conscience was. His mother replied, "Conscience is that little voice inside of you that warns you when you are about to do something bad." At bedtime that night the little fellow knelt beside his bed to pray.

Folding his hands he prayed, "Dear God, please make my little voice loud."

If we fail to respond to this inner warning from the Holy Spirit, the Lord will often send someone to speak with us. Normally it is a person we know and trust, but not always. This person may realize that he is sent from the Lord, but more often than not he does not. Usually he simply feels motivated by his concern for us. Having observed some potentially devastating behavior, he moves to counsel us regarding the danger ahead.

Although the tornado sirens are now screaming shrilly inside our heads, this second warning as often as not falls on deaf ears as well. Being self-willed by nature, it is almost impossible to convince us that we are in any real danger. Now the Lord may be forced to speak in more dramatic ways—through dreams or unusual events. Circumstances may seem to conspire to prevent us from following through with our self-destructive plans. "Therefore," said the Lord, "behold, / I will hedge up your way with thorns, / And wall [you] in, / So that [you] cannot find [your] paths" (Hos. 2:6). It is not anger that motivates Him, but love. More than anything He wants to save us from that finger of darkness that is bearing down upon us.

Unfortunately a warning alone is not enough, as the residents of Jarrell discovered. Following the 1989 twister that took one life, the city fathers installed a tornado warning siren in hopes it would prevent any future fatalities. It did not. On Wednesday afternoon, May 28, 1997, while the siren screamed its incessant warning, at least thirty people perished.

Perhaps the alarm did not sound soon enough. Or maybe those who perished heard the siren in plenty of time but simply failed to respond. After all, tornado warnings from the National Weather Service are not uncommon in that part of Texas, nor is the sounding of the tornado siren. Or more likely they simply had no place to go—no shelter capable of protecting them from a killer tornado of that magnitude. Being unprepared, they died, and a terrible death it was.

Hearing the news reports, I could not help thinking of my friend Bill (Chapter 11). God issued a warning for Bill when He came to me in a dream telling me to warn him not to have anything to do with Ruth. Although Bill would later claim that the warning came too late, after he was already emotionally involved with Ruth, I cannot help but believe there was still time for him to extricate himself. Unfortunately, Bill failed to respond to the Holy Spirit's warning, and like those who perished in Jarrell, Texas, he is suffering the consequences. Obviously an early warning system is of little benefit if you do not seek shelter.

Preparing a Storm Shelter

The time to prepare for temptation is *before* it strikes. Only a fool would try to dig a storm cellar in the middle of a tornado, yet many seem to think nothing of ignoring the reality of temptation until they are in the midst of it. A good place to begin is to establish moral and spiritual standards ahead of time. Few of us are capable of making a spiritual value decision in the heat of temptation. Therefore it is critical to settle the issues before we are tempted. Determine an appropriate response and then respond accordingly when temptation comes.

Sometime ago I was speaking at a men's retreat on this very subject. Following my session, a retired Lieutenant Colonel, a former infantry officer in the United States Army, asked to speak with me. After getting some coffee we moved to a corner table where we could talk privately.

Once we were seated he said, "In the army we prepared a predetermined response for every conceivable tactic of the enemy. Since the most effective military response is often contrary to human nature, we practiced it hundreds of times. These predetermined responses are called *immediate action drills*."

When I nodded, indicating that I understood, he continued. "For instance, when you come under an artillery attack, your first response is to seek cover. Unfortunately that is the worst thing you can do. Unless there is a steel-reinforced, concrete bunker for you to take shelter in, you are going to die. There is nothing in the natural terrain that will protect you from artillery fire. The enemy will seek you out and kill you.

"The army's predetermined response to an artillery attack is to run and reassemble at a given location based on what is called 'clock direction.' Here's how it works. As soon as the attack begins the squad leader calls out the reassembly point—say three o'clock at two hundred meters. Since this response is totally contrary to human nature only hundreds of hours of drills can condition a man to respond correctly."

As he continued to talk, detailing one immediate action drill after another, my mind was racing. When temptation comes, the correct response is almost always contrary to our human nature. "For the flesh lusts against the Spirit, and the Spirit against the flesh, and these are contrary to one another, so that you do not do the things that you wish" (Gal. 5:17).

Could it be that the way to victory lies not in pretending that we are above certain temptations, but in realistically anticipating them? I am not talking about courting temptation but simply preparing for it. Using the army's immediate action drill model we could identify the most common temptations we are likely to encounter in a given situation. Next we could play the tempting scenario out in our mind while allowing the Holy Spirit to inspire us with spiritually sound and effective rebuttals.

An amusing illustration of how this could work comes from a young lady whose father believed in being prepared. When she turned sixteen and started dating, he gave her a quarter. "Whenever you go out with a boy," he told her, "keep that quarter handy. If he tries to get fresh give it to him and tell him to call me."

Needless to say, that was a cute and effective way of dealing with aggressive guys. However his daughter did have the last laugh. On her wedding night her father received a call from his new son-in-law. "Dad," he said, "your daughter just gave me a quarter and said I had to call and get your permission before she will consummate our marriage."

Of course dealing effectively with temptation long term, especially the pressure to participate in premarital sex, requires more than a clever response. In preparing our daughter for those inevitable pressures, her mother and I helped her identify a number of reasons why sex before marriage is not a good idea. Once she had a clear understanding of why it was wrong, we then discussed specific situations and how she could best respond. Armed with her convictions, a well-thought-out argument, and an immediate action plan, she was equipped to deal with whatever temptations came her way.

A Very Present Help

An immediate action plan is critically important in overcoming temptation, but by itself it is not enough. Who among us has not succumbed to temptation in spite of our best-laid plans? Alone we are simply no match for the enemy. We need reinforcements from above.

Thankfully those reinforcements are readily available in the person of the Lord Jesus Christ. Hebrews 4:15–16 declares: "For we do not have a High Priest who cannot sympathize with our weaknesses, but was in all points tempted as we are, yet without sin. Let us therefore come boldly to the throne of grace, that we may obtain mercy and find grace to help in time of need."

God does not help us by sending an angel who has never known the all-consuming passion of temptation's fatal attraction. Nor does He simply dab us with "spiritual" power. Instead He sends His own Son to aid us when the tornadoes of temptation bear down upon us. And because "He Himself has suffered, being tempted, He is able to aid those who are tempted" (Heb. 2:18).

This powerful truth was driven home to me afresh as I considered yet another story coming out of Texas following the killer tornadoes that struck that state on May 28, 1997. Once the storm had passed over Jarrell, it continued on its southward trek, barreling toward Cedar Park, just north of Austin. Along the way it spawned still more ominous funnel clouds. As it neared the huge 55,000-square-foot Albertson's supermarket in Cedar Park, it produced yet another deadly tornado with winds in excess of 150 miles per hour.

Inside the supermarket shoppers watched with near hypnotic fascination as that finger of darkness prepared to seek them out. A few rushed toward the exits, hoping to outrun the giant twister, which was less than a quarter mile away and barreling down upon them with unbelievable speed. Suddenly the store's intercom crackled to life, and a man's voice filled the huge supermarket. "Don't leave this store or you will die," he commanded. "You cannot outrun that tornado. Your only chance of survival is to do exactly what I tell you."

The speaker was Larry Fore, the manager of the Albertson's store and a tornado survivor himself. In 1979 he escaped with his life when one of the deadliest twisters in Texas history smashed Wichita Falls, killing fifty-three and injuring more than two thousand. Now he urged both customers and staff to take shelter in the steel-reinforced meat locker that was located at the rear center of the store.

In a matter of seconds the supermarket seemed to explode as the tornado ripped off huge sections of its 1.5-million-pound roof. Groceries and merchandise went flying, displays were destroyed, and counters and shelving were flung about like a child's erector set. Then as suddenly as it struck, it was over and an eerie stillness settled over the wreckage. Slowly, the door to the steel meat locker was forced open and people began to emerge. Others who did not make it that far crawled out from under piles of debris. Family members clutched one another, thankful to be alive.

Miraculously, not a single life was lost. Thanks to one man's quick action there were no fatalities. The Albertson's shoppers in Cedar Park escaped with their lives, due in large part to the fact that the store manager was a tornado survivor and he knew what to do. Without Larry Fore's clearheaded direction the death toll in Texas may well have been considerably higher.

When the tornadoes of temptation sweep down, threatening to destroy us, we have someone greater than Larry Fore to help us. He is Jesus Christ, Alpha and Omega, the First and the Last, the One who lived and was dead, and behold is alive forevermore. He has survived the greatest temptations known to man. He has conquered all the devil could throw at Him, and now He is present to make us overcomers as well.

Therefore let us say with the Psalmist:

> God is our refuge and strength,
> A very present help in trouble.
> Therefore we will not fear,
> Even though the earth be removed,
> And though the mountains be carried
> into the midst of the sea;
> Though its waters roar and be troubled,
> Though the mountains shake with its swelling. . . .
> The LORD of hosts is with us;
> The God of Jacob is our refuge. *(Ps. 46:1–3, 7)*

Reflecting on Him

1. *What are the atmospheric conditions of your life at this moment? Refer back to the earlier assessment you conducted of your life with regard to the amount of energy you are investing*

in the four critical areas of your career, your relationships with others, your personal satisfaction, and your spiritual walk.

2. *Remember the lieutenant colonel mentioning that the "correct" thing to do was not the "natural" thing to do when under attack? What parallels do you see regarding when we come under the spiritual attack of temptation in terms of the "correct" thing to do not being the "natural" thing?*

3. *How are you preparing today, and each day, for the inevitable tornadoes of temptation you will face? What contingency plans do you have in place for sexual temptation, for the lure of achievement, for the sacrifice of family for career, etc. so that you do the "correct" thing when under fire?*

25

MAKE YOURSELF ACCOUNTABLE

Taking a seat in the chair across from me she nervously straightened her skirt, being careful not to make eye contact. After placing her purse on the floor beside her chair, she clasped her hands in her lap and took a deep breath. Obviously she was nervous, and well she might have been, for she had come for counseling. Baring one's soul to the pastor is never easy, especially the first time.

While waiting for her to work up the courage to begin, I listened to the noisy silence. My secretary's voice, deadened by the closed door, could be heard over the clatter of a distant printer. The muted noise of traffic from the street below filtered into the stillness, and I gradually became aware of a sexual tension. I was not sure of its source, whether it was coming from her or whether it was a product of my own imagination. She had not done anything remotely sexual, nor had I consciously entertained sexual thoughts; nonetheless, the feelings were there.

At last she spoke, and I forced myself to concentrate. With an effort I was able to focus on ministry, but the sexual tension was always present just below the surface—unbidden, unwelcome, but there just the same. Finally the hour was finished, and we closed the session with prayer. After she left I sat at my desk for several minutes trying to make some sense of my feelings. Nothing like this had ever happened to me before, and it left me shaken, frightened.

Walking down the hall I stepped into my associate pastor's office and closed the door. He looked up from his computer screen as I sat down across the desk from him. Without any preamble, I told him what had just transpired and asked him to hold me accountable. Since the lady was scheduled to return for another appointment next week, I asked him to meet with me as soon as her session was over. Looking him in the eye, I said, "If I admit that the sexual tension is still present, or if you sense that it is, insist that I refer her to another counselor. If I refuse to do so, please share everything we have talked about with the elder board." He agreed and we shared a time of prayer before I returned to my office.

As the time for her next appointment approached, I was more than a little nervous. Just before she arrived I called my associate pastor on the intercom to make sure he remembered our covenant. Of course he did and I breathed a silent prayer before beginning the session. It was nothing like the first time. There was not even a hint of sexual tension. I was able to concentrate on ministry with no distractions, and we had a productive session.

Following that experience I came to several conclusions, not all of them flattering. Based on the fact that there was absolutely no sexual feelings present during the second session, I could only conclude that the feelings originated with me. I also discovered that what seems so alluring, so mesmerizing, in the secrecy of the imagination is revealed for what it truly is when it is confessed to another. Temptation flourishes in the dark, but it withers and dies when it is brought into the light of accountability.

I tremble when I think of what might have happened had I not had the kind of relationship with my associate pastor that allowed me to share that experience with him. Perhaps I could have conquered those sexual feelings with God's help alone, but given the proliferation of moral failures within the body of Christ, I did not feel it wise to try. In fact I am convinced that few believers can consistently overcome temptation without a relationship of this kind with a friend, a spouse, or a pastor.

Relationships of this nature are more than good—they are absolutely necessary. They serve many purposes, not the least of which is to provide a safe place where the imprisoning secrets of our hidden life can be disclosed. Freed from our need to pretend, we can finally be about the business of becoming the man or woman we have been called to be.

Choosing a Spiritual Partner

Having decided to make yourself accountable, you now face a critically important decision: choosing your spiritual partner. Of course it goes without saying that he or she should be of your own gender. If you struggle with homosexual or lesbian temptations, it is advisable to include a third person. This minimizes the enemy's chances of compromising the relationship. If you are unsure about whom to choose do not hesitate to seek your pastor's counsel.

Your spiritual partner should be spiritually mature and emotionally whole. The scriptural qualifications for elders and deacons provide some good guidelines. Although most of us fall short of these high standards they do provide an objective way of determining the kind of person who is trustworthy. Consider Titus 1:7–8:

> Since an overseer is entrusted with God's work, he must be blameless—not overbearing, not quick-tempered, not given to drunkenness, not violent, not pursuing dishonest gain. Rather he must be hospitable, one who loves what is good, who is self-controlled, upright, holy and disciplined. He must hold firmly to the trustworthy message as it has been taught, so that he can encourage others by sound doctrine and refute those who oppose it. *(NIV)*

Based on these guidelines you should select a person whose personal relationships are in good order. He or she should model the kind of behaviors you seek to develop in your own life: faithfulness in the things of God, submission to godly authority, spiritual disciplines, trustworthiness, and self-control. He or she should also be well-grounded in the Word of God.

Since you will be sharing the most intimate details of your spiritual life, it is absolutely mandatory that your spiritual partner be a person of uncompromising integrity. One word of caution along this line: *Never trust a person who tells you another person's secrets.* If he or she betrays that person's confidence he or she is likely to betray yours as well. That type of person reveals the things told in confidence as a way of proving his or her importance. The deepest issues of your life become the currency he or she uses to advance him or herself. The wise man in Proverbs tells us to, "avoid a man who talks too much" (Prov. 20:19 NIV).

A Covenant Relationship of Mutual Accountability

The kind of relationship we are talking about is more than mere friendship. It is a covenant relationship in which you voluntarily submit to a preset group of spiritual principles. These principles should include: 1) full disclosure; 2) immediate notification; 3) regular meetings; and 4) spiritual disciplines. Others may be added, but these four are imperative.

1. Full Disclosure

The integrity of this relationship depends upon full disclosure. Its strength lies in the fact that nothing need be hidden. Here we are loved and accepted unconditionally. There is no need to shade the truth or to try to show oneself in a better light. And what a liberating thing it is, for hiding and pretending require a dreadful amount of energy. Covering our sin is a little like trying to submerge a beach ball. You can do it, but if you relax for an instant it comes shooting out of the water.

As we have already noted, sin and temptation flourish in secret, but when they are exposed to the light of Christian fellowship, through confession and mutual accountability, they lose much of their seductive power. Alone we are no match for the enemy, especially if we are battling a long-standing habit or secret sin: but together with a spiritual friend, or friends, we find the strength in Christ to overcome.

When we speak of full disclosure we are not talking about the "dirty details," but the *fact* of our sinfulness or particular areas of weakness and temptation. We do not minimize the seriousness of our sin, nor do we make excuses or otherwise participate in rationalization or self-justification; but neither do we indulge in morbid introspection for the gratification of our flesh. Repentance, not penance, is the way to victory. "He who covers his sins will not prosper, / But whoever confesses and forsakes them will have mercy" (Prov. 28:13).

2. Immediate Notification

One of the great strengths in a covenant relationship of this nature is that it provides an *immediate* source of help. At the first sign of temptation, we notify our spiritual partner so he or she can pray for us. *Often the very act of confessing our temptation defeats it*. And since we have acted speedily it has not had an opportunity to sink its roots deep into the soil of our imagination. If temptation persists we can meet together for counsel, study, and prayer. It is not often that temptation can withstand such a sustained counterattack. "Though one may be overpowered by another, two can withstand him. / And a threefold cord is not quickly broken" (Eccl. 4:12).

3. Regular Meetings

Equally important are the weekly or biweekly meetings. It is here that the spiritual partners look each other in the eye and ask the hard questions—about each other's relationship with God and the significant others in their lives. If one of the partners is battling a besetting sin or a deeply entrenched habit, specific questions regarding those areas should be raised. In addition they discuss their devotional reading and the things the Lord is teaching them. They also discuss their business life and related areas, especially any decisions they might need to pray about. These types of conversations give them an opportunity to examine their lives and to stay focused on the things that really matter.

While meeting with one of my spiritual partners some months ago, I felt compelled to ask him about his marriage. He readily acknowledged some difficulties, and I pressed him further. Leaning across the table I asked him point-blank if there was anyone else in his life. He assured me there was not, but having opened that door, I now had an opportunity to talk with him about guarding his heart, especially when his relationship with his wife was not all it should be.

A few weeks later God spoke to his heart while he was having his morning devotions, bringing to his mind a number of hurtful things he had said and done to his wife during the course of their marriage. It was a deeply painful experience, and he wept before the Lord in deep contrition. As he waited before the Lord, he had a growing sense that God wanted him to wash his wife's feet.

After preparing a basin of water and a towel, he joined his wife in the master bedroom. Before washing her feet he explained what had transpired during his prayer time. Kneeling before her, he took her foot in his hand and began to tenderly wash it, all the while praying silently that the Lord would wash away all the hurt and pain he had inflicted over the years. Taking the other foot he repeated the process. By the time he finished, both he and his wife were weeping, so real was the healing presence of the Lord Jesus.

The weeks following that experience have been a time of profound healing in their marriage. I do not know that our earlier conversation had anything to do with what happened, but I would like to think that it did. Perhaps our discussion opened the door to his heart just enough to let the Lord speak to him. Even if that is not the case, that is the kind of thing that regularly happens when a person enters a covenant relationship of mutual accountability.

4. Spiritual Disciplines

No accountability relationship is complete unless the covenant partners are committed to the spiritual disciplines, especially devotional reading and prayer. By committing to the same Bible reading schedule, they can encourage one another. By sharing many of the same books they can have in-depth discussions that are mutually beneficial. They are also able to be more faithful in daily prayer because they know someone is holding them accountable.

The key here is faithfulness. As we practice the disciplines we open ourselves to the transforming power of the Holy Spirit. Little by little He is changing us from the inside out by conforming us to the image of our Lord and Savior, making our nature and personality unmistakably like His. As a result, temptation loses much of its appeal.

Responsibilities of a Spiritual Adviser

Often an accountability relationship is formed because one of the participants is struggling with a besetting sin. In desperation the person bares his soul and makes himself accountable to a Christian he admires. Not infrequently it is a new experience for that person as well. Though they may be more spiritually mature, it is unlikely that they have participated in a formal relationship of this nature before. That being the case, they may be at a loss to know what is required of them in their new role as a spiritual adviser. The more common responsibilities can be summed up in four words: 1) availability, 2) accountability, 3) transparency, and 4) confidentiality.

Availability

The spiritual adviser is responsible to be available to both God and the person who has made himself accountable. (For the sake of clarity let us refer to him as a *protégé*.) Having accepted responsibility for the care of the protégé's soul the spiritual adviser now makes himself available to God for spiritual battle as the need arises. He puts himself at the Lord's disposal to be used as He sees fit. He will interrupt his work and go to prayer as the Lord directs. He will pray through the night if necessary.

Being available to the protégé means that he may be called upon at any time, day or night. Spiritual attacks often come at the most inopportune times, and he must be ready to step into the breach at a moment's notice. Crisis calls are usually far more frequent during the first weeks of the relationship when the battle to overcome spiritual bondage is in the earliest stages. Once the initial victory has been won and the ground reclaimed, the crises usually diminish. If the spiritual adviser senses the protégé is taking advantage of the situation by becoming overly dependent on him he must be quick to confront him in love.

Accountability

As the more mature believer, the spiritual adviser is responsible to be on the lookout for danger signs and to hold the protégé accountable for his actions. How do we do that? Gordon MacDonald writes,

> We watch a friend's eyes. Abnormal fatigue? Anger? Avoidance of truth? We listen to a friend's words to lovingly discern inconsistencies, attitudes, and negative criticisms of people. We watch spending patterns. Too excessive? Trying to prove something? We note the respect and affection with which he or she treats others. Loving toward a spouse and children? Too harsh? Disdainful? Disrespectful? Too familiar with others? We are sensitive to questionable habits. Substance abuse? Sleeplessness? Workaholism?[1]

Confrontation invariably will be necessary. A relationship seldom achieves its full potential without it; but it is almost always doomed to failure, unless it grows out of a deep trust built on honest communication. Even then, it must be done with sensitivity and tenderness. If the protégé is not convinced of the spiritual adviser's genuine concern, he will likely become defensive and withdraw.

Therefore, it is *extremely* important to take great care to create a safe place—a place of affirmation and acceptance, and a place where the protégé can be assured, again and again, of the spiritual adviser's love and respect. Even then, confrontation will be painful and should be undertaken only after the adviser has carefully prepared his heart before the Lord.

Remember, the ultimate purpose of a covenant relationship is not accountability but nurture. As a spiritual adviser your responsibility is not to make others "toe the line," but to enable them to become all God has called them to be. Spiritual partners are committed to protecting each other through mutual accountability, to be sure. Yet, if that becomes the sole reason or even the primary reason for the relationship, it will not long survive. The bread that nourishes the soul is acceptance and encouragement, not accountability.

Transparency

There is an old adage that says, "Spiritual values are more quickly caught than taught." Nowhere is this more true than in covenant relationships. If the spiritual adviser wants his protégé to be open and transparent, then he must model that behavior. He must take the first step by sharing from his own life. This is what Jesus did—how else could we know of His temptation experience in the wilderness, since no one else was there? He did the same thing in Gethsemane when He told the disciples that His soul was exceedingly sorrowful even to the point of death (Mark 14:34).

Many of the experiences the spiritual adviser will share will be in the past tense simply because the things his protégé is battling involve issues he has already dealt with. Because he has overcome a similar temptation or difficulty, his experience gives the protégé hope, thus reinforcing his faith. It also provides practical insights for helping the protégé deal with his own temptations. And because he knows that his spiritual adviser shares the life experiences that are common to us all, he finds his counsel authentic.

Confidentiality

While there are a number of factors that make it difficult for Christians to participate in covenant relationships, one stands out above all the others: a lack of confidentiality! Painful experience has taught most of us to keep our own counsel. But all of that is changing. Men and women, desperate to overcome temptation and walk in true spiritual vitality, are once again making themselves accountable to one another. At great personal risk they are confessing their sins one to the other (James 5:16) rather than living in bondage. Therefore it is critically important that as a spiritual adviser you hold the confessions of your protégé in absolute confidence. If you betray their trust, "may God deal with you, be it ever so severely" (1 Sam. 3:17 NIV).

The Truth Will Make You Free

Truth telling is seldom easy, but it is the key that unlocks the door to spiritual victory. As long as we deny our struggles and pretend to be something we are not, we will never be free. The person who is trapped in secret sin lives a double life. He appears to be a godly man, a faithful husband and father, but in secret he is something else altogether. Now it is not just his sin that traps him, but his reputation as well. By pretending to have it all together, he cuts himself off from the help he so desperately needs.

In John 4 we have the account of a woman who was trapped by her past. Apparently she developed an elaborate facade that allowed her to function with a degree of normalcy. Unfortunately, it was based on secrets and half-truths, leaving her in constant fear of being found out. Consequently she often preferred her own company to that of others, as is evidenced by the fact that she came to draw water at noon, when it was customary to draw water only in the cool of the morning and evening. It seems she found the hot, noonday sun more bearable than the scalding tongues of the village wags, who came to Jacob's well both early and late each day.

Approaching the well on this sun-scorched day she is surprised to see a weary traveler sitting on the well curb. And even more surprised when He asks her for a drink. Then she said to Him, "How is it that You, being a Jew, ask a drink from me, a Samaritan woman?" (John 4:9).

Thus began the conversation that would change this desperate woman's life. The weary traveler was none other than Jesus Himself, and He told her, "If you knew . . . who it is who says to you 'Give Me a drink,' you would have asked Him, and He would have given you living water. . . . Whoever drinks of the water that I shall give him will never thirst. But the water that I shall give him will become in him a fountain of water springing up into everlasting life" (4:10, 14).

To the woman it sounded nearly too good to be true—to never have to brave either the blazing sun or the biting remarks of her judgmental neighbors. "Sir," she said, "give me this water, that I may not thirst, nor come here to draw" (4:15).

Then came the moment of truth: Jesus said, "Go, call your husband, and come here" (4:16).

This is what she hated about relationships. You could never start clean. You always had to bring your past with you. Her mind was racing. *Is His request a gesture of courtesy, or does He know something?* she wondered. After only the slightest hesitation she said, "I have no husband" (4:17). It is the truth, but it is not the whole truth.

"Jesus said to her, 'You have well said, "I have no husband," for you have had five husbands, and the one whom you now have is not your husband; in that you spoke truly'" (4:17–18).

Then she did what people with a shameful past are apt to do—she diverted attention from herself. "Sir," she said, "I perceive that You are a prophet. Our fathers worshiped on this mountain, and you Jews say that in Jerusalem is the place where one ought to worship" (4:19–20).

Isn't that just like us? Anytime the truth starts to hit too close to home we want to start a theological discussion—something abstract, safe. But Jesus would have no part of it. Without being offensive He turned the conversation back to personal issues: "Woman, believe Me, . . . the hour is coming, and now is, when the true worshipers will worship the Father in spirit and truth; for the Father is seeking such to worship Him. God is Spirit, and those who worship Him must worship in spirit and truth" (4:21, 23–24).

The "truth" Jesus is referring to here is not doctrinal correctness but personal transparency. With unrelenting accuracy He pursues her into the shadows of her past, willing her to come clean with Him. Undoubtedly she longs to lay her heavy burden down, but pretending has become a way of life with her; besides, He might reject her if He knew the whole truth about her sordid life.

Still she is moving toward the truth—the truth about Jesus and the truth about herself. Then she said, "'I know that Messiah is coming' (who is called Christ). 'When He comes, He will tell us all things'" (4:25).

"Jesus said to her, 'I who speak to you am He'" (4:26).

The Scriptures record nothing else of their conversation, but it must have included more, for the woman left her water jug and returned to the city and said to the men, "Come, see a Man who told me all things that I ever did. Could this be the Christ?" (4:29).

What finally allowed her to move from skepticism to saving faith? Not just the fact that Jesus knew all the secrets of her life, though that was convincing indeed. No, the thing that finally got her was the fact that He knew the worst about her and still believed the best. He knew all about the five husbands, the failed marriages, the rejection and the promiscuity; still, He believed in her—why else would He have spent so much time ministering to her? With Him she did not have to pretend. He loved her just the way she was. He knew what she was, but more importantly He knew what she could be. Through the eyes of love He saw her as redeemed— a woman of worth and purity—a child of God. And because He saw her this way *she* was able to see herself that way as well. Now she didn't have to pretend to be respectable. His love had made her all of that and more!

A recovering alcoholic wrote,

> The besetting torture of my life has been a sense of being in the wrong and liable to punishment for it. I have tried many ways of dealing with this mental plague. I have tried bluster, proclaiming that I was not in the wrong at all, and wishful thinking, pretending the haunting feeling wasn't really there. I've tried stern repression, resolving not to let my mind dwell morbidly upon it. I've tried hard work, the pursuit of amusement and diversion, and God knows I've tried getting drunk. Regardless of my evasive maneuvers, there— when the chase was ended—it was, ready to pounce.
>
> It is hard for me to describe the terror that goes with this. I tense up and shorten my breath and feel scared. I go on the defensive at all points, fairly bristling like a mental porcupine, yet with an underlying deeply panicked sense that my defense is not going to be successful. It means ultimatums impossible to meet, ostracism and disgrace and an eternity of unfriendliness.[2]

One night this man could bear the pain of his aloneness no longer. In desperation he risked reaching out through openness and confession. Cutting through all the falsity of his life, his real self emerged. He wrote: "The kindness of God and man made it possible for me to admit wrong. . . . Though the experience is grueling, the reward is a life lived fully and actively before God and man completely without fear."[3]

Such is the power of relationships in which Jesus is present. Freed from the need to pretend, we can bare our souls to one another and receive both acceptance and forgiveness. Once we confess our faults and sins to each other, they will no longer separate us. Now we can worship in spirit—that is, with the anointing—and in truth—that is, personal transparency or truthfulness.

Free at last! Free at last! Thank God almighty we are free at last!

Reflecting on Him

1. *Who do you have in your life, at this moment, that can assist you in holding yourself accountable to God?*

2. *What is the ultimate purpose of an accountability relationship—to prevent someone from sinning, or to facilitate the spiritual growth of another believer so that triumph over temptation is a shared experience?*

3. *What must you start to do in your life so that you can begin to serve in this role for another individual?*

26

HIDE THE WORD OF GOD
IN YOUR HEART

The sun was shining brightly as the president and his entourage emerged from the hotel in Washington, D.C., and moved toward the waiting limousines. Suddenly the brisk March afternoon was shattered by the sharp bark of gunfire. Several shots were fired in rapid succession, scattering the entourage like a covey of startled quail. On the sidewalk three men were down. As one man, the secret service agents closed around the president, hustling him into the bulletproof limo, where he was shoved to the floor. Stomping the accelerator the chauffeur jerked the big car away from the curb. With tires squealing, it rounded the corner and disappeared from sight.

In spite of their quick action, the secret service agents were too late. The president had been shot. For the next several hours anxious Americans huddled in front of their televisions while a team of surgeons fought to save his life. Late that night the weary surgeons issued a terse statement saying that the president was in serious but stable condition.

With President Reagan out of danger the nation's attention turned toward the man who shot him. He was twenty-six-year-old, John Hinckley Jr. The son of a prosperous oil executive, he was raised in a Dallas, Texas, suburb. He was not the victim of child abuse or domestic violence. Nor was he a member of any underground antigovernment organization. In fact there was nothing in his childhood to suggest that he might become a violent criminal. He simply did not fit the profile of a potential assassin.

In the weeks following his unsuccessful assassination attempt, the bizarre story behind his crime began to come into focus. According to the FBI, Hinckley was acting out a romantic obsession involving Hollywood actress Jody Foster. His obsession was inspired by the movie *Taxi Driver,* in which Foster played a young prostitute pursued by a love-crazed cabby. In a desperate attempt to win her love, the cabby assassinated a government official. Apparently, Hinckley mistakenly believed he could win Foster's love by assassinating the president of the United States.

While the Hinckley case is extreme, to be sure, it is also classic. It graphically demonstrates the connection between a person's secret *thoughts,* his deepest *desires,* and his *actions.* The implications are clear: think on something long enough—fantasize about it, feed it—and it will ultimately become overpowering!

> *On the whole, the devotional life is more discipline than inspiration.*

Most of us will never entertain a desire to kill the President of the United States, still, our secret desires are just as prophetic and are the root of all our temptations. According to the apostle James, temptation comes to us through the doorway of the mind. Or as he put it, "Temptation is the pull of man's *own* evil thoughts and wishes" (James 1:14 TLB). That being the case nothing is more critical to overcoming temptation than a renewed mind, "for to be carnally minded is death, but to be spiritually minded is life and peace" (Rom. 8:6).

A person's mind—that is his worldview, his values—is largely formed by the information he takes into it. If he spends the bulk of his time digesting secular material he will have a secular mind, notwithstanding his faith in Christ. Let him fill his mind with the insipid offerings of network television night after night, and it is little wonder that he succumbs to temptation. To complete the picture we must add books, magazines, movies—plus all the various things we listen to and laugh at. Fodder, each and every one, for the carnal mind.

Sooner or later the carnal mind will produce carnal actions. It is inevitable. Proverbs 23:7 says, "As [a person] thinks in his heart, so is he." Which is to say that the thoughts and feelings we harbor in our hearts *inevitably* become the attitudes and actions of our lives. Think on something long enough, and it will eventually become impossible to resist.

In the depths of despair and self-disgust, the wife of a well-known minister attempted suicide. Her life was a mess. She was trapped in a promiscuous lifestyle that included an addiction to drugs and alcohol. How could it happen? How could someone reared in the church and married to a minister become so messed up?

In her case a lot of it had to do with her thought life. She fed her mind a steady diet of sexually stimulating material. The people she admired were not spiritual persons, but bizarre characters like Madonna. In her fantasies she cast herself in similar roles, and it was only a matter of time until her thought life spilled over into reality.

I know her situation is extreme. Still, like the Hinckley case, it graphically demonstrates the connection between our thoughts and our actions. If we do not want to succumb to temptation, we will bring "every thought into captivity to the obedience of Christ" (2 Cor. 10:5).

If we fill our minds with the Word of God, we will find ourselves increasingly resistant to temptation. The Word of God will make us wise, so that we will not be taken in by the tricks of the enemy. "The statutes of the LORD are trustworthy, making wise the simple" (Ps. 19:7 NIV).

The Word of God will make us pure, so that we will not desire the impure offerings of the world. "How can a young man keep his way pure? By living according to your word" (Ps. 119:9 NIV).

The Word of God will transform us. "Do not be conformed to this world, but be transformed by the renewing of your mind, that you may prove what is that good and acceptable and perfect will of God" (Rom. 12:2).

Unfortunately, for all of its benefits, Bible reading is a vanishing discipline. According to Dallas Willard, "The 'open secret' of many 'Bible believing' churches is that a vanishingly small percentage of those talking about prayer and Bible reading are actually doing what they are talking about."[1] Why is this? If the benefits of living in the Word of God are so obvious and the consequences of ignoring it are so grave, why do the vast majority of Christians struggle to maintain a consistent devotional life?

Unrealistic Expectations

Some of the reasons are obvious. Contemporary Christians are literally inundated with distractions. Newspapers, magazines, books, television, movies, and home videos are just a few of the noisy diversions that clutter our already overcrowded minds. What chance does the Spirit's "still, small voice" have against such high-tech productions?

Additionally there's the time factor. When asked, "What is the one greatest obstacle you struggle with in your devotional life?" four out of five respondents said, "Time."

Perhaps behind both time and distractions there lies a third and more fundamental cause: disappointment or even disillusionment. Many Christians approach their devotional life with unrealistic expectations. They expect instant results. Instant insight into the Scriptures. Instant awareness of God's presence. Instant increase in their faith. Instant victory over the weaknesses of their flesh. Not infrequently what they get is instant disappointment. When their expectations are not realized they may become disillusioned.

A productive devotional life is built on consistent discipline. There will be times when you are blessed with a sense of divine presence. At other times the Word of God will open unto you in a special way, and revelation will quicken your understanding. There may even be times when you experience a special manifestation of the sanctifying power of the Holy Spirit, times when the habits of your flesh fall away, but these are the exception rather than the rule. On the whole, the devotional life is more discipline than inspiration. And it is consistent discipline that prepares us for those moments of revelation and presence.

As you prepare for the devotional life it is important to approach it realistically. The amount of time you commit yourself to should be something you can expect to be faithful to each day. Start with ten minutes—not an hour. If you decided to take up running you wouldn't begin with the Boston Marathon. You would probably start with a graduated training program, working up to longer distances over a period of time. Use that same principle for your devotional life.

Most of your devotional time will be discipline without immediate or obvious benefits. Do not let that discourage you. Consider the analogy of the runner again. Early in his training his running is pure drudgery, sometimes it is closer to sheer torture.

His muscles get sore, his feet hurt, sometimes he gets blisters or shinsplints; but over a period of weeks his body rounds into shape. Without realizing it he starts to feel better. Even after he is in shape there will be days when he has to force himself to run. As often as not the actual act of running is more discipline than pleasure.

So it is with the devotional life. The spiritual benefits are seldom immediately apparent. Sometimes after days of Bible study and prayer you feel no closer to God. It seems you are making no progress. Don't give up. Like the runner, your spiritual man is slowly rounding into shape.

Marathoners talk of "breaking through the wall." They run until they are on the verge of collapsing. By sheer determination they press on, and suddenly they are through the wall. They get their second wind, but it's more than that. They experience an almost euphoric feeling, a runner's high. That experience corresponds with those moments in our devotional life when we are literally overwhelmed with the presence of God. It does not happen every time we pray or read the Scriptures, but when it does, it makes everything—all the discipline, all the solitude and sacrifice, all the hours of waiting—worthwhile.

The Discipline of Scripture

When we read the Bible, we do so on at least three levels. By that I mean we read it in order to answer three questions. First, What is the historical setting? What did this passage of Scripture mean to the person who wrote it? What did it mean to his contemporaries who read it? Reading on this level preserves the Scripture's objectivity, its historical perspective. It also focuses its meaning for us—the twentieth-century readers.

The second question is more personal: What does this passage say to me about my spiritual condition, about my life and my standing with God? The Bible is a living book that transcends time and place. God uses it to speak directly into our individual situations. Read it to receive a word from Him.

Some of you can probably remember the old RCA Victrola commercials, especially the one with the dog sitting in front of the speaker horn with his head cocked to one side, a bemused expression on his face. The caption underneath said, "He hears his master's voice." Many of those early phonograph records were of questionable quality. The recorded material had to compete with scratches, background noise, and distortions for the listener's attention. In spite of all of that, the dog recognized his master's voice because he was listening for it.

Reading the Bible can be somewhat like that. The voice of God heard through the Scriptures, comes to us through human hands with many cultural and historical distortions. Some readers get hung up on the history, or the scholarship, or the customs and miss the whole point. But for those readers who want to know God, who want to hear His voice, He is there!

A Chinese Christian once said, "Reading the Bible is like eating fish—you have to watch out for the bones." When you come to something you do not understand, set it aside, like a fish bone, and go on. You would not throw out the whole fish because of a few bones, so do not throw out the Bible just because you cannot understand it all.

The third question is: What does this passage say about God? I am told that in the Library of Congress there is a copy of the United States Constitution, which when viewed from a certain angle, seems to bear a portrait of George Washington, the father of our country. So it is with the Scriptures. When we read them with faith, they are more than just a collection of ancient poetry or proverbs, they are a revelation of God Himself, a portrait of our heavenly Father.

Finally, when you read the Scriptures, act on what you are learning. The Word of God is bread to be eaten, not literature to be admired. Put it into practice, let it change your life. As Richard Foster writes, "When we come to the Scripture we come to be changed, not to amass information."[2]

The Transforming Power of the Word of God

When I consider the transforming power of the Word of God two incidents come to mind. The first is the story of Pitcairn's Island as it is preserved in the *Encyclopaedia Britannica*. Following the famous mutiny on the ship *Bounty*, Fletcher Christian and his men put Captain Bly and his loyal crew adrift. The *Bounty* then sailed for Pitcairn's Island, where the crew wrecked their ship and set about to build a new life. Though they had landed on a virtual paradise, they soon created a "hell on earth."

One of the sailors discovered a way to make alcohol from a native plant. Soon drunkenness and violence abounded. In a short time, all of the native men were dead and all but one of the white men—Alexander Smith. He was left alone with a harem of native women and a crowd of mixed race children.

Several years passed; the children grew up and married, and more children came, and the community seemed to prosper. Many years later the *Topez* (a U.S. Navy ship) landed on the island. They found a seemingly perfect civilization. There was no illiteracy, no crime, no disease, no mental illness. The island was 100 percent Christian. The *Britannica* states that nowhere on earth were life and property more safe than on Pitcairn's Island.

God's past provision becomes the ground for present confidence.

What happened? What changed a "hell on earth" into a seemingly perfect civilization? One day while going through some of the trunks that had been salvaged from the *Bounty,* Alexander Smith had found a Bible. As he read it, faith was kindled in his heart (Rom. 10:17). Then he began reading it to the others, and faith was born in their hearts as well. By putting their faith in the Lord Jesus Christ the entire population of the island found salvation. By reading and applying the principles of Scripture, their entire society was transformed![3]

The second incident is related by Bruce Larson.[4] As a young man he found the devotional reading of the Bible nothing short of frustrating. He made a commitment to read a chapter a day, but found he could not keep it. For a day or two, sometimes even a week, things would go pretty well, then he would go through a dry season when the Scriptures seemed totally irrelevant. Since he did not seem to be getting anything out of his Bible reading, it was hard for him to be consistent.

Finally he met a Christian whose life was so real that he asked him the secret of his vibrant faith. To which the man replied, "Nothing is more important to my walk with the Lord than my daily quiet time. Each morning I begin the day with Bible reading and prayer."

Needless to say Larson was disappointed. He had already tried that, and it had not worked for him. In frustration he shared his experience with his new friend. Whereupon the man replied, "Since I have committed the rest of my life to God I don't feel so frantic to 'grow.' I don't have to 'feel' like I am getting something out of it every time."

He went on to explain that he wanted to reprogram his entire life and perspective so that he could see and think as Christ did. If he could permeate his whole life—the conscious and the unconscious parts of his mind—with the loving perspective of God, then his *natural reactions* might become loving and Christlike. Before that realization he had thought only in terms of his *conscious* life, but upon realizing that our minds are about two-thirds unconscious, he saw that something more than occasional conscious "study and memorizing" was necessary. Realizing that the truth had to pass through his conscious thoughts in order to reach the unconscious part of his mind, he decided that he would begin each day by consciously putting a part of God's Word into his mind. He wasn't going to worry about how "much he got out of it" for that day; rather he was going to trust the transforming power of the Word to do its holy work as silently and as surely as a seed germinates in the darkness of the soil.

Based on that man's experience, Bruce Larson renewed his commitment to spend time reading the Scriptures every day. Although he admits that he has not been perfect in his commitment, the Word of God is doing its holy work. The truth of God's Word is becoming so much a part of his inner being that he often responds with a "scriptural" response without even realizing it. What now seems like "common sense" often turns out to be something that Jesus or Paul said.

The Discipline of Prayer

The disciple who is serious about resisting temptation and living a transformed life will add to his Bible reading the discipline of daily prayer. His prayer life will be both structured and spontaneous. His structured prayer will likely include adoration, confession, thanksgiving, and supplication—what some practitioners call the *A.C.T.S.* of prayer. This makes for a clever acrostic and a handy way to remember it. *A* is for adoration, *C* is for confession, *T* is for thanksgiving, and *S* is for supplication.

By beginning prayer with a time of adoration, attention is focused on the person of God—*who* He is rather than *what* He has done. Adoration inspires faith because it turns our attention away from the circumstances of life and focuses it fully on the Father. Now we worship and adore Him, magnifying His greatness and His glory. We exalt His character, crying, "Holy, holy, holy is the LORD of hosts; / The whole earth is full of His glory!" (Isa. 6:3). We bless His faithfulness, saying "I will sing of the mercies of the LORD forever; / With my mouth will I make known / Your faithfulness to all generations" (Ps. 89:1). We praise Him for His unconditional love (Ps. 89:33; 103:17 NIV), His abiding presence (Matt. 28:20), and His omnipotent power (Ps. 21:13). Once our souls are thoroughly soaked in His eternal greatness we can move to confession and petition without fear.

Step two in devotional prayer is confession. Nothing so hinders prayer as unconfessed sin. In confession, we name our sin and take full responsibility for it. Like David we pray, "I acknowledge my transgressions, / And my sin is always before me. / Against You, You only, have I sinned, / And done this evil in Your sight . . . Blot out my transgressions. / Wash me thoroughly from my iniquity, / And cleanse me from my sin" (Ps. 51:3–4, 1–2).

He who taught us to pray, "Your kingdom come"
also taught us to pray,
"Give us this day our daily bread"
(Matt. 6:10–11).

Sometimes we are not consciously aware of sin in our life so we pray: "Search me, O God, and know my heart; / Try me, and know my anxieties; / And see if there is any wicked way in me, / And lead me in the way everlasting" (Ps. 139:23–24).

I once counseled with a woman who said this second step became a real deterrent to sin for her. It helped her resist temptation, she explained, because she knew if she sinned she would have to face God with her failure the next time she went to prayer. In that sense confession not only cleanses us, but it also makes us accountable.

Anytime I am tempted to think that confession is not really necessary, I go back to 1 John. "If we say that we have no sin, we deceive ourselves, and the truth is not in us. If we confess our sins,

He is faithful and just to forgive us our sins and to cleanse us from all unrighteousness" (1 John 1:8–9).

Step three is thanksgiving. Thanksgiving differs from adoration in that it focuses on what God has done rather than who He is. When we give thanks we carefully count our blessings, we name them one by one, and in so doing we cultivate a spirit of thankfulness and trust. God's past provision becomes the ground for present confidence.

To help me remember specific areas in which I need to give thanks I sometimes pray Psalm 103:1–5:

> Bless the LORD, O my soul;
> And all that is within me,
>   bless His holy name!
> Bless the LORD, O my soul,
> And forget not all His benefits:
> Who forgives all your iniquities,
> Who heals all your diseases,
> Who redeems your life from destruction,
> Who crowns you with lovingkindness and tender mercies,
> Who satisfies your mouth with good things,
> So that your youth is renewed like the eagle's.

Step four is supplication, which includes petition for personal needs as well as intercession for others and the needs of the world. It is a natural outgrowth of thanksgiving. When we remember God's past provision we are inspired to approach Him with our present need. Of course, I am not talking about turning God into some kind of cosmic Santa Claus. But if we pray God-centered prayers, there is always a place for our personal needs. He who taught us to pray, "Your kingdom come" also taught us to pray, "Give us this day our daily bread" (Matt. 6:10–11).

In prayer, as in all of life, there *must* be a balance between daily bread and coming kingdoms. He who spends time in prayer getting to know God and thinking God's thoughts after Him will never be guilty of praying petty, selfish prayers. Yet, on the other hand he will never be embarrassed to share with the Father the concerns of his heart, regardless of how insignificant they might seem.

> Thou art coming to a king
> Large petitions with thee bring,

> For His wealth and power are such
> That thou canst never ask too much.[5]

The One in whose name we pray is "able to do exceedingly abundantly above all that we ask or think, according to the power that works in us" (Eph. 3:20).

For the devotional life to be complete we need to add to our Scripture reading devotional classics and other books that deal with the inner life. It is enormously helpful to learn from the experience of those who have walked this way before us. To the *A.C.T.S.* of prayer we need to add meditation, listening prayer, and a written journal. Be assured that the rewards make it well worth the effort.

Those who have mastered the disciplines of the devotional life know a richness unimagined by the casual pilgrim. They know God, and they know His peace that passes all understanding. Prayer has given their lives a holy center, a sacred place. They have an inner strength that enables them to live godly lives in spite of the worldliness of our present age.

My dear friend Owen Carr is such a man. My life is richer just for having known him. He walks with God and knows Him intimately. When I am with him I feel an unmistakable sense of God's nearness. When he prays there is a childlike intimacy in the way he approaches God. It is readily apparent that he knows the Father and that the Father knows him. Of course that holy intimacy is the product of nearly sixty years of spiritual disciplines, for Owen Carr is a man of prayer and of the Word.

That kind of relationship is available to every one of us, but it can be had only by devoting ourselves to God through a disciplined devotional life. Therefore let us say with the psalmist:

> I seek you with all my heart;
>> do not let me stray from your commands.
> I have hidden your word in my heart
>> that I might not sin against you. . . .
> I rejoice in following your statutes
>> as one rejoices in great riches.
> I meditate on your precepts
>> and consider your ways.
> I delight in your decrees;
>> I will not neglect your word.
> *(Ps. 119:10–11, 14–16 NIV)*

Having committed ourselves to the disciplines of the Word and of prayer, we are open to the transforming power of God's holy presence. Day by day the Spirit does His redemptive work, making us more and more into people of God. This does not make us immune to temptation, but it does enable us to confront it from a position of spiritual strength rather than from one of weakness. And with God's help we are able to overcome every temptation the enemy throws at us. For we are indeed "more than conquerors through Him who loved us" (Rom. 8:37).

Reflecting on Him

1. *Complete a careful review of what "things" you put into your mind on a regular basis. How often are you including the teachings of the Word, the celebration of Christian music, the joy of active prayer with others?*

2. *Take a moment and begin to recite every Bible verse that you can recall (it is not important to have them exactly word-for-word nor do you need to remember the chapter and verse). How many different Scriptures did you remember? Practice this exercise with your family, especially your children, as a means for hiding God's Word in your heart.*

3. *Reread Psalm 119:10, 11; 14-16. I challenge you to say as David said, "I will not neglect your word." If you accept this challenge, write down at least three or four specific ways you plan to pay attention to God's Word.*

4. *Do you recall the simple steps of prayer: Adoration, Confession, Thanksgiving, and Supplication? They provide you with a natural means for developing the discipline of prayer. Please consider keeping a personal prayer journal. One means for doing this would be to use the following four statements as guides for each entry (preferably daily) of your journal. Take a moment and complete each one.*

Heavenly Father, what I admire most about You is

_____.

Dear Lord, I am sorry but I need to tell You

_____.

Jesus, I am so grateful for

_____.

Father, with a humble heart I need Your help with

_____.

NOTES

Introduction

1. The idea for this parable was inspired in part by an essay entitled "Southern Flight" by Robert James Waller. It was published originally in the *Des Moines Register,* Oct. 23, 1988, and later included in a book of essays: *Robert James Waller, "Old Songs in a New Café"* (New York: Warner Books, 1994), 157–64.

Section One: The Truth About Temptation
Chapter 1

1. Richard Exley, *How to Be a Man of Character in a World of Compromise* (Tulsa: Honor Books, 1995), 30.
2. Ibid., 29–30.

Chapter 2

1. William Temple, *Readings in St. John's Gospel* (London: Macmillan, 1963), 24.

Chapter 3

1. Haddon W. Robinson, "Don't Doubt God's Goodness: A Case Study in Temptation," in *Best Sermons*, ed. by James W. Cox (San Francisco: Harper and Row, 1988), 147.
2. Based on information contained in *I Was Wrong* by Jim Bakker (Nashville: Thomas Nelson, 1996) and *Integrity* by Richard Dortch (Green Forest: New Leaf Press, 1991).
3. Robinson, *Don't Doubt God's Goodness*, 48.
4. "Stunned by an Inside Job," *Leadership* 8, no. 1 (Winter 1987): 102.
5. Ibid.
6. Dallas Willard, *The Spirit of the Disciplines* (San Francisco: Harper and Row, 1988), ix.
7. Ibid., 4.

Chapter 4

1. Robinson, *Don't Doubt God's Goodness,* 151.
2. Ibid.

Section Two: The Three Faces of Temptation
Chapter 5

1. David L. McKenna, *The Jesus Model* (Waco: Word, 1977), 71.
2. Myron S. Augsburger, *The Communicator's Commentary*, Vol. 1, *Matthew* (Waco: Word, 1982), 49.

Chapter 6:

1. Dick Gregory, quoted in Robert A. Raines, *Soundings* (New York: Harper and Row, 1970), 94–95.
2. Dietrich Bonhoeffer, quoted in Robert Raines, *Creative Brooding* (New York: Macmillan, 1966), 33–34.

Chapter 7

1. Based on information contained in Paul Lee Tan, *Encyclopedia of 7,700 Illustrations: Signs of the Times* (Chicago: Assurance Publishers, 1979), 824.
2. C. S. Lewis, *Mere Christianity* (New York: Macmillan, 1976), 81–82.
3. Rolf Zettersten, *Dr. Dobson: Turn Your Heart Toward Home* (Dallas: Word), 111.
4. Ibid, 111–12.

Chapter 8

1. Based on information contained in Tan, *Encyclopedia of 7,700 Illustrations*, 167–69.
2. Norval Geldenhuys, *Commentary on the Gospel of Luke* (Grand Rapids: Eerdmans, 1979), 162.
3. The material for this section on John Alexander Dowie was gleaned from Roberts Liardon, *God's Generals* (Tulsa: Albury, 1996), 21–43.
4. Ibid, 39.
5. Richard Foster, *Money, Sex and Power* (San Francisco: Harper and Row, 1985), 178.
6. "I Made Mistakes," *Christianity Today,* 18 March 1988, 47.

Chapter 9

1. Foster, *Money, Sex and Power*, 240.
2. Jim Bakker, *I Was Wrong* (Nashville: Thomas Nelson, 1996), 544.
3. Ibid., 543–44.
4. Foster, *Money, Sex and Power*, 223.

Chapter 10

1. McKenna, *The Jesus Model,* 79.
2. Ibid., 89–90.
3. Fred Craddock, *When the Roll Is Called Down Here*, Preaching Today, Tape No. 50, 1987.

Section Three: The Seven Stages of Temptation
Chapter 11

1. EMERGE Ministry is a Christian counseling center in Akron, Ohio, that specializes in helping clergy couples in crisis.
2. Francis Thompson, *The Hound of Heaven* (Westwood: Revell), 18.

Chapter 12

1. Gordon MacDonald, *Rebuilding Your Broken World* (Nashville: Thomas Nelson, 1988), 53.
2. Ibid., 53.
3. Oswald Chambers, *My Utmost for His Highest* (Westwood: Barbour and Company), 79.
4. Charles Blair with John and Elizabeth Sherrill, *The Man Who Could Do No Wrong* (Lincoln, VA: Chosen Books, 1981), 231.
5. Thomas à Kempis quoted in Keith Miller, *Habitation of Dragons* (Waco: Word, 1970), 110.

Chapter 13

1. Tan, *Encyclopedia of 7,700 Illustrations*, 1447.

Chapter 14

1. Tan, *Encyclopedia of 7700 Illustrations*, 1668.
2. Ibid.

Chapter 15

1. H. B. London Jr. and Neil B. Wiseman, *Pastors at Risk* (Wheaton: Victor Books, 1993), 79–80.

Chapter 16

1. John Steinbeck, *Of Mice and Men* (New York: Viking Press, 1971), 79–80.

Chapter 17

1. John K. Ryan, trans. *The Confessions of St. Augustine* (New York: Doubleday, 1960), 69–72.
2. Ibid.

Chapter 18

1. Richard Exley, *Perils of Power* (Tulsa: Honor Books, 1988), 117–18.
2. Tan, *Encyclopedia of 7,700 Illustrations*, 1260.

Section Four: Sexual Temptation
Chapter 20

1. Name Withheld, "The War Within: An Anatomy of Lust," *Leadership* (fall 1982), 41–42.
2. Dietrich Bonhoeffer, quoted in Bob Benson and Michael W. Benson, *Disciplines for the Inner Life* (Waco: Word, 1985), 59–60.
3. Richard Foster, *Celebration of Discipline* (San Francisco: Harper and Row, 1978), 127.

Chapter 21
1. Carlfred Broderick, *Couples* (New York: Simon and Schuster, 1979), 163.
2. R. Kent Hughes, *Disciplines of a Godly Man* (Wheaton: Crossway Books, 1991), 32.
3. Richard Dobbins, "Saints in Crisis," *Grow*, 13, no. 1, (1984), 4, 6.
4. Walter Wangerin Jr., *As for Me and My House* (Nashville: Thomas Nelson, 1987), 196–97.
5. Ibid.

Chapter 22
1. Harold Kushner, *When All You've Ever Wanted Isn't Enough* (New York: Simon and Schuster, 1986), 3.
2. "A Talk with the MacDonalds," *Christianity Today*, 10 July 1987, 39.
3. Ibid., 38.
4. *U.S. News and World Report*, October 25, 1982,"Mid-life Crisis—Is it Avoidable?" Interview with Daniel J. Levinson, psychologist, 74.
5. Many of the insights for this discussion of David and midlife were inspired by John Claypool, *Stages: The Art of Living the Expected* (Waco: Word, 1977).
6. Kenneth L. Chafin, *The Communicator's Commentary* , vol. 8, *1, 2 Samuel* (Dallas: Word, 1989), 301.
7. H. Norman Wright, *Seasons of a Marriage* (Ventura, CA: Regal Books, 1982), 62.
8. Ibid., 64.
9. Ibid., 57.

Section Five: Overcoming Temptation
Chapter 23
1. R. Kent Hughes, *Disciplines of a Godly Man,* 81.
2. Richard Exley, *The Making of a Man* (Tulsa: Honor Books, 1993), 145, 149.

Chapter 24
1. John Gardener, quoted in MacDonald, *Rebuilding Your Broken World*, 74.

Chapter 25
1. MacDonald, *Rebuilding Your Broken World*, 204.
2. Gordon C. Hunter, *When the Walls Come Tumblin' Down* (Waco: Word, 1970), 67.
3. Ibid.

Chapter 26
1. Willard, *The Spirit of the Disciplines,* 186.
2. Foster, *Celebration of Discipline,* 60.

NOTES

3. Based on information in Keith Miller and Bruce Larson, *The Edge of Adventure* (Waco: Word, 1974), 70.
4. Ibid., 81.
5. J. Wallace Hamilton, *Where Now Is Thy God?* (Old Tappan, NJ: Revell, 1969), 47.